IDENTITY
& where
it comes from

Courtney Weir

FOREWORD BY PASTOR ERIC SWITHIN

müllerhaus
[LEGACY]

TULSA

The truth is I prefer movies over books. And, if I must read, I prefer fiction over nonfiction. However, in the book *Identity and Where It Comes From*, Courtney Weir has found a way to draw the reader into a nonfiction masterpiece like I've rarely encountered before. In my opinion, she has provided the reader with the most raw, colorful, engaging, sentimental and thought-provoking Bible study tool on the subject of identity that has ever been written.

The dominant theme in this heart-stirring study is found at the crucial intersection of God's sovereignty and our personal identity. Simply stated, Courtney helps her reader separate spiritual fact from fiction regarding *whose* we are and *who* we are in Christ.

She accomplishes this in three ways: first, by engaging her reader in interactive exercises; second, by asking questions that require deep reflection; finally, by providing practical steps that can immediately be applied. Her colorful word pictures communicate truths we so often hear but typically miss. Somehow, she is able to help bridge the eighteen-inch gap between our heads and hearts.

It's clear that the Holy Spirit gets credit for this book because it somehow manages to speak to both me (a forty-year-old full-time minister) and a young teenage girl who might be wrestling with anxiety and depression.

This book is useful for Bible studies, Sunday school curriculums, sermon content or for personal growth. It is for anyone who has asked questions similar to:

- "Why did God make me like this?"
- "Why does God care about what I say, think or do?"
- "Am I living in my old identity or out of my new identity?"
- "How do I identify, defend myself against and fight the lies that I so often believe about who I am destined to be?"

Courtney's conversational writing style is best enjoyed slowly like a fine meal. It is simply too rich and life-giving to be skimmed.

Once again, in partnership with God's spirit, Courtney's writing has challenged, entertained and helped me move closer to the heart of Jesus.

—Eric Swithin,
Executive Director of Outdoor Adventures
OUTDOORADVENTURES.ORG

Creator of *The Fatherless Epidemic*
FATHERLESSEPIDEMIC.MOVIE

Identity and Where It Comes From
Courtney Weir

Müllerhaus Publishing Arts, Inc.
DBA Müllerhaus Legacy
5200 South Yale Ave, Penthouse | Tulsa, Oklahoma 74135
www.MullerhausLegacy.com

ISBN-13: 978-1-951700-19-5
LCCN: 2022902352

Scripture in this book is taken from the NASB unless otherwise indicated.

Scripture taken from the NEW AMERICAN STANDARD BIBLE®, Copyright © 1960, 1962, 1963, 1968, 1971, 1972, 1973, 1975, 1977, 1995 by The Lockman Foundation. Used by permission.

Scripture taken from the HOLY BIBLE, NEW INTERNATIONAL VERSION®. Copyright © 1973, 1978, 1984 by International Bible Society. Used by permission of Zondervan Publishing House. All rights reserved.

Scripture taken from the *New King James Version*. Copyright © 1979, 1980, 1982 by Thomas Nelson, Inc. Used by permission. All rights reserved.

Scripture taken from the Modern English Version. Copyright © 2014 by Military Bible Association. Used by permission. All rights reserved.

Every effort has been made to trace the ownership of all copyrighted material included in this publication. Any errors that may have occurred are inadvertent and will be corrected in subsequent additions, provided notification is sent to the publisher.

Cover and Interior Design by Kristin Stroup and Laura Hyde | Müllerhaus Legacy
Edited by Jessica Barnes | Story-Driven Editorial

Printed in the United States of America.
2 3 4 5 6 7 8 9 10   2023

CONTENTS

CHAPTER 1
Designed by the Master

Once upon a time, there was a girl named Courtney. And she had everything going for her. A great family, a wonderful church, friends, and she was going off to college for the first time. And then, about halfway through the semester, she came down with a crippling case of depression.

She went home, quit school, and spent the next ten years trying everything to get better. And only got worse. And that's when thoughts she did not want and could not control started sneaking through her head.

I'm worthless.

I'm useless.

I'm a failure.

A mistake.

A waste of space.

I don't deserve to be breathing other people's air.

It would be best if I just crawled away into a corner and died quietly so I don't bother anybody.

These thoughts didn't come from her parents, who were the most supportive people in the world (okay, yes, this is a story about me. Love you, Mom). These thoughts didn't come from my church. These thoughts didn't even seem to be coming from me. And yet here I was thinking them. And starting to wonder if I should act on them.

So, the therapist I was seeing at the time gave me a list of good, positive affirmations, things I should practice saying to myself in the mirror. Things like "I matter." "I have value." "I'm good at things." Not only did this not work, it made things worse.

Depression never drove me to the brink of suicide. Anxiety never drove me to the brink of suicide. Lies did. Lies about who I am. When I believed I was worthless and that my family and the world at large would be better off without me, that's when I sat there on my bed, pill bottle in hand, considering how best to get it done.

Some people believe that exploring the question of identity is a soft or self-indulgent topic. That, at best, it only serves the purpose of making people feel better about themselves, and, at worst, it glorifies the sin of pride. I used to think that. Not so much anymore.

Others believe that the question of identity is simply a choice. That I decide who I am, everything from race to gender. Or that those are artificial constructs and I can define myself entirely apart from such things. Saying positive things in the mirror makes it so, simple as that.

Tried it. Didn't work.

Needless to say, there is some debate on the subject of identity. But no matter how gnarly the topic, it needs to be addressed. It matters who we are. This is a question that desperately needs to be answered.

But if I am not the ultimate authority on who I am, and if, God forbid, society is not the ultimate authority on who I am, and if my therapist can't for the life of her tell me who I am, then who am I? Who has the answers? Who can smash the lies parading through my head and get me to set down the pill bottle, get up off the bed, and live a life worth living?

In my experience, there is only one source of truth— the unadulterated, pure kind that you can take to the bank. The stuff that doesn't change on you year to year and generation to generation. The stuff that is solid and lasting and firm enough to build a life on top of. The stuff that can pull you out of the confusion and give you a safe place to stand.

"You will pull me out of the net which they have secretly laid for me... O LORD, God of truth."[1] "Your word is truth."[2]

In the realm of big questions that a person has to answer for themselves, right on the heels of "Who am I?" is the question "Where do I come from?" and I don't think we *can* answer the first without the second. Only one place has the answer to that question.

"In the beginning, God created the heavens and the earth. Then God said, 'Let Us make man in Our image, according to Our likeness.' God created man in His own image, in the image of God He created him; male and female He created them... The LORD God formed man of dust from the ground, and breathed into his nostrils the breath of life; and man became a living being."[3]

Now, before we go much further than that, we should probably address the fact that there is some debate about Genesis 1. Is it literal or is it a metaphor? Did God actually form Adam out of the dust of the ground and breathe into him the breath of life, or did God begin the great process known as evolution, which eventually resulted in human beings?

For many believers, it makes no difference. God, being God, could just as easily have set the dominoes falling that led to the creation of Adam and Eve as He could have designed and fashioned them by hand. It makes Him no less their Creator, and their lives would be no less miraculous or intentional. If this is you, read on and don't worry about it. As long as you can accept God's Word, Genesis 1 included, as *true*, whether it's literal or not, then we are on the same page and can move forward together.

But for others, whether God created exactly the way He described in Genesis 1 or whether He used evolution to do it makes all the difference in the world. If God designed me, then I am intentional, purposeful, valuable, loved. If I evolved, then I am an accident, potentially a mistake, a product of random chance. How then do we hope to answer the question "Who am I?" or move forward on the same page if we can't even agree on page 1?

If you believe you exist by cosmic accident, then please check out the appendix ("The One Thing You Don't Mess With") before moving on. If you believe you can ignore the naïve homeschooler who never learned about evolution in school and just skip on to the application, I'm afraid you'll spend way too much time rolling your eyes at me. It might be worth a peek at the appendix to save yourself some aggravation. But from here on in, we will assume two things: Who I am is a question best answered by God; and God's Word is to be taken at face value.

"In the beginning, God created the heavens and the earth. Then God said, 'Let Us make man in Our image, according to Our likeness.' God created man in His own image, in the image of God He created him; male and female He created them... The Lord God formed man of dust from the ground, and breathed into his nostrils the breath of life; and man became a living being."[4]

This is where we come from. More importantly, this is *who* we come from.

My brother was recently looking to buy himself a house, and he found this great little fixer-upper perfectly in his price range, right in the neighborhood he wanted to live in, with great proximity both to our sister's house and the Subway (the restaurant, not the transportation system). But as he looked into it further, he found out who the builder was, and my grandfather, who was in the business years ago, warned him that that builder was known to brag about how cheaply he could build a house, and that if you pulled one nail from the house, the house would fall down.

It didn't matter how perfect the house seemed in all other respects. If that guy was the builder, the house was a death trap. Needless to say, my brother passed on the house.

If the builder is shoddy, the house is shoddy. If the maker is sloppy, the product is sloppy. If the creator is skillful, the creation is flawless. The character of the maker determines the quality of the made.

God's Word puts it this way. "Does a fountain send out from the same opening both fresh and bitter water? Can a fig tree, my brethren, produce olives, or a vine produce figs? Nor can salt water produce fresh."[5] What comes out of the source is a reflection of that source. Nothing can come from a source incompatible with its nature.

I have a God who is all-powerful. With God, all things are possible,[6] no purpose of His can be thwarted,[7] and nothing is too difficult for Him.[8] This is the God who founded the earth on nothing,[9] who raises and destroys nations,[10] who controls the hearts of kings.[11] This is the God who has one hand on the sparrows as they hop across the ground and the other on the constellation He leads across the sky and never loses His grip on either.[12]

This is the God whose voice shapes reality. If He orders it to exist, it exists by the sheer power of His voice on the blueprint of His imagination.[13] This is the God whose voice controls reality. If He commands the sun to shine or the moon to tug on the sea or the wind and the waves to rise or be still, it happens, because nothing in all of creation can resist the voice of Almighty God.[14] This is the God who sends demons running for cover with a single word.[15]

I have a God who is all-knowing. He sees hearts,[16] reads minds,[17] and knows futures.[18] He knows all,[19] sees all,[20] and there is nowhere on earth God is not present.[21]

What God starts, He finishes.[22] What God plans, He accomplishes.[23] What God promises, He provides.[24] What God says, He will do.

And God is good. What He creates is good.[25] His intentions are good.[26] What He plans is good.[27] The results are good.[28] This is the God who is the definition, template, standard, and measure of love itself.[29] This is the God who is too just to allow sin to go unpunished, too merciful to allow that punishment to fall on His people, and too good to allow His people to perish. And that goodness sent Jesus Christ to the cross.[30]

If this is the character of the One who made me... what does that make me?

If the God who designed me is good, then only good things can come from Him. And I came from Him. His mind designed me, His hands sculpted me, His breath breathed life into me, and by His heart, I am loved.

A perfect God cannot make worthless creatures. A wise God cannot make faulty creations. A superior God cannot make inferior products. And my God doesn't make mistakes.

I am not an accident. Not my existence, not my nature, not my character, not my strengths or weaknesses or eccentricities. It is no accident that I am who I am, how I am, the way I am. The God who only produces good saw every circumstance I would ever encounter, every obstacle I'd ever have to overcome, every person I'd ever interact with, and designed a blueprint for me that is perfect. And, in His power, He fashioned me exactly according to that blueprint. I was created this way on purpose and for a purpose.

I am not a mistake. I do not exist by mistake. God doesn't make those. *I* do. I make mistakes all the time, but somehow even my mistakes fit into the intricate plan God has for my good.[31] And though my many mistakes have culminated in a record of sin so long only the death of God's own Son could wipe it out, God does not regret my creation, my existence, my birth, or my life. Rather, He delights to trade His Son's life for mine,[32] so that He may finish the process He started and bring me to a home He's prepared for me.[33]

I am not a failure. When God begins an endeavor, He has every move mapped out before He begins. The very last day I'll ever live on this earth was chronicled by God before He ever put pen to paper to sketch out the blueprints for me.[34] What God plans, He carries out, and carries out to completion.[35] And He will not give up on a thing until it is finished. At no point does God write me off as a failed experiment, a good first effort He can improve on for the next attempt, a cute anecdote He'll tell the angels about when He recounts the early days of creating out of His parents' garage. I am the crowning glory of His creation, the achievement He brags about to those angels.[36]

This is where I come from—*Who* I come from. And this is who I am. Under no other conditions could I say such things about myself. Made by anyone less, alive by coincidence or accident, I would see my failures and call myself a failure. Why wouldn't I? How else would I judge myself? I would see my mistakes and believe myself to *be* a mistake. But I am not. Because I am made by the Creator.

But it gets even better. God did not simply invent a template and create me according to it.

He *is* that template.

When God was creating this world, He said to Jesus and the Holy Spirit, who were also creating alongside, "Let Us make man in Our image, according to Our likeness."[37]

Odd, because God is spirit.[38] He has no actual, physical likeness to copy. But when God breathed something of Himself into that first human being and called him a living soul,[39] He set you and me apart from every other piece of His creation.

"Then God said, 'Behold, I have given you every plant yielding seed that is on the surface of all the earth, and every tree which has fruit yielding seed; it shall be food for you.' Then the LORD God took the man and put him into the garden of Eden to cultivate it and keep it."[40]

Nothing is more beautiful *to me* than nature— unspoiled, vast, green, beautiful nature. Fields that go on forever. Forests that block out all but perfect shafts of sunlight as they light upon the mossy rocks. Waterfalls that are so perfect they can't possibly be real. Canyons of amazing reds, oranges, and whites at sunset.

But there is nothing so beautiful *to God* as people.

No, I don't suppose towers of steel and alleyways lined with dumpsters are God's crowning achievement, but people, most definitely. Nature, on the other hand, was given to Adam and Eve to be their sustenance, their shade, their medicines, their shelter. They were ordered to cultivate it, to shape it to those needs. Being reckless and irresponsible with nature is not good, or what God commanded. But the greatest natural resource, the most irreplaceable thing on planet earth are the people who live on it. Nature, God said, was "good."[41] People, God said, were "very good."[42]

When God decided to create in His image, He said, "Let them rule over the fish of the sea and over the birds of the sky and over the cattle and over all the earth, and over every creeping thing that creeps on the earth." And when God sent Noah out from the ark along with all the animals he'd stashed on the thing, He said, "The fear of you and the terror of you will be on every beast of the earth and on every bird of the sky; with everything that creeps on the ground, and all the fish of the sea, into your hand they are given. Every moving thing that is alive shall be food for you; I give all to you, as I gave the green plant. Only you shall not eat flesh with its life, that is, its blood." So, presumably, chicken is good, just make sure you fully cook it so you don't get salmonella.

There's nothing wrong with being a vegetarian—Daniel actually got very good results from that particular lifestyle[43]—but the God who created salads also invented steaks. And He put animals on this earth for our benefit. If riding horses is useful, ride a horse. If milking cows is useful, milk away. Grill them steaks.

And if the relative value of humans and animals was in question, God Himself comes down and kills some of the animals He Himself had made, tanned their hides, and made clothing for Adam and Eve.[44] This was not a trade of animal life for human life. This was animal life to provide privacy, to give us warmth, to keep us protected from mosquitoes and thistles.

"Are not two sparrows sold for a cent? And yet not one of them will fall to the ground apart from your Father. But the very hairs of your head are all numbered. So do not fear; you are more valuable than many sparrows."[45]

God did not create us as two-legged animals, as one of many species on this planet, the one that just happened to have opposable thumbs, figure out how to use tools, or come up with languages to communicate and coordinate our efforts. We are not just the dominate form of life or the top of the food chain. We are set apart. Special, to God Himself.

Jesus, the Creator who came and lived among His creation,[46] demonstrated exactly what God thinks of what He made. Jesus was a carpenter (requiring the sawing down of trees at some point, I imagine), and did quite a bit of fishing (requiring, duh, the killing of fish), but when it came to human beings, He laid down His life for us.[47]

What Jesus did for humankind is so incredible, so impossible to grasp, that when the story of His sacrifice was handed down to us, angels were wishing to get a clear glimpse of it. They longed to look into this salvation that we have been freely given. They will never know what it is to be loved as we are, and that makes us a subject of envy. By angels.[48]

If Revelation 12 is to be understood as a description of the fall of Satan,[49] a full third of all the angels in heaven joined Satan and were cast down with him when he rebelled, and it is them that hell is waiting for.[50] And yet, when Jesus came to save, He did not put on the flesh of an angel, walk a mile in their shoes, and die in their place. He did that for humankind.[51] And because of that, He can help us when we are tempted, He hears us when we pray, and He comes to our aid—something He has never done once for an angel.[52]

When an angel was giving John, Jesus' disciple, a tour of heaven, John responded by bowing down to worship him. And the angel told John, "Do not do that; I am a fellow servant. Worship God."[53] And yet Jesus told John this: "No longer do I call you slaves... but I have called you friends."[54] That is something no angel in heaven can claim.

"When I consider Your heavens, the work of Your fingers, the moon and the stars, which You have ordained; what is man that You take thought of him, and the son of man that You care for him? Yet You have made him a little lower than God, and You crown him with glory and majesty! You make him to rule over the works of Your hands; You have put all things under his feet."[55]

Everything God made, He made perfect. Everything God does is good. But when God created in His own image, when He breathed into human beings the breath of life, He made something truly special, something that nothing else compares to. Everything else that God made, He made by the Word of His power.[56] He spoke, and there it was. Not so with me.

"Then God formed man of dust from the ground, and breathed into his nostrils the breath of life; and man became a living being. The LORD God caused a deep sleep to fall upon the man, and he slept; then He took one of his ribs and closed up the flesh at that place. The LORD God fashioned into a woman the rib which He had taken from the man."[57]

When I was growing up, my family loved visiting Silver Dollar City. It's a theme park where, alongside the roller coasters and funnel cake carts, were the demonstrations of old-timey processes like candle making or basket weaving or glass blowing.

One of our favorites was watching the potter take a lump of clay and turn it into a pot or a mug or a plate ready for the kiln. But when you're three feet tall standing around watching pottery be made, you get very impatient with the potter, because he's not exactly making the pot the way he should be.

I remember he'd press his fingers into the center of the lump with the wheel spinning and pull the sides of the pot up until it almost looked finished, then he'd slowly smash the thing back down, then pull it up again, and add some water, and again, and again. And every time I'd think he was just about done, he'd take it back down to something resembling that useless lump again, all so he could get the consistency just right before shaping it. We asked him why he kept doing that, and he said that if the clay was too dry, it'd crack. If it was too wet, it wouldn't set properly. No matter how good it looked, only the potter, whose fingers were gunked with the stuff, knew what was right for that particular pot.

Isaiah 64:8 says, "But now, O LORD, You are our Father, we are the clay, and You our potter; and all of us are the work of Your hand."

God did not simply speak us into existence (though I'm sure He could have). Instead, He chose to get His hands dirty. To have flecks of us all over His apron. To work His fingers raw and cold until we were just right—the right consistency, the right shape, the right size and wall thickness to hold whatever beverage or tealight we were meant to contain. We are God's crowning achievement, the only one He got down in the mud for, so that He could fashion it with His own hands. And to a one, we have declared that our Potter got it wrong.

"Woe to the one who quarrels with his Maker—an earthenware vessel among the vessels of earth! Will the clay say to the potter, 'What are you doing?'"[58]

"What are you doing?" The question we have all asked God at one point or another. Perhaps we do not like our purpose. Perhaps we think He made a mistake when He made us. But at some point, each of us has demanded to know what God was thinking when He made us this way.

"Who are you, O man, who answers back to God? The thing molded will not say to the molder, 'Why did you make me like this,' will it? Or does not the potter have a right over the clay, to make from the same lump one vessel for honorable use and another for common use?"[59]

I've struggled with depression my entire adult life. Good things happen and I can't seem to be happy about them. Exciting things are coming up and I can't seem to look forward to them. Sadness happens and I can't seem to push through it. Hurt happens and I can't seem to overcome it. *Why did You make me like this?*

Anxiety comes hand in hand with depression for me.

I want to get out and do something, but I end up closing my mini blinds and hoping no one knocks on my door. I find something I'm really good at but somehow put all this pressure on myself and constantly question if I can really do it. I finally crest one mountain, and instead of the relief I'd hoped for, I find another mountain. *Why did You make me like this?*

I'm not great with people. It takes so much energy to interact with people. I'm constantly second-guessing my every conversation. I feel like a bad friend, pretty much always.

Why did You make me like this?

I must be careful to never blame God for sin—He is not the tempter.[60] And if I take "the way God made me" too far and use it as an excuse for sin, that is not the design of the Potter, either.

But my God did not give me the happy, bubbly personality that my mother has. He did not give me the social, people-person gene that my sister got. I am not the laid-back, easy-going person that my brother is—but that's okay. God made me *this* way, and if I demand to know "What are You doing?!" "Why did You make me like this?!" then this is what I am saying:

My God makes mistakes.

My God does bad work.

My God doesn't know what He's doing.

It works both ways. If the character of the Maker determines the quality of the made, then when I disparage, belittle, or devalue something God made—*me*—I also disparage the character of the Maker.

Every time the thought "I'm worthless" crosses my mind, it leaves this imprint on my heart: God does bad work. Every time I think "I'm useless," it implies that God is limited and can't do miracles with anything less than perfect tools. Every time I think "I can't do this," I end up believing that maybe some things are impossible with God.

Who I am doesn't just matter to me. It matters. It all matters.

There is an assumption that who I am is due to genetics, the coincidence that was my parents meeting and how their DNA happens to combine to make up me. There is an assumption that who I am is due to environment, my upbringing. Where I happen to live, what school I happen to go to, the things that happen to me as I grow up, what I happen to grow up with (or without), and who is raising me.

But God has left none of this to random chance. Sure,

He uses any and all of these things to make the unique person that is me. But these are all ingredients that God Himself has measured and carefully combined so that I would be *this*.

God did not wind this world up like a giant watch and let it tick away while He sat back and watched for the last several millennia. He is intimately involved with the design of each person, and what I do matters to Him.

"O Lᴏʀᴅ, You have searched me and known me. You know when I sit down and when I rise up; You understand my thought from afar. You scrutinize my path and my lying down, and are intimately acquainted with all my ways. Even before there is a word on my tongue, behold, O Lᴏʀᴅ, You know it all."[61]

Ironically, one of the most common things to feel as a human being is the feeling of being alone. To feel like no one understands, like no one gets me. Like I'm the only one who's ever felt what I feel and who thinks the way I think. "Don't think you know me." "Don't pretend to understand me." Because no one can.

And yet, God does. Not just because He is God, sitting up there on His throne, all-knowing and all-wise. But because He has searched me out. Taken the time and effort to get to know me. My thoughts, He understands, even when I don't. My words, He knows, even before I do. He is "intimately acquainted" with me, with everything I do, and why.

"You have enclosed me behind and before, and laid Your hand upon me. Such knowledge is too wonderful for me; it is too high, I cannot attain to it."[62]

God isn't just watching every single thing that happens to me, but He is also protecting me every step of the way. He's guarding me with His hands out in front and wrapped around behind, so nothing sneaks up on me unawares. So nothing happens that He does not ordain.[63] So nothing gets to me that He has not planned for my good.[64] He has laid His hand over me so that come hell or high water, I am protected.[65]

"Where can I go from Your Spirit? Or where can I flee from Your presence? If I ascend to heaven, You are there; if I make my bed in Sheol [the nether world], behold, You are there. If I take the wings of the dawn, if I dwell in the remotest part of the sea, even there Your hand will lead me, and Your right hand will lay hold of me. If I say, 'Surely the darkness will overwhelm me, and the light around me will be night,' even the darkness is not dark to

You, and the night is as bright as the day. Darkness and light are alike to You."[66]

There is no inner city so abandoned that God is not there. There is no middle-of-nowhere so far that God cannot find your address. There is no jungle so dense, no desert so vast, no ocean so deep that God cannot hunt you down and find you. In the place so deep, so dark, so cold, and so intensely pressurized that only blind fish slither along its bottom, yep. God's there too. Oh, and death. You could be on life support, given hours to live, braindead and already gone, and God does not let go or lose track of you.

There is no getting outside His reach. There is no life so lost that God can't find it. No sin so bad that God can't forgive it. No time too many that God gives up on it. He is God. Nothing escapes Him.

"For You formed my inward parts; You wove me in my mother's womb. I will give thanks to You for I am fearfully and wonderfully made; wonderful are Your works, and my soul knows it very well."[67]

God reached down and knit me together. Lovingly, carefully, intentionally, with all of my future in mind. God personally got involved in my making. I am not a copy of a copy of a copy, a duplicate of every other person ever born since the time of the first template that God made. I am not interchangeable with anyone else, nor am I expendable. I do not come off an assembly line. I am a one-of-a-kind artisanal work of a God who did not just create my race in His image or form my people with His hand, but personally crafted *me*, just me, with His own hands.

This is why I am "fearfully and wonderfully made." I was not hastily thrown together. I was not knit mindlessly while God was watching Netflix. I was made fearfully, cautiously, because He had to get me just right. With great care and attention, with specific intention and great love, God made me, and His work is wonderful.

Another translation of Scripture says of God, "You are fearfully wonderful." And it all comes out to the same thing. Because God is fearfully wonderful, something to reverence and revere, someone before whom your breath catches and your mouth drops open, everything He makes is also wonderful. Is also jaw-droppingly amazing. He is God, and He made me. So, what does that make me?

"All the days ordained for me were written in Your book before one of them came to be. How precious to me are your thoughts, O God! How vast is the sum of them.

Were I to count them, they would outnumber the grains of sand—when I awake, I am still with you."[68]

Before I was born, before I was conceived, before I had one day written in the history books, God had written my history, my future, had filled in my day planner with everything I would ever encounter or do or say or think. My every microsecond is accounted for by the God who does all things well. My every moment is filled with His goodness, from before I even existed.

I suppose that God, being God, could have written my history, knit my essence, and gone on with more important things, but one translation of this verse is "How amazing are your thoughts concerning me."[69] "How vast is the sum of them. Were I to count them, they would outnumber the grains of sand."[70]

I have no idea how many grains of sand are on the seashore. But I also imagine it would take a lifetime to count, if for no other reason than because every tide would shift things around and make you lose count and have to start over. God has more thoughts *about me* than it would take my whole life to count. I am not an afterthought to Him. A project He began and then lost interest in. A name in a ledger, lost among a million others. He thinks about me.

He thinks about what's best for me. He calculates what's best for me. And He does what's best for me.

"Search me, O God, and know my heart; try me and know my anxious thoughts; and see if there be any hurtful way in me, and lead me in the everlasting way."[71]

Before we go any further, I have to ask a question: When you hear that God knows your every thought, that there is nowhere you can possibly go to escape Him, and that He has a detailed plan for you, does that fill you with comfort, or with fear?

Believe it or not, both are valid, depending on where you stand with God. For while all people are created in His image, and every one of us is formed by His hand, and while each person is knit together with love, the future we have in store for us is not all the same.

Once upon a time, God created a perfect world, and two perfect people in it. But with a single choice to disobey the single command that God gave them, Adam and Eve's perfect nature got corrupted. And that's the nature we've all been born with since.

Since then, we as a people have discovered many, many ways to violate the character and the law of God. And God, being God, can't just let that go.

Enter Jesus. God knows exactly what His justice would do to us[72]—hell, torment forever—and, unwilling that that should happen to any of us,[73] He exacted His justice on Jesus instead, because Jesus could take it.[74] And Jesus, indestructible as He was, came back from the dead with new life to share with everyone who wants it.

Simple, right? And everyone everywhere would surely want this resurrected life, this heaven-bound eternal life. And yet this is where things get truly heartbreaking for the Creator who knit my soul and lovingly planned my days.

There are two types of people. There are those who agree that, yes, I have defied You, ignored You, disobeyed You, and earned hell for myself, and please, please, yes, I want the mercy and new life You offer. And there are those who shrug off the whole offer. Perhaps they believe God doesn't exist. Perhaps they don't believe God has to be just. That if He is good, He wouldn't send people to hell. Perhaps they believe the whole thing is so metaphoric it means virtually nothing. Perhaps they've never been warned in so many words. It doesn't matter the reason. Unless God's offer is accepted, they are what God calls "vessels of wrath, prepared for destruction."[75]

All us pots are made to contain one of two things: wrath, filled up to the brim, or mercy, overflowing and abundant. God is extremely patient, letting all these vessels of wrath have their day so that He can make His offer of mercy to as many people as possible. "And He did so to make known the riches of His glory upon vessels of mercy, which He prepared beforehand for glory."[76]

Which pot are you?

Which do you want to be?

God knows my every move. If I am a vessel of wrath, then my sins are being catalogued. My record is getting longer. My punishment is on its way. And my sins cannot be forgotten.

But if I am a vessel of mercy and God knows my every move, then I am known by somebody who understands me. Someone who gets me. Someone who sees the good, the bad, and the ugly, and loves me anyway. I am never alone.

God has wrapped His hands around me, and I cannot escape His reach. If I am a vessel of wrath, then His justice is inescapable. My punishment is inevitable. Reminders are everywhere. And I am doomed.

But if I am a vessel of mercy and I cannot escape God's hands, forgiveness is inexhaustible. Second chances are abundant. Life holds no fear, because no place—location or situation—is outside His loving control. He turns the darkness into light, and the good stuff, the bad stuff, it's all the same because He has a good plan for all of it.[77]

God has numbered my days and planned out my moments. If I am a vessel of wrath, I am headed for a future that includes hell, and nothing I encounter along the way is promised to be particularly good.

But if I am a vessel of mercy and God has planned out my moments, I am headed for a future that includes heaven. And *everything* I encounter along the way is promised to be good.[78]

Everything we discuss from here on out will apply to those God calls "vessels of mercy." To those who have received God's offer of salvation. If that isn't you, or you're not sure, please stop and get that straight before you go on. There are no magic words to pray (if there were, mine would certainly not have qualified). There is no list of things to have a perfect understanding of so that, voilà, you're saved (if there was, I'd have been saved ages ago). Chapter 3 describes salvation in much more detail, but it all comes down to this:

"For by grace you have been saved through faith; and that is not of yourselves, it is the gift of God; not as a result of works, so that no one may boast."[79]

If you deny you need saving, you're refusing that gift. If you intend to earn it for yourself, you're denying that it *is* a gift. Both things will keep you from ripping open the wrapping paper.

But if you realize that you are a sinner in need of saving, incapable of saving yourself, then Jesus delights to save. It's His favorite thing to do.

Many people imagine salvation to be a get-out-of-hell-free card, a heaven ticket that they tuck away safely for the day they need it. But it isn't. Salvation takes a person who has been created in the image of God and formed by His hand and turns them into someone even more spectacular.

Michelangelo, perhaps the most famous sculptor of all time (I say this because he's literally the only one I've ever heard of), said that when he sculpted, the statue was inside the stone the whole time, and he just carved away what wasn't the statue. And what he ended up with was a masterpiece.

When Jesus offers salvation to a person, He is offering it to a person encased in stone, all of that beautiful, incredible design that God put into me, buried under layers of gunk. And the moment that offer of salvation is accepted, Jesus gets to chiseling.

"For we are His workmanship, created in Christ Jesus for good works, which God prepared beforehand that we would walk in them."[80]

I love the word the New Living Translation uses. "For we are His 'masterpiece.'"

I don't understand art (like I say, I know the name of precisely one sculptor). Novels, poetry, sure. I get story-type art. I see the beauty in a perfectly structured story, in a beautifully arced character, in a plot twist no one saw coming, but in hindsight is so totally inevitable you wonder how you didn't see it. A perfectly crafted sentence? My heart beats faster as it does in the presence of chocolate. But, hey, I'm a writer. Maybe if I was a sculptor or a painter, I'd get it.

What makes one painting worthless and another priceless? What determines that this is just the finger painting done by the neighbor kid down the street, and this one here is worth ten million dollars?

When I was little, my mom kept an empty pizza box in the house. Every time one of her children would make a construction-paper-and-crayon masterpiece, she would *ooh* and *ahh* and put said masterpiece into said pizza box.

Never to be heard from again.

Now, I'm sure she didn't know we were wise to this scheme. But there is not enough fridge space in the world for every crummy thing I ever drew for my mother. So, she'd keep maybe one thing to remember my lack of talent by, and the rest would go into the box, and, periodically, the box would be emptied into the trash.

I always assumed that my value to God was purely sentimental. I'm His kid. He loves me. So, when I present my pathetic little stick drawing of a life to Him, He proudly displays it on His heavenly fridge. But, as I learned early on, sentimental value has its limits. And no one other than a proud parent would ever look at my life and think it a masterpiece.

I clearly never learned the definition of *masterpiece*.

Lit. a piece done by a Master.

I'm sure there are things you learn in art class about what sets paintings apart from each other. Composition, maybe? The colors, the brushstrokes, some level of realism? And yet, when it comes right down to it, none of these things make a masterpiece.

I could take a photocopy of said masterpiece or plunk a master forger right down in front of the thing for hours so that he copied it perfectly, and both would contain every bit the composition, colors, realism, brushstrokes and what-have-you, but they would have none of the value of a masterpiece. Why? Because they were not painted by the master and are worth no more than the canvas they're printed on.

If the life I offer to God is drawn by me, then my value is only sentimental, and only to the one who loves me. I hold no value anywhere else but on His fridge. Not to any other person, museum, or catalogue.

But if my life is painted by Him, it is a masterpiece, and holds actual, real value. Whether you are an art lover, a collector, a museum curator, or a black marketeer buying guns and a painting is easier to transport than fat bundles of cash, I have value, because the whole world recognizes that if the master painted it, it has value, and that value is incalculable. So, even if I am a Picasso, disproportionate and confusing, I was painted by the Master, and so I look like what I'm supposed to look like. I am what I'm supposed to be.

And I am priceless.

LIVING THE TRUTH

What thoughts go through my head about me? Where do they come from? Does God agree? What then should I do with those thoughts?

Draw a line down the middle of a page, and on the left side, make a list of who God is (it doesn't have to be exhaustive, just a decent list of who I know God to be). If this is the character of the One who made me, what does that make me? Write that on the right side of the page.

What do I like about how God made me? What do I not like about how God made me? In what way have I said to God, "Why did You make me like this?"

What does my opinion about myself say about God? What should my opinion be of God? What should my opinion be of me?

Read Psalm 139. When I read that, am I filled with comfort or with fear? Why? Where do I stand in relation to God? Is that where I want to be?

Am I a masterpiece? Am I treating myself that way? In what ways am I devaluing or damaging the masterpiece that is me? In what ways am I hiding away and wasting the masterpiece that is me? In what ways am I displaying the masterpiece that is me so that its value is taken full advantage of? In what ways could I be displaying the masterpiece that is me that I'm not currently doing?

CHAPTER 2

The First Casualty of War

O n every TV show I've ever watched, if they want to use a quote about war, they quote Sun Tzu, who was, apparently, the greatest war philosopher to ever philosophize about war. And he said something to the tune of "know the enemy, know yourself, and you will win a hundred battles."

You and I are at war with someone. Have been since the day we were born. Despite being created in God's image, formed with His hand, and—assuming you are also a vessel of mercy—a masterpiece painted by the Master Himself, you and I do not automatically have a charmed life where everything goes perfectly and we see ourselves with 20/20 vision. Instead, we are embroiled in a fight for our lives. For our very identities.

Jesus Christ has assured us that the war is already won. When Satan and his armies line up against God and His armies, the carnage is completely one-sided and, frankly, anticlimactic as no one is a match for God.[81] When Jesus rescues a person from the kingdom of Satan and transfers them to the kingdom of God, brings them from darkness to light and makes them one of His, nothing in this world can snatch that person out of His hand.[82]

But when it comes to the daily struggles, the individual battles, the question of whether we will push forward or be pushed back, I believe Christians lose a lot of battles because we don't know the enemy, and we don't know ourselves.

But in case the enemy is unclear—and let's face it, he loves to be. He loves to obscure his intentions behind layers of other things and dress himself up as an angel of light[83]—God has pointed out for us exactly who the enemy is in Ephesians 6.

"For our struggle is not against flesh and blood, but against the rulers, against the powers, against the world forces of this darkness, against the spiritual forces of wickedness in the heavenly places."[84]

Contrary to popular opinion, the enemy we are up against when it comes to our identity is not a superficial, looks-obsessed society, or bad parents who tell us we'll never amount to anything, or school bullies who try to shame us into submission, or work rivals who sabotage us at every turn. Our enemy is not flesh and blood. It's the devil himself.

Let's assume for a moment that Sun Tzu was right. Let's assume that he did not just write about war but possibly at some point in his life won those hundred battles he was always bragging about. Maybe we should take his advice and get to know our enemy a little bit better. And the first time Satan comes on the scene is right there at the beginning in Genesis 3.

If God was communicating His thoughts, His Word, His story to us in the age of Hollywood instead of the age of stone tablets and papyrus scrolls, might He have made a movie instead of a book? So, in an effort to get as clear a picture of this as we can, let's use God's Word as the screenplay and imagine us a movie, shall we?

Let me set the stage. God plants a garden right at the confluence of four sparkling, sun-kissed rivers. Imagine the branches of the trees hanging low over the water, gurgling brook sounds, tweeting birds, brightly-colored fruits hanging on every branch. Deer and bunnies hop through the underbrush, and curled around a branch would be a truly gorgeous... well, snake.

Now, please remember that our universal dislike of snakes likely *comes* from this event, rather than pre-dating it. So, when our lovely heroine dances onto the scene, tending the garden as she was asked by God to do, she does not, unfortunately, shriek, "Adam! Get the garden hoe!"

"Now the serpent was more crafty than any beast of the field which the LORD God had made. And he said to the woman, 'Indeed, has God said, "You shall not eat from any tree of the garden"?'"[85] (By the way, the voiceover for the snake is done by James Earl Jones in my version of the movie.)

Again, unfortunately, Eve did not shriek, "Aaaah! It can talk! God! Smite this slimy thing!"

Instead, she starts to civilly converse with the devil in disguise. "The woman said to the serpent, 'From the fruit of the trees of the garden we may eat; but from the fruit of the tree which is in the middle of the garden, God has said, "You shall not eat from it or touch it, or you will die."'"[86]

Now, the discerning movie viewer would then screechily rewind the film to earlier in the day, when God actually warned about the tree in question. I'm picturing a really huge, sprawling tree that shadows the clearing it's in, right smack-dab in the middle of the place, and Adam looking up at the looming branches as the voice of God booms down with the sunbeams, "From any tree of the garden you may eat freely; but from the tree of the knowledge of good and evil you shall not eat, for in the day that you eat from it you will surely die."[87]

Perhaps something got lost in translation. Adam still had all his ribs at this point, so he must have relayed the message to Eve, perhaps as they were leaving the house for the day, Adam going to cultivate the back forty with lunch pail in hand, warning Eve over his shoulder, "Oh, and there's this tree and God said we're really not supposed to touch it..."

Obviously there's a bit of creative license going on in the telling of this story. But that's kind of the point. Creative license was taken by the snake, when he, voice full of mock disdain and skepticism, asked if God really prohibited them from eating from *all* the trees of the garden. Creative license was taken by Eve when she repeated, supposedly word-for-word what God said, and took God's prohibition even further than He did by saying they couldn't touch the tree either. And very possibly creative license was taken by Adam when he repeated God's warning to her, all of which left Eve with a very big problem.

She wasn't entirely sure what God said.

There is no more dangerous question in all of creation than "Did God really say...?" Satan, the father of lies,[88] need not even bother with a lie if he can only get us asking, "*Did* God really say?" Because that leaves us open to phase 2.

"The serpent said to the woman, 'You surely will not die!'"[89]

I can just see the snake recoiling, hissing out a gasp of shock. No, surely not. God wouldn't do *that* to you.

And, as Eve is standing there, frowning, trying to remember exactly what God did say and whether it actually made sense for Him to have said something so unreasonable as that, Satan goes on to phase 3. And I can just hear him, car-salesman smooth, brushing over the whole controversy with a reasonable alternative to the very unreasonable warning from God.

"For God knows that in the day you eat from it your eyes will be opened, and you will be like God, knowing good and evil."[90]

Ah, and now it all makes sense. God, the great, the awesome, the only, wants to keep all the power to Himself. He wants to keep the knowledge hidden that Eve so very much wants to have—or at least she does now that she was made aware of it. Her happy little life in paradise was now dismally lacking, and her God, the one she'd so naïvely trusted, was holding out on her. After all, she could see with her own eyes that the fruit was "good for food, and that it was a delight to the eyes, and that the tree was desirable to make one wise."

So, "she took from its fruit and ate; and she gave also to her husband with her, and he ate."[91]

When God warned Adam not to eat of the tree, He claimed that they would surely die "in the day that [they] eat of it."[92] And yet, if Eve lived to be as old as her husband, she made it another nine hundred years after this. She saw her great-great-great-great-great-great-grandchildren be born.[93] So was God maybe going a little overboard when He said they would die that very day?

And yet something did happen that very day. Immediately. As she stood there, horrified realization turning that mouthful of fruit to sawdust in her mouth, juice still dribbling down her chin, in that moment, the person she was—her very identity—shriveled up and died.

Not much is directly told to us about Eve before this moment. In fact, the first words recorded out of her mouth were in conversation with the devil.[94] We know a little bit more about Eve after this happens, but for the most part, who she was and what she was like is a mystery to us. So, let's take what we do know about Eve, and see if we can pinpoint exactly who died the day she ate of the fruit.

"And the man and his wife were both naked and were not ashamed."[95]

Somewhere in my childhood brain, the one that wore shorts and a T-shirt over my swimsuit, I assumed that they were both being very sinful wearing nothing, and because they had yet to eat of the knowledge of good and evil, they were oblivious. Uh, no.

You've got God, who looks at the heart,[96] and Adam, who had every right to be looking, and enjoying, and whatnot. And there was no puffed-up pride at looking good and catching her husband's eye, because there was no pride in this world yet. The world had yet to be infected with sin, so nothing pre-fruit was sinful.[97]

They say beauty is in the eye of the beholder. When my dad casually mentions that he's always thought so-and-so was pretty, I realize, hey, she's got Mom's smile, or Mom's hairstyle, or Mom's eyes. Every time I've ever heard Dad comment on someone as beautiful, she in some way resembles the person he considers to be his ideal, the standard and template for what beautiful looks like for every other woman.

Eve, by design, must have been the standard and template for what beautiful would henceforth look like. Think about it. God, knowing Adam's every need, desire, and opinion, fashioned a woman specifically to be his "help meet."[98] The one who would specifically meet his every need, not as his servant or property, but as his perfect match. That was her very definition, what she *was* as her essence. If Adam had an ideal in mind, she met it. Probably, knowing God, she surpassed it. And when God finished her, He stood back and "behold, it was very good."[99]

New generations of the iPhone are supposed to be better and better, more bug-resistant, with faster download speeds, and each generation is an improvement on the one before it. Yet all are a version of the one that came before. But when God is the template for creation, Generation One, if you will,[100] and He creates man and woman in His image,[101] and each generation after that is in the image of the generation that came before,[102] then may I suggest that a copy of a copy of a copy of a copy of a copy is not an improvement on the original? In fact, every generation out from the original perfection that is God is going to be less beautiful.

Roughly halfway between Eve and the women of today, Abraham and Sarah sojourned in Egypt, and Abraham was so worried about Sarah catching Pharaoh's eye and tempting him to knock off her husband so he could have her to himself that Abraham asked Sarah to lie and claim to be his sister instead. And guess what? Pharaoh did indeed take note of the eye-catching beauty that was Sarah and want her for himself.[103]

Did you know she was sixty-five years old at the time?[104] How many women of that age catch the eye of the most powerful man on earth, when he could have *anybody*? Compare today's women back to Sarah and track that trend back to Eve and without Scripture ever saying it, I feel confident in suggesting that Eve was the most gorgeous woman to ever walk our planet.

And this woman, who walked in the sight of God and her husband with nothing whatsoever to be ashamed of, looked down the second she ate of that fruit and immediately she was ashamed and felt the need to cover up all the beauty that God designed in her.[105]

Did she suddenly sprout warts? Get cellulite? Grow haggard and wrinkled? I feel like God might have mentioned it if she had. But what actually happened was worse. Without changing one iota, she suddenly saw a whole different person in the mirror, one not endowed with the beauty designed by the eye and hand of the Master sculptor, but one in desperate need to hide behind anything that could disguise her.

Before this, there was nothing whatsoever that could hurt Eve. The garden was never too hot or too cold. If the spiders and bugs and snakes were venomous, they would never have dreamed of biting her, and I don't think they'd have been venomous at this point anyway (why bite something unless to kill and eat it, and there was no death pre-sin[106]). She could walk barefoot and never step on a single thorn or thistle.[107] She would never starve or need to stock up for winter. Everything she needed literally grew on trees. And God Himself, great Creator, loving Father, fast friend, declared her "very good."

There was both literally nothing to fear in the whole universe for her and no such thing as fear.

In verse 6, she eats the fruit. In verse 7, she is crippled by shame. And in verse 8, she feels for the first time the horrible grip of fear. "They heard the sound of the LORD God walking in the garden in the cool of the day, and the man and his wife hid themselves from the presence of the LORD God among the trees of the garden. Then the LORD God called to the man, and said to him, 'Where are you?' He said, 'I heard the sound of You in the garden, and I was afraid.'"[108]

As this was the world's first game of hide-and-seek, Adam and Eve weren't very good at it yet. For instance, when It yells, "Where are you?" you're not supposed to yell back the answer.

But humankind has gotten better at acting out of fear. And it all started with this. *Before* the ground, the snake, and the vegetation were cursed to cause pain and danger and lack of food, Eve became afraid. And she directed that fear at God.

And do you know what God, the One she feared and hid from behind the trees He created to give them shade and sustenance, did as soon as He found them?

He killed one of His own creatures to improve on the totally inadequate coverings they'd made for themselves. And He promised to send His own Son in sacrifice for their sin. Their problem, solved in the same breath in which He told them they had a problem.[109] That's what she was hiding from. That's who she feared.

Identity is the first casualty of sin. Not reputation. Long before God went walking in the cool of the day and asked Eve if she ate that fruit she'd been told not to eat, she was filled with shame, gripped by fear, and had completely lost who she was.

And when identity is destroyed, purpose goes out the window.

Eve had the world's only perfect marriage. She and Adam were made for each other—literally designed by God with each other in mind. They were personally brought together by the hand of God, who walked Eve over to Adam and put her hand in his.[110] Soulmates by design.

She was designed to be a perfect fit for Adam, for them to live their lives together like a hand in a glove.

The God who designed the garden to meet their every physical need designed marriage to fulfill their emotional needs. Their marriage predated the arrival of jealousy, resentment, competition, and selfishness into this world. Adam would never belittle her or bully her or abuse her. Eve would never nag him or be let down by him or feel like he wasn't pulling his weight in the marriage. Life was good.

Then one little conversation with one little reptile...

"To the woman [God] said, 'I will greatly multiply your pain in childbirth, in pain you will bring forth children.'" Yes, we have Eve to thank for that too. "Yet your desire will be for your husband, and he will rule over you."[111]

The literal translation is that Eve will desire to gain control over her husband. And he will rule over her unrighteously. Enter jealousy, resentment, competition, and selfishness. Enter belittling, bullying, and abuse. Enter nagging.

When Jesus wishes to describe His relationship with His people to us so that we peons will understand it, He describes Himself as the bridegroom, going to build onto His Father's house a place for Him and His beloved to live together forever.[112] When God wishes to describe His people's relationship to Him, He speaks of them as His wife and He as her husband.[113]

Marriage is the first picture God ever paints of salvation. This is how He tells me who He is and who I am and who we are in relationship to each other. Is there a more important picture to paint? Eve's purpose wasn't just to be a good wife. It was to show every subsequent generation what it meant to love your God. And the picture she paints instead is rebellion and obstinance, imagining that she knows better than her husband does. To lead instead of follow, to rule instead of rest, to nag instead of partner. To constantly be in conflict and a tug-of-war over control, a wife who wants to run over her husband, whose husband then rules her with an iron fist.

No wonder humankind sees God only as a distant tyrant who takes our freedom and imposes His will on us. No wonder people are not eager to accept God's marriage proposal.

Can you see why Satan bothers attacking our identity? It isn't a matter of feeling good about ourselves. It's a matter of lifelong purpose and whether or not we spend our lives fulfilling it, or whether we spend our lives unfulfilled, out-of-step, constantly feeling like we're missing something. Because we are missing something: the purpose God designed us to have.

They say truth is the first casualty of war. I don't know who "they" are or what prompted them to say it, but they're right. In the very first war fought by the very first Good versus the very first Evil, truth was the first casualty.

Allow me to explain what truth Satan attacked.

We call God the God of truth. The God of all wisdom, perhaps. Like God is simply looking down on this world and accurately conveying what He sees. Basically, that God is a God of truth because what He says lines up with reality.

But the very first thing that happens on the very first day of all of history is that God said, "Let there be light." Only there was no light when He said it. Not only did it not exist as a tangible thing, it did not exist as a concept. No one had ever thought of it before. But God spoke, and now, suddenly, there was light.[114] God is not a God of truth because—or only because—what He says lines up with reality. He is a God of truth because when He speaks, reality lines up with Him.

Imagine this: God, looking at the world after He made it, sees a blue sky. If God were to offhandedly comment that the sky is red, oops. Lo and behold, the sky would suddenly be red.

How then does this God exaggerate? Prevaricate? Obfuscate? Let alone lie?

The Bible says God cannot lie.[115] I would have thought that it would say God *does* not lie—a choice He makes. But He cannot lie. Lying is a choice He cannot make.

When words come out of God's mouth, they shape reality. When He says something is so, it *becomes* so. Just because He said it. This is who God is—the Way, the Truth, and the Life. He is truth because truth is defined by Him. It lines up to who He is, what He says. That is how our world exists in the first place.

Can you imagine how much planning it would have taken to get the world right on the first try? Okay, yes, it was God. I imagine what He actually did was decide, "Let's make the world," and then He did. But the number of variables that all have to be right for this world to function at all, let alone well, is staggering.

If the earth was a little closer to the sun, we'd burn. If it was a little farther away, we'd freeze. If the earth's axis was tilted a little more or a little less, seasons would go crazy and we'd drown in melted ice caps or some such thing.

If ice sunk in water instead of floating on top of it, the oceans would freeze solid, the water cycle would stop, rain wouldn't happen, crops wouldn't grow. We'd die, basically.

If insects didn't like the taste of nectar, flowers wouldn't be pollinated and they'd go extinct. If flowers went extinct, insects would too. Then, I suppose, birds would as well, and who would poop tree seeds out in the sun where the shade of their own parent trees wouldn't kill them as saplings? Then where would we be?

My favorite example is one from an episode of *The Magic School Bus*. Ms. Frizzle's class visited the Amazon (the jungle, not the website) to see an investment that had been made on behalf of the class in cocoa trees (from whence comes chocolate). But whoever owned the plot of land where their cocoa trees were really disliked all the mud, so he'd put down artificial turf. Which made all the warthogs migrate elsewhere so they could wallow in the mud like they wanted. Which sent the swarms of insects that buzz around on top of warthogs to fly off as well. Which meant they weren't pollinating the cocoa flowers, which killed all the chocolate!

My point is that if something wasn't the way God designed it, the world would end. And why does God bother getting every element of His created world to work together? The water cycle, photosynthesis, the food chain, everything? Why did He plant a garden in the best spot among four rivers and water it every morning? So He could plop two people down in the middle of it and shower them with His overabundant kindness day after day after day.

Paul, writing about the Holy Spirit, says He "intercedes for the saints according to the will of God." What might the will of God be? "And we know that God causes all things to work together for good to those who love God, to those who are called according to His purpose."[116] Ephesians tells us that God "works all things after the counsel of His will." To what end? "To the end that we who were the first to hope in Christ would be to the praise of His glory."[117]

When God does something, He does it unconstrained by any outside influence. He simply does it because He is God and He can't help but be Himself. So why does He do what He does? To save, to love, to work all things for our good.

And into this incredible world, designed for the people God created to live in it, Satan slithers up and suggests that the God of truth is a liar, that He does not have Eve's best interests at heart, and that the one fruit that she should not have is in fact the one thing she needed.

"You surely will not die! For God knows that in the day you eat from it your eyes will be opened, and you will be like God, knowing good and evil."[118]

Sounds good, doesn't it? To be like God? To know good and evil? God's clearly keeping this good and beneficial knowledge all to Himself. This secret knowledge must be great if He wants it so bad He won't share it. What a miser God is! How stingy! A Scrooge who lets go of nothing unless someone pries it out of His hands. He's holding out on me. His so-called generosity clearly has a limit. Whatever goodness He offers is held in tightly-gripped hands. So much for the God who claims to *be* love.[119]

And, if God is holding out on me, then He must be lying to me too. After all, He claimed eating the fruit would kill me, and clearly that's not the reason. It's probably not even true. What a liar God is! Exaggerating the consequences of something that's not even bad! Placing all these scary warnings when behind the warning signs is actually knowledge—that's supposed to be a good thing! Half-truths and buried motives and protected knowledge that He doesn't want me to know. What kind of God is this?

And then, if God is lying to me about something good He doesn't want me to have, then, clearly, His commands and warnings and instructions aren't for *my* benefit. They're not for *my* protection. It's all about Him! So that He can be the only One who's powerful and all-knowing and whatever else. He's just trying to keep me down, to keep me from coming up to His level. It's not about me at all! It's just a smokescreen so God can keep pretending to be something special while I sit down here, His little stooge, naïvely believing everything He tells me. How selfish God must be!

When Satan sets out to tell a lie, he really goes to town. And with a single sentence, Eve believed all of it. And the moment she did, God's glorious creation felt shame, knew fear, and lost her purpose.

Did you catch that? Satan lied about God, and it was *Eve's* identity that suffered.

What does that tell me about my identity? Perhaps that it stands squarely on who God is. And if God's identity gets obscured, mine gets obliterated.

The truth is that every good and perfect gift comes from God.[120] God gives only good gifts to His children.[121] Everything God does toward me is done with goodness in mind.[122] And based on the fact that He sacrificed His Son Jesus for the good of His people, there is absolutely no good thing in the universe that our good God would withhold from us.[123]

The truth is that God cannot lie.[124] The truth is that, unlike people, God does not change His mind.[125] This is the God who knows the end from the beginning.[126] Who knows the hearts of all men.[127] Who knows the plans He has for me[128] and has made those plans good.[129]

The truth is that everything God has said to me, everything He has done in regard to me, He has done *for* me, to the end that we who were the first to hope in Christ would be to the praise of His glory.[130]

The truth is, if God is Creator,[131] then I am fearfully and wonderfully made.[132]

If God is the Potter,[133] then I am a vessel of mercy prepared beforehand for glory.[134]

If God is the giver of life and breath, then I am held by the hand.[135]

If God is inescapable, then I am never alone.[136]

If God is a warrior who saves, then I am an object of His delight, rejoiced over with singing.[137]

If God is everlasting, untiring, the Creator of the ends of the earth, then I am strong and soar on wings like eagles.[138]

If God is sufficient in His grace, then even when I am weak, I am strong.[139]

If God is truth,[140] then I am privy to information so good I am envied by angels.[141]

If God is my Savior, I am redeemed, ransomed, precious in His sight, honored, and loved. There is nothing in this world left to be afraid of.[142]

If God is Redeemer,[143] then I am rescued from the domain of darkness and transferred to the kingdom of His beloved Son.[144]

If the King of King and Lord of Lords[145] rules a kingdom not of this earth,[146] then I am a citizen of heaven.[147]

If Christ is raised from the dead, I walk in newness of life.[148]

Because He lives, I will live also.[149]

If God is rich in mercy, then I am made alive, raised with Christ, and seated with Him in the heavenly places.[150]

If God is love, then I am His beloved.[151]

If God is a good Father,[152] then I am a rightful child of His.[153]

If the Lord is my Shepherd, I shall not want.[154]

If the Father is greater than all, then no one can snatch me out of His hands.[155]

If the Lord is faithful, then I am protected from the evil one.[156]

If God does not fail,[157] then the good work begun in me will be carried on to completion.[158]

If no purpose of God's can be thwarted,[159] then I will be glorified, even as I have been foreknown, predestined, and justified by the blood of Christ.[160]

If Jesus overcomes,[161] then I am an overcomer[162] who eats of the tree of life, who cannot be hurt by the second death. I am given a new name and authority over the nations, clothed in white garments, and my name is indelibly etched in His book of life. I am claimed before God and an assembly of angels, allowed to sit on His throne. I am an heir to the spring of the waters of life and a child of God.[163]

If God is for us, then who can be against us?[164]

If God is God, then I am His and He is mine.[165]

Jesus said there are two types of people in this world. There's the wise man who builds his house on the rock, and there's the foolish man who builds his house on the sand.[166] Now, I don't know if the wise man dug a giant crater down to find the bedrock, cleared out all the sand and dirt, brushed off the rock, and planted his house down there in the hole, or whether he just drilled pylons all the way down to that bedrock. But I'd bet the latter.

From the outside, the houses couldn't have looked any different. Both sitting there innocently on top of what appeared to be sand, nice and square, strong and safe, as the sun beat down and the birds tweeted cheerily. Perfectly the same. Until the weather turned.

When the rain falls and the floods come and the winds blow and slam against those houses, one stands and one falls. It's only then you know the difference.

If you were to go to a secular therapist, they're likely to give you a list of positive mantras to say about yourself. If the therapist is a Christian, they might give you an "identity in Christ" list, verses like the ones used above, all telling me good and lovely things about myself for the purpose of making me feel better about myself.

But who I am is nothing more than topsoil, that upper layer of sand upon which the foolish man built his house. If all I've got is who I am—true or not—Satan

needs nothing more than a good mudslide and my identity erodes and washes away. But connect all the state-
ments about who I am to who God is, and I won't have to
fear the drought or the wind or the storm or the lightning
strikes or even the tornadoes that rip trees out by the
roots, because the bedrock does not move.

Psalm 1 describes the blessed man, the stable man,
the solid man, the one who cannot be moved by drought
or storm. "He will be like a tree firmly planted by streams
of water, which yields its fruit in its season and its leaf
does not wither; and in whatever he does, he prospers."[167]

If all I had was a nice list of who I am, it would be
like trying to plant that oak tree in two inches of topsoil.
Topsoil is good. It's got nutrients. It's necessary for the
health and growth of the tree, but it can only support a
tiny, baby sprig with a leaf on top. If I want something
immovable—tree or house—I have to go deeper. Past all
the lovely things I'd like to believe about myself, through
the character of Jesus who changed me, the salvation that
remade me, to the character of the God who chose to save
me in the first place.

The great thing about a good, biblical "who I am" list
is that Satan doesn't usually attack when I've got an hour

to devote to in-depth Bible study. He usually attacks when I'm doing something else, like eating, sleeping, breathing, etc. So, when Satan comes at me and all I've got is thirty seconds between parking the car and grabbing a grocery cart, why not go to my "who I am" list, the one I've taped to my mirror and taken a picture of with my phone?

Hillsong United sings a song with the lyric, "Let the devil know, 'not today.'"[168] That list is a great thing to shove in the devil's face, rub his nose in, and use to say, "Not today."

I'm not falling for your lies today because I'm a child of the King. You can't get me with that "you're not good enough" malarkey because I am an overcomer. You are crushed under my feet today, snake.[169] I'm going shopping.

But these will never be and *can* never be just words to me, a list of unconnected, foundationless topsoil or great will be my fall.

Looking to myself for self-confidence is a house that's solidly secured as a unit, walls to ceiling and floors, yet unconnected to the ground—a trailer, not a house. There's a reason tornadoes do more devastation to trailer parks than any other place. It's almost as if tornadoes aim for those things, knowing nothing's nailed down.

Satan aims for what is not nailed down, and when he does his devastating work, I'm left having to scrap it all and start over because there's nothing left to rebuild from. It's how he got Eve. He lied about God, and she lost herself. Satan can't lie to me about me until I've lost sight of my God. But to get myself back, I cannot go looking for me. I must start looking at Him.

If Sun Tzu is right, then I need to know my enemy—the devil, the deceiver, the one who comes to steal and kill and destroy, the murderer from the beginning.[170] But I also need to know myself. Who am I? Know God, and I will know this. Know this, and I will win a hundred battles.

LIVING THE TRUTH

In what area of my life do I find myself asking, "Did God really say?" What does God really say about that? How can I remind myself of this so that I can get traction and move forward, rather than spinning my wheels in confusion?

What do I see that is "a delight to the eyes, desirable" that I do not have? What is the truth about God, according to Matthew 7:11 and Romans 8:32? What then can I conclude about the thing I want but still don't have?

What lie have I believed about God? How does that make me feel about God? What is the truth? How does that make me feel about God?

Who does God say I am? How do I see myself instead? What truth about God would set right this faulty view of myself?

What do I usually remind myself of when my identity is in question—when I find myself depressed or anxious or beating myself up? How well is it working? How well are my reminders anchored to the bedrock?

How well do I know bedrock truth? What can I do to get to know that truth better? What quick reminders stand on this truth that I can easily pull out whenever my identity is under attack? How can I put these at my fingertips so they're memorable and easily accessible?

CHAPTER 3
Useless, Meet Priceless

I intended to start this book at the very beginning—at the "in the beginning God created the heavens and the earth"[171] part. But in all actuality, there was something that happened *before* the beginning.

Yes, I know. Shouldn't the beginning be... the beginning? But if history were a novel, this would be the prologue. If history were a movie trilogy, this would be the prequel. If history is written by God, then God did some brainstorming before He ever put pen to paper and spoke into the darkness, "Let there be light."[172] And here's what happened.

Before God gathered dust off the ground and made a human being with it, before He breathed into that man the breath of life, before fashioning Eve out of a rib and declaring them both to be "very good,"[173] He "chose us in

Him before the foundation of the world, that we would be holy and blameless before Him. In love He predestined us to adoption as sons through Jesus Christ to Himself, according to the kind intention of His will."[174]

Before I was born, He chose me. Before my parents were born, He set His affection on me. Before my great-great-greats were born, God decided I would be His, all His, so that He could dump bucket loads of kindness on me.

Why? Have you ever wondered? What did God, sitting back at the before-the-beginning place when as yet there was nothing, see when He looked through the ages at little ole me?

He must have seen someone pretty great, yes?

"There is none righteous, not even one."[175]

Okay, then maybe He saw someone who, while not *good*, per se, really wanted to be. Someone who was searching.

"There is none who understands, there is none who seeks for God."[176]

Fine. But I must have had potential. Otherwise why would He choose me?

"All have turned aside, together they have become useless."[177]

Did I stumble upon some goodness by accident?

"There is none who does good, there is not even one."[178]

And if that weren't bad enough, God does not particularly hold back in His description of what He found people on earth to be like. In case it wasn't already painfully apparent. "Their throat is an open grave, with their tongues they keep deceiving, the poison of asps is under their lips; whose mouth is full of cursing and bitterness; their feet are swift to shed blood, destruction and misery are in their paths, and the path of peace they have not known. There is no fear of God before their eyes."[179]

This is what happened to humankind—all of humankind—the moment Eve handed the fruit to Adam and he took a bite. Adam and Eve's nature changed so that they were no longer the perfect people God created them to be, but rather sinners. And that is something they passed on to every one of their children, and their children, and their children, on down to us. This is what the enemy accomplished with one lie about God.

What was God to do? And what on earth was God thinking when He chose to save any of us from this? Especially considering the price?

In order to redeem a person, to change their nature, to save their soul, the price was a trade. The perfect for the imperfect. The incorruptible for the corrupted. The blameless for the one totally to blame. And the only Person who fit the bill was Jesus Christ—perfect, incorruptible, blameless. And in order for Him to trade places with us, He had to die, specifically the worst death that humankind had managed to invent—crucifixion, where Jesus was nailed up to a cross to suffocate to death in the place of the people who actually deserved it.

"What was God thinking?" is not really a safe question to try to answer. My brain might explode. Though I suppose if I was God and I was bound and determined to save us (for no rational reason that any human can discern), I would try something a little less drastic than the cross.

Despite our complete lack of anything resembling goodness, there is something inside us that is screaming out, "There is a God! Pay attention!" Romans 1:19–20 says, "That which is known about God is evident within them; for God made it evident to them. For since the creation of the world His invisible attributes, His eternal power and divine nature, have been clearly seen, being understood through what has been made." And the reason for this is painfully obvious. "So that they are without excuse." God gave us a little warning light in our brains so that when all us idiots wander straight into hell, we realize, "Yeah, I should have seen this coming."

And to the casual Bible reader, it appears that, for a time, God left His corrupted little population to figure out right and wrong for themselves. Hoping that little warning light would go off and they'd figure out, "Duh. Murder and greed and deceit are really bad ideas, and maybe we should try some kindness and maybe give thought to somebody other than ourselves for a minute." Spoiler: They did not.

In fact, if this was an experiment God was running, keeping tabs on His little subjects, here would be the dismal result: "Then the LORD saw that the wickedness of man was great on the earth, and that every intent of the thoughts of his heart was only evil continually."[180]

I can't even imagine a world in which this was the case. Even Ted Bundy had to think something like, "Hmm, I should pick up a gallon of milk" at some point. These people thought *only* evil. Continually.

So, God put eight people in a boat and flooded everything else. This time, He clarified, "Okay, here's right, here's wrong. Thou shalt. Thou shalt not."[181]

That didn't turn out much better. God sends judges, each of whom is supposed to lead the people back to Him. He replaces bad kings with good ones. He sends prophets, all meant to warn the people like visible, audible warning signs, saying, "Don't go that way! Hell is down there!" And when all is said and done, "There is no faithfulness or kindness or knowledge of God in the land. There is swearing, deception, murder, stealing and adultery. They employ violence, so that bloodshed follows bloodshed. Therefore the land mourns."[182]

And when all else failed, God sent Jesus. The last, best, and only hope. And here's what's truly crazy. If I was God, I would have tried anything and everything—including giving up entirely—before sending my son to die for those people. But none of the experiments God ran, if I can use that term, were in any way meant to save His people. And they were never, ever expected to work.

God knew from the beginning that despite our lack of excuse, none of us would do good or choose God. God knew from the beginning that no matter how clear the boundaries, no matter how carved-into-stone those laws were, there would never be any fear of God before our eyes. God did not hold off so long in sending His Son because He hoped He wouldn't have to, but because we needed to know what God knew all along: that we could not save ourselves.

"Now we know that whatever the Law says, it speaks to those who are under the Law, so that every mouth may be closed and all the world may become accountable to God; because by the works of the Law no flesh will be justified in His sight, for through the Law comes the knowledge of sin."[183] "Therefore the Law has become our tutor to lead us to Christ, so that we may be justified by faith."[184]

Remember the "before the foundation of the world" moment? The one in which we were chosen? Something else happened during that prequel, that prologue, that moment before time began: Jesus Christ was crucified.[185] Yes, Jesus died two thousand years ago, after two millennia of the downward slide into every thought only being on evil continually. After two more millennia of the Law being violated and His people being unfaithful. After all that, Jesus came, and He died. But when God decides something will happen, it is done, in that moment, and before the foundation of the world, Jesus was crucified, sacrificed, sentenced to die for people yet to be born.

And before we were ever aware of just how desperate our situation was, God was promising Jesus,[186] so the second we knew we were hell-bound and helpless, we would also know there was a Savior, and His name is Jesus Christ.

Jesus—perfect, flawless, sinless, blameless, God-in-human-flesh—died the most excruciating death that humankind had yet devised. Literally. The word *excruciating* comes from the word *crucifixion*. The worst we could devise, and that wasn't even the worst of it. Sin must be punished, and as neither you nor I would survive the wrath of God, Jesus picked up our sin off of us and wore it to His death, where God poured out all of heaven's wrath and that of hell onto His own Son.

As much as Jesus' death was a demonstration of the extent and breadth of God's love,[187] as much as it was justice meted out against the God of Mercy,[188] it was also the very real cost of an actual transaction. A ransom paid.[189] A debt paid in full.[190] A slave bought back.[191]

For years, my dad was a real estate appraiser. It was his job to go into a house before it went on the market and determine its value. Some of it was tangible—houses with crumbling foundations were less valuable than ones with strong foundations, and houses with two-and-a-half bathrooms were more valuable than one with a single bath. But no matter how much evidence my dad would give on why a house was worth a certain amount, he could not convince a bank of what a house was worth unless he proved it using "comps." Comps were houses of the same size in the same neighborhood with similar amenities that had recently sold. If people are willing to pay X for that house, they will pay X for this house.

Price has always been determined, in part, by what people are willing to pay for a thing. Even though there has never been any proof that having powerlines in your backyard causes health problems, people see powerlines and get a little squirmy about it, and no matter what the powerlines do or don't do to the actual value of the property, people will always pay less for a house with powerlines than they will for one without them. Therefore, because people will pay less, the house is worth less. Even though it shouldn't be.

You and I *should* be worth... wait, let me calculate... carry the one... nothing. At some point, no matter how famous or masterful the Builder was, it costs more to renovate a run-down house than it costs to tear it down and start over. And it cost way more to renovate me than I was ever worth.

It is important to remember that no human being is worthless. From the moment we are conceived to the moment we breathe our last breath, whether that breath is aided by machine or not, there is no person and no point at which that person is worthless. Nothing God designed ever was. Created in God's image, formed by His hand, and died for by Jesus Christ,[192] there is no one—believer or unbeliever—who has no value.

But then the house that was made by God was hit with the big wrecking ball of sin. So, while God's fingerprints are still on it, it's totally useless as a house. The occupants would be rained on. The furniture would be stolen. It's totally uninhabitable. Worse, it cost more to renovate us than it would to scrap us and start over.

So, no. Not worthless. But not worth it, either. Because the price that was paid for the wreck of a house that is me was Jesus Christ.

Let us just for a moment calculate the value that is Jesus. Ha, okay. I recognize the futility of that endeavor, but humor me. How do we determine the value of something a little more objectively?

- Purity.

Any number of substances from gold to drugs are valued based on purity. If you have a substance that is considered valuable, like gold, you want to be sure how much of the rock in your hand is actually gold. If it's alloyed with lesser metals, it's less pure, and less valuable. And if I have my TV trivia correct, that's why all the drug dealers on the shows taste the white powder before paying for it, to make sure it's good quality cocaine and not cocaine plus baby formula or some such thing.

Jesus is described as "holy, innocent, undefiled, separated from sinners and exalted above the heavens."[193] This is nice if He lives on your street, or you're buying a table and chairs from His carpentry shop, or you're spending a day fishing with Him and hearing His stories. But this is essential if He's considering being a sacrifice for your sin.

The bar is perfection. The requirement is total sinlessness. Absolute pure goodness. Anything less is less than required, and the very best substitute humankind could offer was only ever accepted as a temporary IOU, a promise of the sacrifice to come.[194]

- Scarcity

When something is unique, one of a kind, its value skyrockets. When there were only ever six of a type of car ever made, collectors clamor for it. When so-and-so's rookie baseball card becomes impossible to find, it becomes ridiculously expensive. When animals that used to roam the continents in packs are now down to a few thousand, suddenly the world cares. Why? Because they're cute or useful or valuable? Not so much. No one notices until they're few and far between. And when they are, they are considered of such value that you can't build on their habitat or endanger their eco-system. But spiders? They're everywhere. Sure. Squash the buggers.

In Greek mythology, and in Egyptian mythology, gods were a dime a dozen. But in reality, "there is one God, and one mediator also between God and men, the man Christ Jesus, who gave Himself as a ransom for all."[195]

One. In all the world, in all the universe, there is one. Only one. I'm not sure there's any other totally unique thing in the universe. There is no valid way to even put a price on a thing there is only one of. And He, by virtue of sheer uniqueness, the most valuable thing in the universe, chose to barter His life away as ransom. For me.

- Availability

Supply and demand, folks. The ratio of how much there is to how many people want it determines a thing's value. Gas prices go up and down because availability of supply is always changing. I imagine fax machines are going pretty cheap these days because nobody wants them.

With the whole of the human race across history headed straight for hell (I cannot even calculate the immensity of that number), and a single sacrifice, Jesus Christ, the only hope for any of us, imagine the price. Imagine one dose of a cure for a worldwide pandemic from which no one ever recovered. Imagine one seat in the lifeboat when the whole world is going under. Imagine one fallout shelter when the bombs are falling. One hope when the end comes. That's Jesus.

So, when Jesus, the one hundred percent pure, one-of-a-kind, only-hope-for-humankind, the One whose price is literally beyond calculation and is therefore definitively *priceless,* signs His life over in exchange for me...

What does that make me?

No, I may not have five bathrooms and granite countertops, and, yeah, my foundation may be crumbling, but this is what the market says I'm worth. This is what God says I'm worth. Because this is what He paid.

Many Christians dislike God's description of what people, pre-salvation, are like. They think that dwelling on the no-good, dirty, rotten sinner passages lead to wrong thinking, bad feelings about oneself, or even self-hatred. But the cure to self-loathing is not a recitation of positive mantras. It's dwelling on the truth.

And the truth is, Satan tells both lies. He tells me that I was originally good, full of potential, deserving of what God has to offer, and therefore God chose and saved me—or worse, that I saved myself. And he tells me the opposite. That I am still the dirty, rotten sinner I always was and will never change.

Both are lies.

There's this card game called Pitch that my uncles have been playing since way back when they were fraternity brothers together. It's a team game, and you keep score, and after every hand, one of them usually recites the score, so that each team knows how many points they need to make up and how critical it is that they get the bid on the next hand. And, invariably, when one of them is losing, when the deficit is growing, when it's starting to look too late, they will utter this phrase: "I've seen sicker cats than this get well."

Perhaps the phrase came about when my uncle was in veterinary school. Perhaps it's been around so long none of them knows where it's from. But it means that I've come from further behind than this. I've made up a greater deficit than this. I've snatched victory out of the jaws of a worse defeat than this one, and it's not over yet.

The lie of my original goodness, childhood innocence, or buried potential may sound good on the surface. It may appear to bolster my self-confidence, allow me to see myself as not all bad, and give me hope, but while that is what Satan promises, what he delivers is the exact opposite.

If I believe that God looked through time and saw some promising quality in me, then what happens when life goes sideways and I'm not making good on that promise? If He picked up on my potential and plucked me out of the pack, then I have to live up to that potential. If I in any way contributed to God's choice to reach down and save me, then my salvation is partially dependent on me. And if my salvation is in any way dependent on me, then I can lose it.

If God's love of me is in any way based on my nature, on my character, on my behavior, then God's love is not unconditional, and it will fluctuate with my successes and failures. If God's choice of me is due to me, then I can do something that makes Him think better of the whole plan and change His mind. If my salvation is in any way dependent on me, then woe is me for I am undone.

But, if God looked through time and saw someone useless, but conferred on me the value of priceless, then there is nothing I can do to undo His love for me. There is nothing I can do to invalidate His choice of me. If there is nothing I can do to save myself, then there is nothing I can do to lose that most precious salvation. And there is no place I can go too far for God to keep coming after me with His love. No matter what state I'm in, no matter how far I've fallen, no matter how far I've run from God's grace, *no matter what,* I can always say, "I've seen sicker cats than this get well."

God has brought me from further behind than this. God has made up a greater deficit than this. God has snatched victory out of the jaws of a worse defeat than this one, and it's not over yet.

The truth is, I can never sink lower than the place I was when God found me. I was dead. There is no sicker cat than that. And when I was dead, He made me alive.[196] What can I do now that puts me at too far gone? What sin can I commit, what failure can I fall into, what mistake can I make, what life can I live that God cannot forgive? That God cannot overcome? That God cannot turn around and turn into good?[197] Is there a more positive, bolstering mantra than this? "But God demonstrates His own love for us, in that while we were still sinners, Christ died for us."[198]

On the other hand, do not sink into the lie that you have no value *now*. The moment Jesus signed over His life in exchange for yours, He set market value for you at beyond price. AND NOW YOU ARE. "Therefore if anyone is in Christ, he is a new creature; the old things passed away; behold, new things have come."[199] You were designed to bear the image of God[200] and in Christ, you have been redesigned to look increasingly like the incomparable Jesus Christ who lives in you.[201]

Before God breathed into Adam the breath of life, he was no more than a two-legged animal. Before God put into him the life that only God can give, Adam was nothing special. Simply the last in a long line of really cool things that God created. But when God breathed life into him, something happened, and he became incredible.

The fall, sin, and the corruption of the world turned a once-living being into someone who was, for all intents and purposes, dead.[202] A walking corpse. Bound for hell. Still walking, still talking, no idea it was already decomposing on its feet.

But God chose to take that dead, rotting corpse that was me and breathe new life into it. Once again, God breathed something of Himself into me. The life that was His Son, Jesus Christ. Jesus died so that He could take the old rotting corpse to the grave with Him. He lives to ever make intercession for me.[203] And He has taken up residence in this newly re-alivened person.[204] Suddenly I have all the capability, responsibility, and, indeed, inevitability of fulfilling the incredible purpose God once and for all intended for me.[205]

When my brother, sister, and I were little, we had this big backyard to play in, and behind that was the fence, and behind that, a vast wilderness. It was a huge tangle of trees and underbrush and it felt like it went on forever. Since growing up and driving past the neighborhood again, I realize the endless forest was maybe a block deep, but when you're three feet tall, it was the edge of the world. Off the edge of the map, and beyond that were monsters.

Adventuresome children that we were, we'd venture out into the great unknown to pick up fallen branches to build forts in the backyard, but there weren't really any landmarks out there. No giant boulders to mark space by, no creeks to reorient to, no huge fallen logs to tell us we'd gone too far. The only way to know where you were, how far you were from home, or which direction you were going was if you could look out past the treetops and see the roof-line of the house. Otherwise, you could get lost forever and ever and nobody would ever find you (so it seemed).

No matter the topic, whether it's some deep theoretical discussion or some modern social issue, we cannot venture into the tangle of all the lies Satan has surrounded us with if we don't have sight of salvation. That is our starting point, our compass point, our landmark, our home. We start there, and that is where we go back to at the end of the day, because without that, we will be lost.

Satan has surrounded us with lies. He wants us to veer off one side into pride and ego, puffing ourselves up with nice-sounding platitudes that make us feel good but may or may not be true. He'd like us to forever wander in the land where worth is based on our actions, on people's opinions, on our own opinion—all of which has us lost in insecurity and self-loathing, leaving us trapped. If we want to answer the big tangle of a question, "Who am I?" we have to start with the cross.

So, let's look back at salvation. Let's start there. Let's keep track of it over our shoulder as we wade into the underbrush. Let's get back there at the end of the day, because at the end of the day, that's the only thing that matters.

There are many beautiful, glorious descriptions of salvation in Scripture, but one of the best, most bolstering, encouraging, heart-soaring, delightful ones is Ephesians 2:1–10. It's one of those you can't just read but have to camp out on and sink your teeth into. I hope you brought your appetite.

"And you were dead—"

Okay, pause the movie. "Were dead." Did you catch that? Past tense. "Were" dead. Not "are dead" or "will be dead" or "have been dead for the last decade." "Were." Past tense. To be dead in the past tense means that, in the present, I'm alive. And nobody is alive after they "were dead."

Do you know how many places in the known universe the phrase "were dead" can justifiably be used? Vampire books and stories of people who were shocked by a defibrillator. That's it. "Well, they *were* dead, but now..."

Once upon a time, we were dead. Rotten from the inside out. Nothing left to do but to donate our organs and use us as a cautionary tale to others. That was us. We were dead. Once. But no longer.

"And you were dead in your trespasses and sins, in which you formerly walked according to the course of this world, according to the prince of the power of the air, of the spirit that is now working in the sons of disobedience. Among them we too all formerly lived in the lusts of our flesh, indulging in the desires of the flesh and of the mind, and were by nature children of wrath, even as the rest."

There's not even the fantasy that we were once innocent children who gradually became corrupted by society or ruined by our parents or jaded by experience. Nope. This was our nature. Not worth the salvage costs. Nothing under all the gunk worth the effort of saving. Nothing before all the gunk worth remembering and pitying and diving in for. From our inception, we were children of wrath. Destined for it, simmering in it, living it out with every heartbeat. From the moment of our first breath, our first kick inside our mothers, our first heartbeat, the first moment of our conception, we were wrathful little ingrates destined for hell. Lovely, isn't it?

Absolutely it is. Because that, too, is past tense.

"But God—"

Okay, yes, this is my favorite phrase in all of Scripture. The train is derailing and heading off a cliff, BUT GOD is flying to the rescue, cape fluttering out behind Him. The fire is blazing out of control and there are still people in the house, the firefighters can't go in, BUT GOD rolls up in His Batmobile. The earth splits, the sky turns dark, the Son of God breathes His last, BUT GOD. The forces of hell are amassed, the world is ending, the final battle is approaching, and everyone left on earth is assembled to destroy the King of Kings and Lord of Lords. BUT GOD. When you hear that phrase, triumphant orchestral music plays and the battle is over before it starts.

You were dead in your sins, useless, corrupted by nature, rotten from the inside out. BUT GOD.

"Being rich in mercy..."

Do you know of any other attribute of God He is "rich" in? I know of none, and I did check. Two thousand years ago, when Ephesians was written, there was "poor," meaning you did not have enough to eat today. There was "middle class," meaning if you work today, you eat today. And there was "rich." You have more than what you need.

God is more merciful than the ginormous amount of mercy it would take to forgive the sins of the world. He overflows with it. Oozes with it as He walks down the street. It tumbles out of His arms as He struggles to contain it. It overflows. He can't help it. He doesn't want to.

And with all this abundance of mercy—which will never run out or reach its limit, which I can never exhaust or frustrate or terminate or invalidate or push away—God has set His sights on me, and here He comes, immense and looming, mercy tumbling free.

"But God, being rich in mercy, because of His great love with which He loved us—"

Apologies. We may never finish. Did you catch that? Why does God love me? Why does He shower me with mercy? Because of His great love. He loves because He loves.

On one episode of *The Andy Griffith Show*, Sheriff Taylor goes out to mediate between two feuding hillbilly families, the Wakefields and the Carters. And he sits down with the patriarch from the Carter family on the guy's front porch to find out what started the feud and therefore if there was a way to end it.

Why are you feuding? Because they're Wakefields. But why do you have a problem with the Wakefields? Because we're feuding. But why are you feuding? Because they're Wakefields.

As you can imagine, this being a comedy, it went around a few times. But there was a point under there: It was what it was. It had no inciting incident, at least not one anyone remembered. And because it had no beginning, the feud couldn't be ended.

God's love had no inciting incident, no beginning. Why did you shower your mercy on me? Because I love you. Why do you love me? Because I showered mercy on you. Yeah, but why did you shower mercy...? Because I love you. It is what it is. No beginning, and therefore no end.

Okay. Back to the passage. "But God, being rich in mercy, because of His great love with which He loved us, even when we were dead in our transgressions—"

HOLY COW, can you believe that? He loved me when I was dead! Ah, but because we were dead, He "made us alive together with Christ (by grace you have been saved), and raised us up with Him, and seated us with Him in the heavenly places in Christ Jesus—"

It's not my fault, I swear. If Paul would just put a period in his very long run-on sentence, I wouldn't have to keep interrupting him.

Raised us up with him. Seated us with him. Also past tense. And yet this hasn't happened yet.

Someday, I will be seated in heaven. Someday, when this body dies and I am buried, I will be raised, alive again, and this time forever. Hasn't happened, but when God declares a thing, it is as done a deal as any deal is done.

"So that in the ages to come He might show the surpassing riches of His grace in kindness toward us in Christ Jesus."

Finally! The great big "why" behind it all! Why did God shower His mercy on me? Why does He love me with such a great love? Why did He sacrifice His priceless Son for useless me? So that in the ages to come He might show the surpassing riches of His grace in kindness toward us in Christ Jesus.

He was merciful so He could be loving so He could be gracious so He could be kind. And as He sits there on His porch in His overalls explaining this with a wide-eyed expression to the sheriff, He is simply baffled that the sheriff can't get this.

This is who God is. This is who *I* am. The cycle never ends.

"For by grace you have been saved through faith; and that not of yourselves—"

As if we could possibly imagine it was. After all we know about ourselves pre-Christ? Was there ever any hope that we, somehow, could accomplish this?

"It is the gift of God; not as a result of works, so that no one may boast."

I've got nothin'. I never had anything. Nothing but the greatest price conferred on me by the God who way overpaid for me. No result of anything I think, say, or do, but as a simple gift, no strings attached. No boasting. Just basking.

"For we are His workmanship, created in Christ Jesus for good works, which God prepared beforehand so that we would walk in them."[206]

I don't even have to map out a course. He's got that too. A carved-out path and all I need do is stumble along, hand in His, knowing He's got a plan and it is a good one. I am, after all, a masterpiece. Priceless, beyond calculation, and to say I look like a million bucks would be an understatement.

Feeling good about yourself yet?

No, that may not be the point, but it is the inevitable conclusion of knowing and living the truth. You cannot hate what God so abundantly loves.

I keep thinking I'm going to get tired of this. That I will explain salvation one too many times and it will finally be old hat. And boy was it, when it was just a list of facts one had to recite to properly share the gospel with somebody. But when salvation became more than words to me, when it became life and breath to me, I cannot seem to get enough of it, and no matter what topic I'm discussing or issue I'm struggling with, it always circles back around to this.

"Who am I?" is a big, gnarly one. It's one of the biggest questions we can ask. But if we can get sight of salvation, and keep sight of it, then we will not get lost. We will not fall into the trap of falsely puffing ourselves up or harmfully puncturing ourselves out of some sort of belief that's what humility is. We will not spend our lives evaluating our worth by our actions or others' opinions, and we will not waste our lives hiding our light under a bushel because we think we don't measure up.

If we start the day at salvation, keep it in sight as we travel, keep orienting ourselves to it as we explore, and map everything we find in relation to that, then we will always be able to find our way home. And we may just find the answers we're looking for.

LIVING THE TRUTH

What kind of person was I (specifically, not humankind in general) before God saved me? What (specifically) were all the results of my attempts to fix me (assuming I even knew I needed it)?

What situations make me feel I've lost my salvation? What do I imagine makes God love me less? At what times do I feel like God's favor is lifted from me? Compare these times to what I was like before I was saved. What does that tell me about God's love? His choice of me? My standing with Him?

Read Romans 3:10–18. What of this still applies to me? In what ways am I acting like it does? What in my life would change if I truly believed *I* had changed?

What issue do I currently find to be a great, big tangle of confusion? How does salvation affect the discussion? If I continually reminded myself of salvation during this discussion, would the issue still seem as critical? What of this issue might salvation untangle?

What is my "But God" moment (salvation or otherwise)? What disaster, by all rights, should have happened? What happened instead? Find someone and tell them about it. (Blame this book if "Hey, I just wanted to tell you about a 'But God' moment I had" doesn't roll off the tongue.)

When do I tend to see good things in my life as "of myself"? How does that make me feel? How might life change if I saw those good things as "gifts from God"? How can I remind myself that they are gifts from God?

CHAPTER 4
Summed Up in One Word

W hen God introduced Himself to Moses, He called Himself "I AM WHO I AM."[207] As names go, it's a bit of a mouthful, and weird to say in English. It comes from the Hebrew word HAYAH, meaning "to be." Basically, "it is what it is." The self-existent one. I am... Me.

With this name, God compares Himself to no one. His identity relies on nothing. He is relative to no other created thing. He simply is. The thing on which everything else is built, to which everything else is compared, around which everything else revolves.

When God gave Moses a set of laws for Israel to follow, He asked for many things, among them, sacrifices. But after a while, He gets fed up with them and says, basically, you've got the sacrifice part down, but you're totally missing the point. I don't actually *need* sacrifices from you. "For every beast of the forest is Mine, the cattle on a thousand hills. I know every bird of the mountains, and everything that moves in the field is Mine. If I were hungry I would not tell you, for the world is Mine, and all it contains."[208]

God has no need of us. He exists quite independent from us. He requires no service or sacrifice. So... what are we here for?

Have you ever wondered why God created in the first place? Why, in the middle of all the infinite, timeless nothing that He existed in, did He decide to speak into the darkness, "Let there be light"?[209] Before that, everything was perfect. God, His Son, and the Holy Spirit existed in perfect harmony, in perfect love. Not a single moment or aspect fell short of perfection.

And then God created us. We destroyed nature.[210] We destroyed ourselves.[211] And when God sent His very own Son to save us, we destroyed Him too.[212]

You and I caused Him no end of grief and trouble. We cost Him His Son. And before He ever spoke this world into existence or formed us with His hands, He knew exactly what the price would be to redeem the creation He was about to make. So... why?

I have a guess. Admittedly, it's only a guess, and though I have verses to back up bits of this argument, I do not know of any Bible verse that comes out and tells us why God chose to create in the first place. But here's my guess:

God is love.[213] It is not just a description of Him, but the definition of Him—His very identity. This is who He is. But what is love without someone *to* love? I think God created because while He does not need us, He does absolutely need to be Himself. And Himself is love.

God loves His Son, Jesus.[214] And He always loved Him, even before there was a world to shower His love on. And Jesus prayed that we would know the love and unity that He shared with the Holy Spirit and His Father.[215] So there was love before there was us. But even before us, there was love *for* us, because He planned out the entire universe in my favor. Out of love for me. Planning to give Himself up for me.

And God, speaking to Jesus, said, "It is too small a thing that You should be My Servant to raise up the tribes of Jacob and to restore the preserved ones of Israel; I will also make You a light of the nations so that My salvation may reach to the end of the earth."[216]

Remember, this is a nation who were so numerous you could just as soon count the stars or the grains of sand on all the beaches of earth as you could count these people.[217] But God looks at this innumerable multitude, and—*huff of frustration*—no. It's too small. Is it possible that God created the world and everyone in it simply because before the world was, His love had too small a stage?

God cannot be contained. His goodness is too much. His love is too expansive. He had too much of Himself not to share who He is (love itself) with the world.

He created me so that He could love. He just couldn't help Himself.

That's my theory, anyway.

So, there is a reason that God sat down with a wad of clay, plopped it onto His potter's wheel, and began to create. But when He formed that clay pot, He also created it with a specific purpose in mind. I am not simply meant to sit there under the faucet of God's love, filling until I overflow. I am made to fulfill a purpose.

There are certain words that Christians use a lot that I'm afraid I've never really understood all that well, mostly because other people don't really use them. You won't find them thrown about on the jobsite or on social media. They're words only Christians use, so without some sort of context, they become almost placeholders. Unfortunately, one of these words is the very reason we exist.

"For you have been bought with a price: therefore glorify God."[218]

The word *glory* or *to glorify* is found all over Scripture, and it's used by Christians all the time. But what does it mean? Answer: many, many things. You'd need a Greek dictionary to make a full list. So, I went on a quest to sum it up, to make it simple, if such a thing can be made simple. And based on the definitions I've heard from reputable sources, the ones found in three different Greek dictionaries, and the way the word itself is used across the pages of Scripture, here's what I've come up with:

"Glory" is God on display. Therefore, "to glorify" is to put God on display.

Who God is—shouted from the mountaintops. His character shining through the clouds so that no one can miss it. God's identity revealed.

God is God. He can't be less than who He is or other than who He is. And so everything He creates is therefore a product of who He is, and each thing He creates inevitably will be a representation of His nature. A product of His character. An example of His identity.

Made to put Him on display.

"The heavens are telling of the glory of God; and their expanse is declaring the work of His hands."[219]

Everything God is (the glory of God) and everything God does (the work of His hands) are put on display by what He has made. However, I cannot imagine the heavens sitting down and brainstorming how to best splash God's character across the sky. They don't roll out of bed with a sigh and blunder about for a cup of coffee to fortify themselves for another hard day of revealing who God is. They don't sweat and tire and exhaust themselves trying to do a good job today. Because it's not their *job*. It's their nature. Their identity. What they are made to be. They can't help but declare God's handiwork, because they *are* God's handiwork.

Even broken, even messed up, even cursed,[220] this is what creation does, every day. It can't help itself.

Romans 1 says that what humankind knows about God—dare I say, *everything* humankind knows about God—is written across creation for all to see. "For since the creation of the world His invisible attributes, His eternal power and divine nature, have been clearly seen, being understood through what has been made."[221]

One would think that God, being God, would not need us to put Him on display. After all, He's God. But much of who God is is actually invisible, and so God (though He does not need us) chooses to use His visible creation to put the invisible on display.

All of creation does this. From the depths of the ocean to the farthest stars that no telescope can yet capture. From the driest deserts to the wettest rainforests to the coldest tundra and the highest mountain. From ostriches to horses to fire-breathing dinosaurs, to the angels in heaven, and the people on earth.[222] Every bit of creation. After all, everything that comes *from* Him points *to* Him.[223] That's just the way it works.

And yet, of every glorious thing in creation, God has His favorite. The billboard He likes the best. The place He chooses to display Himself most prominently.

Us.

We are the vessels of His mercy, the trophies of His grace, the light of the world, the city on a hill.[224] God's most incredible display of Himself—the message of salvation, the cross of Christ—He did not entrust to angels. He entrusted that to us.[225] And at the moment that salvation was accomplished, God only allowed the earth and sky to declare it because His favorite instrument was unfortunately silent.

When God's people say nothing and God's glory isn't being displayed, when the Son of God is being murdered and no one utters a word, even the rocks themselves will cry out.[226] The earth itself will split open, the graves will spit out those interred in them, and the earthquake will go down in history, the evidence still visible to tourists two thousand years later. Why? Because the very ground God made can't help itself. When the Son of God is treated as a criminal, God's glory must be known, and rocks, which are normally silent things, can't keep their mouth shut any longer. *Alright, we've had enough of this. Time to do what we're made for.*

But as God's crowning creation, I am meant to shout louder, to shine brighter, to beckon more insistently than anything else God made, and He would rather hold up His hand to silence the rocks so that I might shout His praises. Even broken, even messed up, even cursed, *this is what I'm made for.*

Romans 1:20 claims that God's "divine nature" is clearly seen in what has been made. I always assumed this verse referred exclusively to grass, trees, stars, sky, etc. But only one part of God's glorious creation ever received that "divine nature."

Us.[227]

God created me so that I could put Him on display. I just can't help myself.[228]

"Whether, then, you eat or drink or whatever you do, do all to the glory of God."[229]

Having been redeemed by Jesus Christ, having been molded as a vessel of mercy, and as a masterpiece that God is continually crafting to perfection, it is my nature to put God on display. It is my purpose to put God on display. In every single thought, word, attitude, and action.

And yet is that something I can claim? That my *every* action has always been a glorious billboard for the character of God?

Uh, no.

One of the first verses I ever learned was Romans 3:23, and I don't think I ever understood it until now. "For all have sinned and fall short of the glory of God."

The word *sin* means "to miss the mark." Like in archery, when you hit slightly off-center, or perhaps miss the target altogether, or, embarrassingly, the arrow arches gently and pathetically out of the bow, poking into the grass at your feet. Way out there is what you're aiming at, and you just... fall short.

If "glory" is God on display, and our purpose is "to glorify," to put God on display, then this is where we miss the mark as human beings. This is where we fall short.

God is perfect. We are imperfect. God is holy. We are compromised. God is righteous. We are sinful. God is just. We are corrupt. God is forgiving. We hold grudges. God is love. We hate.

Sin is sin, not because God sat down one day, took suggestions from the angels, and composed an arbitrary list He then sent down to us. Sin is sin because it goes directly against who God is. Because it goes directly against who I am meant to be. And when I go against who I am designed to be, it hurts me and it grieves God. No wonder He made a "Thou shalt not" list. No wonder He gave us lists of what *does* honor His character. It's the only time we'll ever feel right or happy.

Thank goodness that even in our unforgiveness, God's forgiveness of us still puts Him on display to a watching world. Even in our sin, God's grace gets center stage. In our failure, God's power is made known. And in our weakness, He is strong.[230] And yet, because sin hurts me, I do not want to simply wallow in it, allowing it to trap me, to harm me, to destroy me.

So, what do I do with it?

My dad owns a mini storage facility. We live in Colorado, but the mini storage in is Oklahoma, so dad has a manager, Miss Sheila, who runs the place for him while he's away. And since the day he built the thing, he has had no end of bad luck with the gate. It'll get hit by lightning and the fancy mechanism that raises and lowers it won't work and people can't get in to get their stuff. Someone will be pulling a U-Haul trailer and they're not used to pulling a trailer, so they run into the gate and now it's bent and won't go up or down and, again, people can't get their stuff. Whatever the issue, it's always expensive and it's always a pain.

One day, Miss Sheila calls Dad to inform him that the gate's broken again. My dad's first thought is, "Oh dear, here we go again." She tells him she came in and found it bent, so of course Dad figures that without anyone seeing it happen, they won't be able to track down the person who did it. By now, he's already calculating how much this is going to cost him and whether he needs to drive all the way to Oklahoma to handle this himself.

But before he can say any of this, Miss Sheila informs him that she figured out which customer it was, tracked the guy down, and his insurance is going to pay for it. Wonderful! Dad thinks. He'll contact the gate repair and replacement people, get an estimate—but no, she's not finished. Miss Sheila has already gotten the estimate, hired the people, and the gate is being fixed as they speak.

So, here is where my dad is beginning to wonder why exactly she is calling him if there's nothing left for him to do. In truth, she called him because there's a check in the mail from the guy's insurance company and she didn't want Dad to find it and wonder what it was for.

When I sin, there's a moment when I realize I've done it again. Crashed into the gate. The Holy Spirit, the One whose job it is to tell me when I've done something wrong, could call me up and say, "Look what you've done. Again? Seriously? You realize how much this is going to cost, right? Customers can't get in and get their stuff.

We'll be closed for half a day to get this fixed!" But that's just not His style.

The Holy Spirit will never point out the broken gate, yell at me, and tell me I'd better come up with a way of paying for that. He'll never dump a pile of tools on my foot and throw up His hands, expecting me to figure out a way to fix a gate I'm not qualified to work on. He'll never pull up the records of the twelve other times the gate's been broken this year and demand to know why I haven't gotten my act together yet.

No. When the Holy Spirit calls to inform me the gate's broken, He does it to let me know the grace is in the mail and He just wanted me to know what it's for.

When I sin, Satan would like me to do one of two things: embrace the sin or beat myself up over it. But God says both these things are wrong, and He says it in the space of a single verse: "Do you think lightly of the riches of God's kindness and tolerance and patience, not knowing that the kindness of God leads you to repentance?"[231]

I should not take God's grace lightly, choosing guilt and self-recrimination. Because it's His *kindness* that leads to repentance—not bashing myself over the head with my wrongdoings.

But, on the other hand, I should not take God's grace lightly, just ignoring the broken gate, letting customers line up outside, unable to get their stuff. After all, the kindness of God leads somewhere. Repentance. The gate needs fixing.

One of the biggest tangles in the wilderness of identity is what to accept, embrace, and celebrate as "Me!", the glorious person God created, and what to take note of, get the gate repair people out for, and work toward changing, as it is not at all who I am supposed to be.

So, if I am sitting here, an honest self-appraisal in my hands, a big long list of who I am and what I'm like, then what of this do I embrace, and what of this do I endeavor to change?

Fair question. I'm glad you asked.

I am not a fan of computers. Some things a computer does, it's supposed to do. And some things the computer does, it is *not* supposed to do. Whenever I'm trying to learn a new program, I seem to find all sorts of glitches, and when I go to the all-knowing internet for my answers, all I find is more people who have the same problem but no one who has the answers.

Computers are supposed to be simple. According to my father, who really does know all, computers only do what they're programmed to do. Period. So why are they always crashing and glitching and slowing to a screeching halt and losing my files? Because, at some point somewhere, somebody engineered a virus, and it got into the system and now all computers everywhere are subject to glitches.

The computer, therefore, is still following its programming. Only now, some of those orders are coming from someone wanting only to cause mischief and mayhem.

You and I were originally designed by God, a God who does all things well, who does all things perfectly, who does not make mistakes. And yet, *we* do make mistakes. How? Because, long about the time a snake slithered into the garden and two people ate the wrong fruit, a virus was introduced, and now all people everywhere are subject to sin. We're still following our programming, but not all of it is original programming, done by God. Some of it was introduced by a slimy troublemaker only wanting to steal and kill and destroy.[232]

I have no idea how actual antivirus software works or how professional computer geeks go in and fix the problem, but I have to imagine that eventually they have to go way down deep in the code to determine what is original code and what is virus. What is original design and what is corruption.

Anytime I look in the mirror or examine my behavior, I'm going to see two things: God's original design (the way He made me to be), and a corruption of that design (the virus that is causing glitches, which God calls sin). The trick is to figure out which is which, then call up the heavenly IT department and hand over my hard drive for a thorough scrubbing every time I realize I'm glitching, and to embrace that original design, that which God has made me to be and made me to do.

On every TV show I've ever seen where two hackers are going at it, one trying to break in and one trying to block the hack, invariably one of them recognizes the other either by the style of hacking code or by some signature they embed in the code. Apparently, even when all you're typing are backslashes and strings of nonsensical abbreviations, your own unique flavor bleeds through, and someone who is familiar enough with your work will always be able to tell it's you.

My factory settings, my original coding, is all God. His handiwork, His brainchild, His artistry. And if I go digging through my root code looking for God's signature, His style, His flavor bleeding through, then I will know what of me is original programming and what is not.

Which begs the question: What is God like? What *is* His signature?

Unfortunately, this world is not short on opinions on what God is like. Study the religions that have existed throughout history and you will literally come up with every picture, description, and characterization in the book. Survey the religions that are still around and still have followers, and you will still have every version of God that's possible to come up with. Limit your survey to Christian denominations and you will still have so many answers that you will want to throw your hands up in despair.

If you have a picture in your head of who God is, go looking and someone somewhere will validate it. If you have a picture in your head of who God is, go looking and someone somewhere will deny it vehemently. There's a reason religion is one of the two topics you do not bring up at family gatherings: Everyone has an opinion, and nobody agrees. If you want opinions, go online. But if you want answers, there's only one place to look.

Originally, God walked among humankind. We would not have had to question who He was because He would have been right in front of our faces. His voice in our ears, His works on display. Originally, God's creation, us included, would have reflected Him perfectly. We would not have had to wonder what God is like because creation was quite obviously shouting it from the mountaintops. Originally, you and I would have had 20/20 vision when it comes to seeing God. No guesswork, no difference of opinion, no confusion. We would not have had to theorize what God is like because we would all see exactly, no exaggeration, no understatement, no misunderstanding, no mistake.

But creation was corrupted and God could no longer walk among us like He did. And every set of eyes clouded over, turned nearsighted, and went blind.[233]

So, how do we know what God is like—let alone what we are supposed to be like?

Well, God, knowing our dilemma, decided to describe Himself as clearly as possible, so that there would be no misunderstanding. So that we would not see His work only from our limited perspective and have to guess at His intentions or motives. So that we would *know* who He is. And so, bypassing all the corruption and confusion, God wrote down an autobiography—truth, perfectly recorded, all from His own untainted perspective.[234]

God wrote down His story, His heart, His thoughts, His intentions, and His actions, so that there could be no mistaking who He is. That written-down character sketch of God is called the Bible.

Unfortunately, the eyes of every person who picks up that perfect book are still one hundred percent blind. That's where the Holy Spirit comes in.

When Jesus came down from heaven to walk upon this earth, He came "as a light to the nations, to open blind eyes, to bring out prisoners from the dungeon."[235] He came "that He may give eternal life. This is eternal life, that they may know You, the only true God, and Jesus Christ whom You have sent."[236] And when He left this earth, He left behind a Helper, the Spirit of Truth, who, along with letting us know the grace is in the mail when we sin, would also be there to open our eyes to the truth, to what God *is* like and what life *should* be.[237]

So, with God's perfect words in our hands and the Holy Spirit opening our eyes to finally see, you and I have a chance to know God. To know who He is, what He's like, even, on occasion, how He feels and what He thinks. Once I know that, I know also who I am supposed to be.

For instance, if God is truth,[238] then honesty is my original coding.[239] If I am a liar, I have been infected with a virus.[240]

If God is holy,[241] then purity is in my very nature.[242] Moral compromise is a corruption of that nature.[243]

If God is faithful, a keeper of promises,[244] then I am designed to do the same.[245] Cheating and betrayal are a corruption of that design.[246]

If God is a God of second chances,[247] then I am wired to forgive.[248] Holding a grudge is a glitch.[249]

If God is love,[250] then kindness and understanding are my default setting.[251] Hatred and judgment are aberrations.[252]

And yet "who God is" is a vast topic that would take an eternity of study. In the words of the Apostle John at the end of his biography of Jesus, "And there are also many other things which Jesus did, which if they were written in detail, I suppose that even the world itself would not contain the books that would be written."[253] And in the words of the hymn writer, "Could we with ink the ocean fill and were the skies of parchment made, were every stalk on earth a quill and every man a scribe by trade, to write the love of God above would drain the ocean dry, nor could the scroll contain the whole though stretched from sky to sky."[254]

Just to demonstrate, I looked up the phrase "God is" in a concordance, and this is the list I came up with. Notice this is by no means an exhaustive list of who God is, because it does not take into account phrasing like "holy is the LORD"[255] or "The LORD, the LORD God, compassionate and gracious, slow to anger, and abounding in lovingkindness and truth."[256] I've even trimmed out some repeats, and it's still a pretty long list:

- God is the God of gods and the Lord of lords, the great, the mighty, and the awesome God who does not show partiality nor take a bribe. (Deuteronomy 10:17)
- God is a dwelling place, and underneath are the everlasting arms. (Deuteronomy 33:27)

- God is gracious and compassionate. (2 Chronicles 30:9)
- God is greater than man. (Job 33:12)
- God is mighty but does not despise any; He is mighty in strength of understanding. (Job 36:5)
- God is exalted in power; who is a teacher like Him? (Job 36:22)
- God is our refuge and strength, a very present help in trouble. (Psalm 46:1)
- God is the King of all the earth. (Psalm 47:7)
- God is my helper; the Lord is the sustainer of my soul. (Psalm 54:4)
- This I know, that God is for me. (Psalm 56:9)
- God is my stronghold, the God who shows me lovingkindness. (Psalm 59:17)
- God is to us a God of deliverances; and to God the Lord belong escapes from death. (Psalm 68:20)
- God is good to Israel, to those who are pure in heart. (Psalm 73:1)
- God is the strength of my heart and my portion forever. (Psalm 73: 26)
- God is the Judge; He puts down one and exalts another. (Psalm 75:7)

- God is a sun and shield; the LORD gives grace and glory; no good thing does He withhold from those who walk uprightly. (Psalm 84:11)
- God is in the heavens; He does whatever He pleases. (Psalm 115:3)
- God is compassionate. (Psalm 116:5)
- God is my salvation, I will trust and not be afraid; for the LORD God is my strength and song, and He has become my salvation. (Isaiah 12:2)
- God is ruler over the realm of mankind and... He sets over it whomever He wishes (Daniel 5:21)
- God is righteous with respect to all His deeds which He has done. (Daniel 9:14)
- A jealous and avenging God is the LORD; the LORD is avenging and wrathful. The LORD takes vengeance on His adversaries, and He reserves wrath for His enemies. (Nahum 1:2)
- God is in your midst, a victorious warrior. He will exult over you with joy, He will be quiet in His love, He will rejoice over you with shouts of joy. (Zephaniah 3:17)
- God is true. (John 3:33)
- God is spirit. (John 4:24)

- God is the one who justifies. (Romans 8:33)
- God is faithful. (1 Corinthians 1:9)
- God is not a God of confusion but of peace. (1 Corinthians 14:33)
- God is a consuming fire. (Hebrews 12:29)
- God is opposed to the proud, but gives grace to the humble. (James 4:6)
- God is Light, and in Him there is no darkness at all. (1 John 1:5)
- God is greater than our hearts and knows all things. (1 John 3:20)
- God is love. (1 John 4:8)

I am reminded of the story of the three blind men and the elephant. One touches his trunk and announces the elephant is a hose. One touches his tail and announces it's a rope. Another touches his leg and says it's a tree. All of the verses listed above do one thing: they tell us *something* about God. They give us a quick glimpse out of the corner of our eye, a single touch with one finger. Perhaps if I spent a lifetime blundering along the elephant, running my hands along it from piece to piece, I might eventually form a picture in my head of what I'm touching. And with a long enough list of what God does, or a long enough list of His attributes and characteristics, or a long enough encyclopedia of His names, perhaps I might put together a patchwork God at some point. But it would always be faulty and missing something because none of these things give me the whole.

Except the last one.

"Love" is not an adjective. It's not a description, one in a long list of things that God is like. "Love" is a noun. If you want to get technical, a predicate nominative rather than a predicate adjective. Something that defines rather than describes. This is what God is, top to bottom, trunk to tail, A to Z. God is love.

So here I am, little ole me, blundering along, blind and trying not just to know God but to put Him on display, and I have stumbled upon the very thing—the only thing—that sums Him up completely.

In addition to being full of descriptions of God, the Bible is also full of ways that I can hit the mark. Commands to obey, ways to put each of these characteristics of God on display. And just as the entirety of God is summed up in one single word (love), every command in Scripture is also summed up...

... in that *very same word.*

Once upon a time, a lawyer, perhaps blundering around blindly like the rest of us, just needed things to be simple (perhaps the first and last lawyer in history who did), and asked Jesus "'Teacher, which is the great commandment in the Law?' And He said to him, "'YOU SHALL LOVE THE LORD YOUR GOD WITH ALL YOUR HEART, AND WITH ALL YOUR SOUL, AND WITH ALL YOUR MIND." This is the great and foremost commandment. The second is like it, "YOU SHALL LOVE YOUR NEIGHBOR AS YOURSELF." On these two commandments depend the whole Law and the Prophets.'"[257]

Wait a second. What happened to righteousness and discipline and service? What about all the other aspects of God? Truth and justice and the holiness that is a consuming fire? If we neglect all that, we'll become soft. We'll miss truth. We'll be tickling people's ears and simply telling them what they want to hear instead of what they *need* to hear.[258] It's too easy. "Love." How nice, how quaint. How utterly missing in the entirety of God!

And yet, Jesus Himself claims that the entire Word of God is summed up by a single word: love.[259] Putting on display the one aspect of the character of God which sums Him up entirely.[260]

Allow me to demonstrate.

The purpose of an electrical cord is to take power from the source to the people, to light their homes, to run their devices, to enable them to live at the most efficient level possible. But an electrical cord is made up of two parts, the conductive part that is the wire, and the non-conductive part that is the rubber coating.

We are supposed to put God on display. We are called to take God's words, His ways, everything that empowers a life, and carry it from the source—God—to the people who need it. And we are called to do it in two parts: "Speaking the truth in love."[261] In truth, which is the wire, and in love, which is the rubber coating.

The purpose of the metal wire is to conduct power, but the purpose of the rubber coating is to ensure that that's all it does and to keep it from doing that which it's not supposed to do, such as setting fires and frying pacemakers.

There are two dangers that are warned about in Scripture. The first is to have love without truth.[262] This is to have an empty rubber sleeve with no wire inside. The lights won't turn on, the computer won't charge, and there is no power to the life. The other danger is to have truth without love,[263] to have the wire without the rubber coating. One is useless, harmless, ineffectual. The other is painful, harmful, deadly. Both are a failure to take the powerful truth of God and the powerful love of God and get them to a lost and dying world. Both are a failure to perform the function that we as Christians are meant to perform.

If the Bible warns about both dangers, then what am I to do? If neither is godly or an accurate display of Christ, then where am I to land? Where do I fall if I cannot walk this tightrope?

Choose love.

No one ever shied away from an empty rubber tube, but one zap from a naked, unprotected wire—truth without love—and people will jerk their hand back, wincing in pain, and stay as far away from the power cord (Christians) as they can get. And worse yet, unprotected by love, truth shorts out, and because there is a short in the wire, the power never reaches its intended destination, never accomplishes its intended purpose, and fails to light up a life. It only sets fires and stops hearts.[264]

If I am naked truth, then I must do more than coat myself with love in order to be the instrument of glory that God made me to be. Now I must coat myself in love and then go about healing the hurt I have inflicted before the people I wish to reach are willing to get anywhere near me again. And only then can I hope to convey God's glory to a desperate people.

But if all I am is an empty rubber tube, empty of truth but full of love, then my task is simple. Begin to thread the wire of truth through my life and, lo and behold, those around me are still in perfect position to receive the power that runs through me, having never run away in the first place. They receive the truth because they have learned not to be afraid of the Christian who loves.

If all I care about is truth, love comes hard. I will see every sin and hate it, every failure and judge it. I will see the great chasm of difference between me and them and lift my voice loudly to God like the Pharisee in the temple to thank Him that I am not like this sinner.[265]

But if all I care about is love, truth comes easy. What else would I tell the hurting but the truth because it is the truth that heals? What else would I tell the imprisoned but the truth because the truth sets free?[266] What else would I tell the lost but the truth? Because only the Truth knows the Way, and the Way brings Life.[267]

I wish to speak truth, and I wish to do it out of love. I do not want to sacrifice one for the other. I do not wish to choose one over the other. Nor do I wish to neglect any of the marvelous and multifaceted aspects of the character of God, nor a single command of Scripture. But if I am still learning, if I am still growing, if I am still immature, if I have yet to achieve that perfect synthesis of truth and love and everything else that was Jesus Christ walking on this earth, then I choose love. Not at the expense of the truth, not to the exclusion of the truth, and not in opposition to the truth, but because there is no better conduit for the truth.

I choose love because Jesus did in going to the cross. In emptying Himself of so much of what makes Him God,[268] in allowing lies to win the day and truth to remain silent,[269] He chose love above all. I choose love. When love demands I speak, truth will be what comes out. And when love calls for silence, I will keep my mouth closed, because with or without words, nothing speaks louder than love.

If "love" is who God is, summed up in one word, and "to love" is the command that sums up all others so that I can put the immeasurable, incomparable God on display, then no wonder "they will know we are Christians by our love."[270]

"We love, because He first loved us,"[271] so maybe the best way to obey this command and fulfill our purpose is to first know, as completely and fully as possible, God's great love for us. When I know God's love, it is transformative, overwhelming, and overflowing. Love—on every level and for every person whether family, friends, strangers, or enemies—will be inevitable.

So... maybe I *am* meant to simply sit under the faucet of God's love, filling until I overflow. After all, what puts God on display better than that?

No book of any size could ever capture God completely. No eyes, no matter how wide opened they may be, will ever see God in His entirety. No life is long enough to possibly display God fully. But this is where we start. The only place to start. So, sit under the faucet with me and prepare to overflow.

If, in the cacophony of news and noise and social media and busyness and all the things clamoring for your attention, only one verse of Scripture has ever reached your ears before now, it was probably John 3:16. And there's a reason for it. That verse is bursting with something mind-blowing.

"For God so loved the world, that He gave His only begotten Son, that whoever believes in Him shall not perish, but have eternal life."

We only really have the one English word to say *world*, but in the New Testament, there is more than one Greek word that gets translated that way. And since the New Testament was written in Roman times, one of those words was the one Romans used for the Roman Empire. The known world. The conquered world. To the edge of the map. Beyond that, there be monsters. Well, actually, beyond that were the "barbarians." They didn't count as people. They didn't count as part of the world. Uncivilized savages. Not worth mentioning. Just a slight obstacle in the way of expanding the borders of the world that counts.

That is not the word God used to describe the extent and reach of His love.

The word God uses is *kosmos*. As in "cosmos." The biggest, broadest term possible. Not planet. Not galaxy. Not this particular universe in the multiverse (if you subscribe to such things). There is no limit or border to this word. There are no people beyond its reach. The love that sent Jesus Christ to the cross excludes no one. Everybody, saved or not, going to be or not, is included in this love of God.

But here's what's crazy: God's love only gets bigger from there. And if you want to get in on that, on the immense riches of grace that only grow from there, then you have to get in on the ground floor and embrace the love Jesus had for you that sent Him to the cross to take your sin and give you life. You accept that marvelous gift of salvation and it only gets better from there.

Every year when I was a child, my parents would take me, my brother, and my sister to the Tulsa State Fair. We'd watch the barrel racing and the calf roping and never ride the rides because they cost money. But our favorite part was walking through the booths and watching all the demonstrations (mostly because those buildings were air conditioned).

Romans 5:8 describes the cross as the "demonstration" of God's love. "But God demonstrates His own love toward us, in that while we were yet sinners, Christ died for us."

When the folks at the Tulsa State Fair "demonstrated" the Vitamix blender, they'd mix up something tasty and pour it into tiny little cups and give them out as free samples. Basically saying that here is just a taste of what you can expect if you buy this blender.

All my life I imagined the cross to be the pinnacle of God's love, the peak of it. God's love builds up to it and that's the cap on God's love. But if that is His demonstration, if that is the sample of what we can expect from the love of God, it is unimaginable what we're in for.

Romans 8:32 posits a question. If God gave us His Son, what won't He do? What won't He give—and freely? There is no length too far that God would not go. Jesus introduces God's love to us in the best way possible, letting us know exactly what kind of new morning mercies we can expect every day from here on out.

Ephesians 2:1–7 says that God raised us from the dead so that in the ages to come He could shower us with His greatness, with His kindness, with all the riches of His love that overflow from that first act of love that was Jesus.

Jesus giving His very life, accepting all the wrath of God, dying in our place—this is just Him setting the bar. This is His opening act. This is the free sample. Just a taste. A promise of bigger and better things to come. The groundwork on which a life of God loving us would be built. This is only the beginning.

And why did God love me? Why would He give His Son for me? Why would He want to call me His bride, take me home with Him, carry me over the threshold, and build me a house? Why would He want to spend forever... with *me*?

This is what God said to Israel: "The LORD did not set His love on you nor choose you because you were more in number than any of the peoples, for you were the fewest of all the peoples. But it is because the LORD loved you and because He kept the oath which He swore to your fathers."[272]

God didn't love you and choose you because you were something. He made you something because He loved and chose you. God loves and chooses you because you are chosen and beloved. God, the self-existent one, can have no other reason for His favor than that He feels favorably toward someone.

He chose to love us before we'd ever done anything.[273] And He chooses to love us in spite of all the things we've done.[274]

There's a song popular on the radio called "Good, Good Father." The chorus goes, "You're a good, good Father. It's who You are... And I'm loved by You. It's who I am."[275] That always bugged me because I always felt that being loved by God, that's who *He* is. The love of God is not a function of who I am. It's a function of *His* character, His choice to love me when I was not lovable. And that's true. He doesn't love me *because* of who I am, but He does love me. And that makes me who I am.

Think about a child who grows up in the foster system, the bad side of the foster system. He's always wondering why his parents gave him up, why they didn't love him, what he did wrong. He's bounced from place to place. Sometimes he's treated okay, sometimes neglected, sometimes abused, and he's never sure how long it will last and what the next place will be like. Sometimes he's only tolerated because of the government check the foster parents receive. And sometimes he's more trouble than he's worth and, for whatever reason, "it just didn't work out," and he's on to the next place.

Love for this child would be conditional—as long as he's well-behaved, not too much trouble, and worth the paycheck, he's allowed to stay. Love for this child would be temporary. As soon as he's eighteen, it's over. No one's going to look out for him, nobody cares what happens to him, and he's got to provide a roof for his own head and food for his own table because nobody's getting paid anymore. Love for this child would be limited. He's loved enough to be fed and clothed, for a roof to be put over his head and school supplies to be purchased. But a child needs more love than that. A person needs more love than that.

On the other hand, you've got a child who grows up with both his parents and they love him. They support him. They encourage him. They tell him he is loved and that they are proud. No matter what he brings home on his report card or how many times he messes up, they still love him, and he still knows it.

While there are exceptions to every rule, there is a vast statistical difference between the kind of life and future the second child will have over the first. The first child, who grows up with love that is conditional, temporary, and limited, will likely end up on the streets, on drugs, in a gang, in prison, or dead. The second is graduating college, holding down a job, and starting a family of his own. Why?

Because as we're growing up, our brains are wiring themselves, and every experience directs how that wiring goes. And, as an adult, that wiring determines your personality, your decision-making processes, your thought processes, your emotional makeup, and so on.

And I would suggest that the chief factor in how your brain wires itself is whether or not you are loved. The person you are is different when you are loved. Your behavior is different when you are loved. Your future is different when you are loved. *You are different.*

I am loved by You. It's who I am.

Because I am loved by God, my brain is wiring itself differently. Because I am loved by God, my behavior is different. Because I am loved by God, my future is bright. I am loved by God, and that's what makes me who I am.

Do you want to know who you are? Summed up in one word?

You are loved.

We could stop there. That is a rather cataclysmic collision of me and the Almighty, a rather end-all statement that would silence the voices and suck the fear out of the storm. It's big. It's one thing to *be* loved. It's another to know it.

There are foster kids who, after being unloved for years, end up in a good home but can't bring themselves to believe it. And, expecting it to end, they keep on acting like love is temporary or selfishly motivated or conditional, and they keep on going like they're not loved. EVEN THOUGH THEY ARE.

So, having spent years as an enemy of God, on the wrong side of His justice, I am now at the place where salvation is mine and God's love is just pouring over the side, dousing me and overwhelming me, but am I acting like I'm loved, or am I acting according to the old wiring? Am I still trying to do all the right things and avoid messing up too badly because I'm afraid the love of God will reach its limit? That it will fade or diminish because I'm not living up to His standards? Am I acting out, misbehaving and testing all the boundaries because I'm certain I can't be loved, I don't deserve it, and it'll end eventually, so why bother? Am I letting the lies of Satan define me instead of letting myself be defined by the love that is mine? Do I believe this truth—I'm loved by You; it's who I am?

The Apostle Paul said in Ephesians 3:18–19 that he was praying something inconceivable for the Ephesians. Something utterly impossible. Something beyond imagining.

"That you... may be able to comprehend with all the saints what is the breadth and width and height and depth, and to know the love of Christ which surpasses knowledge, that you may be filled up to all the fullness of God."

Did you catch that? That they may know that surpasses knowledge. That they would know the unknowable, understand the inexplicable, grasp the unfathomable, take hold of the inconceivable. But as anyone who's watched *The Princess Bride* knows, the inconceivable has happened.

God has done the inconceivable when He gave us His Son—pretty words, aren't they? "Gave us His Son." As if He handed us a nice, prettily-wrapped gift rather than slaughtering His very own Son for our salvation. This is inconceivable. But He asks us to do the inconceivable when He tells us, almost dares us, to go ahead and try to get our arms around the size of it.

It's impossible. But that's okay. If there is nothing so formative as being loved, then there is nothing so trans-formative as knowing it. It's the greatest, most wonderful thing I'll ever fall short of achieving. The best goal I'll never reach. The best prize I'll never get my hands around. And it's one endless pursuit I'll gladly spend my life on. After all, it's who I am.

LIVING THE TRUTH

What is my favorite attribute of God? What about it do I love so much? Assuming that attribute isn't love itself, how does God's love influence that attribute? Does applying God's love to God's fill-in-the-blank change how I understand God?

How do I define *glory* or *to glorify*? Does that line up with "God on display" or "to put God on display"? Does that understanding of the word change my efforts to glorify God at all? If I saw glorifying God not as my job but as my nature, how would my day-to-day life change?

In what ways do I miss the mark that is the glory of God? What would God look like on display in those areas?

How would I describe my character, my coding? (Make a list.) What items on that list have God's signature style on it? What items on that list are virus glitches? Are there any parts of God's signature style that I'm not embracing? Are there any virus glitches that I am?

In what areas of my life am I finding it a struggle to glorify God? How long have I struggled with those things? Give this a try: For a set amount of time (a week, a month, a year), replace those efforts with love, beginning with sitting under the faucet of God's love for me. How did it go? Did this in any way affect those ways I've been struggling to glorify God?

In what ways do I act like the beloved child of God I am? In what ways am I still acting like that foster child who isn't sure? What in my life would change if I *knew* I was loved unconditionally, unreservedly, unfathomably?

CHAPTER 5

The Day I Died

Something happened to me on the road between Santa Fe and Pagosa Springs. I could show you the spot on the road, the place where the road rises to circle a half-mountain of red rock and scrub brush, the place where the side of the road fell away into a canyon on the other side. Yeah. I could show you the place.

Because it was in that spot that I died.

I was driving alone, in between radio stations, where the Christian music faded into static and I was left with nothing but my thoughts. I was distraught, depressed, close to suicidal, and fearful that, with a mountain on one side and a canyon on the other, I might just decide in a split second to end it all and take myself and my car over the side rather than grit my teeth and make it home again. So, I pulled over with the intent of pulling out my laptop and drowning my sorrows in a downloaded movie. The thing would not turn on.

My only recourse, my last and final option so that I was not alone with my self-destructive thoughts, was prayer. And God hadn't been listening lately. Heaven was a steel door that nothing penetrated, and my prayers never made it out of my car.

Until this one: God, don't save me now, or I'll think I did something right.

Allow me to describe who I used to be. I was trying. I was fighting. I was desperately attempting to save myself, to find the answers, to pray the magic words (hint: the above would never qualify). I wanted salvation and could not find it. I wanted faith and could not conjure it. I needed grace and could not earn it. I was lost.

And yet, upon those ridiculous words, I died. Every attempt at a perfect prayer died on my lips, every effort toward saving myself was given up as lost, and every answer I ever thought I'd found dissolved into more questions.

But grace was real, faith happened, and salvation was mine.

That day in March 2017 was the day I died. And it was the day that someone else came alive. Someone brand new.

So, if Old Me was struck dead and left in a grave on the road between Santa Fe and Pagosa Springs, then who was it who sniffed, wiped away the tears, and tentatively drove home? If I died, who lives?

That is the question I wish to answer. Not just for myself, but for you. If this moment has happened for you, if somewhere out there lies a grave where Old You was buried, then who are you now?

When I was a kid, I lived with a perpetual record hanging over my head. It might have been invisible, but it was very real. My sins went onto that record. My embarrassments, my failures, my faults. So did my accomplishments, but they didn't seem to carry much weight against what weighed me down.

I was plagued by the record of my sins, literally nauseated by it, and it would never let me forget it was there, watching everything, never forgetting, never erasing or changing. I would feel guilty, sick to my stomach, ugly and failing as long as the record showed a mistake. But after a few weeks or months, after dozens of acts of goodness, kindness, and accomplishments, that mistake would sort of fade. Or at least I imagined it did. I could feel proud, safe, happy about myself as long as the recent history overshadowed the bad stuff.

I remember this one moment, I couldn't have been much older than ten, and I was standing behind Mom's van and had this thought: "I actually feel okay right now. There's nothing to feel guilty for." I noticed it and remember it to this day because that *never* happened. I lived in constant desperation to please the God I'd offended, with a constant need to make up for my sins. I had to make it right and couldn't.

What a horrible, horrible way to live.

Ten-year-old me wasn't imagining that record hanging over her head. Colossians tells me that it was very real.[276] Old Me was right to be plagued by guilt, overwhelmed with shame, and filled with fear. Fast-forward a decade and a half and the record was far longer and darker, the guilt, fear, and shame so bad that suicide was looking attractive.

But something happened to that record on the day I died. You see, this moment—the day I died—was described long before it ever happened. In Galatians 2:20, it says, "I have been crucified with Christ; and it is no longer I who live, but Christ lives in me; and the life which I now live in the flesh I live by faith in the Son of God, who loved me and gave Himself up for me."

When Jesus, the Son of God, loved me and gave Himself up for me, it was not only His hands and feet that were nailed to the cross. In Roman times, when a criminal was crucified, they nailed a plank above his head inscribed with his crimes. And as the timid little law-abiding citizens would walk into town on the way to buy groceries, they'd see the criminals bleeding and dying and gasping for air on the side of the road, and those citizens would know exactly what led this person to be hanging on a cross. A pretty effective way of keeping the population in line.

But when Jesus was nailed to the cross, there was a bit of a hiccup in the legal proceedings. When it came time to nail His crimes above his head for the sake of the education of the public on what was and wasn't acceptable to the Roman Empire, they didn't really have anything to write. So, they went with "Jesus the Nazarene, the King of the Jews."[277] This didn't sit well with the Jews themselves, since they wanted nothing to do with Him, but by the time they complained about it, it was too late, the thing was nailed up there and they went with it.

And along with it, nailed to the cross so that every passerby would know exactly what led Jesus to be hanging on a cross, was *my* record, the very one I'd carried around for years.

"Having canceled out the certificate of debt consisting of decrees against us, which was hostile to us; and He has taken it out of the way, having nailed it to the cross."[278]

I don't know what actually happened to the planks upon which were inscribed the crimes of the condemned. I imagine they were pried off and tossed into a scrap heap so the upright tree part of the cross could be used for the next guy. Perhaps they were used as firewood—after all, they would have been considered worthless afterward. The crime was paid for. No more need for the plank. I don't really know. But I do know what happened to my plank, inscribed with my sins.

It has never been heard from again.

Whatever guilt I ever felt, Jesus died to expunge it.[279] Whatever shame I knew no longer belongs to me and I am free of it. Whatever fear I ever had has been cast out by perfect love.[280] Whatever condemnation I faced has been faced already, and ahead of me is only peace.[281] This is what it means to have my record nailed to the cross.

People speak of clean slates as if that is the highest level of clean I can hope for. To have what was previously written of me, known of me, done by me, erased so I can start over. Clean slate.

The problem with a clean slate is that as time goes on, even a clean slate will be written on. And I am far from perfect. How long do you think it would be before my slate is once again full of sins? My recent history just as checkered as my distant past? My record, perhaps shorter, but filling up once again with my crimes?

In the Old Testament, high priests would offer sacrifices for sin. Once a year, they would declare to the people that we're all good for another year. But then the next year begins, and the record starts to be written on again, and once again there had to be a sacrifice. Not anymore.

There's this protection that we have in America called double jeopardy. It means that once your debt to society is paid, you can never be sentenced again. You can never be punished again. The crime is paid for. It's gone.

My debt to society has been paid. My debt to God has been paid. And it wasn't a few years in prison. It was a death sentence. And since that sentence has already been carried out, double jeopardy applies, and I can never be charged again.

"For it was fitting for us to have such a high priest [Jesus], holy, innocent, undefiled, separated from sinners and exalted above the heavens; who does not need daily, like those high priests, to offer up sacrifices, first for His own sins and then for the sins of the people, because this He did once for all when He offered up Himself. Therefore He is able also to save forever those who draw near to God through Him, since He always lives to make intercession for them."[282]

When Jesus died, He did not just put away past sins. He put away all sins. Jesus died. Once. And that covered all of it. Past, present, future, all of it. When He comes back a second time to take us all home, there will be no mention of my record, no need for Him to take all the stuff I've done since and get rid of it again, eyes rolling as He rips the record up and gestures me through the pearly gates. It's done. Over. Double jeopardy applies. After all, once a death sentence is carried out, what more can you do? And all that can be done for the punishment of sin has been done.

Another problem with a clean slate is that there's nothing written on it. As a writer, I can tell you that very little is as daunting, frustrating, and stressful than staring at a blank page with the need to fill it with something worthwhile. Is that what I have been left with? A blank page for me to fill?

If the question is "Who am I?" and the answer is that I've been given a clean slate, then I am, in essence, an unwritten story. An unknown quantity. As of yet, a nothing. No, perhaps I am not a death-row criminal deserving of hell, but a lifetime of accomplishing absolutely nothing is not exactly something to brag about either. Who am I? Absolutely nobody! Yea!

But that's not what happened when my record got nailed to the cross. See, Jesus Himself had a record too. Thirty-three years of living on this earth as a human being, and every single action, word, thought, motive, and attitude were inscribed onto His record. Since that's nothing to kill Him for, it didn't get nailed to the cross in any sense.

So, what happened to it?

Jesus didn't just come to this earth to die. He also came to this earth to live. God could have inserted Jesus into Judean society as an adult. He could have walked out of nowhere up to the Jordan River where John the Baptist was preaching and Jesus' life could have started with the proclamation, "Behold, the Lamb of God who takes away the sin of the world!"[283] And yet it didn't. Why did Jesus have to be born here on this planet, spend thirty years quietly and patiently biding His time, working in His dad's carpentry shop, and making no fuss?

"Therefore, since the children [believers, us] share in flesh and blood, He Himself likewise also partook of the same. Therefore, He had to be made like His brethren in all things, so that He might become a merciful and faithful high priest in things pertaining to God, to make propitiation for the sins of the people. For since He Himself was tempted in that which He has suffered, He is able to come to the aid of those who are tempted."[284]

Jesus had to have a human life so He could take on human sin—my record, nailed to His cross.

But Jesus also had to have a human life so that He could live a life of righteousness here on this earth—His record, attributed to me.

"Although He was a Son, He learned obedience from the things which He suffered. And having been made perfect, He became to all those who obey Him the source of eternal salvation."[285]

"For the law of the Spirit of life in Christ Jesus has set you free from the law of sin and death. For what the Law could not do, weak as it was through the flesh, God did... so that the requirement of the Law might be fulfilled in us."[286]

Everything the law requires has been fulfilled by Jesus Christ living an obedient, perfect life. What good does that do me? All the good in the world, because what Jesus did has been credited to my account.

"[God] made [Jesus] who knew no sin to be sin on our behalf..." This, we already know. My record, nailed to His cross.

"... So that we might become the righteousness of God in Him."[287]

This is new. His record, credited to my account.

If heaven could be earned, God would look at my record and see that I earned it. If perfection could be achieved, God would look at my past and see that I achieved it. If there was a bar to reach, God would look at my history and see that I reached it. Because that's what He sees when He looks at His Son.

When God looks at me, He sees Jesus' record. He sees what Jesus did, as if I was the one who did it. He sees who Jesus is, as if I am the holy, blameless person His Son was on this earth.

Here's what's truly crazy: God's vision is not blurry. It is not inaccurate. It is not blinded by love or sentiment or wishful thinking. God does not wear rose-colored glasses. He sees what is actually there. His vision is 20/20. His vision is X-ray vision. He sees all the way beneath the surface, past the façade, beneath the exterior to the very heart, to the core of my bones, and when He looks, He sees perfectly.[288]

When God looks at me and calls me blameless, I am blameless. When God looks at me and calls me His, I am. When God looks at me and sees Jesus, it is because Jesus has taken me over. What God says I am, I am.

I wish this meant that everyone who saw me suddenly did a double take. "*Courtney*? Is that you? What happened to you? You look so different!" PS. Sometimes they do that. But usually not.

I wish this meant that everyone who knew me suddenly had a totally different opinion of me, forgot the past, forgave the wrongs I did them, discounted the person I was, and saw the new me as if I always was, like God does. But that rarely happens.

I wish every unbeliever who saw me came up and asked where I got what I have, how I became who I am, and followed me back to the source of this new life I am living. And while it is a delight when that happens, it's not a daily occurrence.

But the good news is while I may have to put up with people's opinions of me, I do not have to believe people's opinions of me. And I am certainly not defined by it. If God says I am new, then I am new.

So, whose opinion am I going to adopt as my own? God's—who sees perfectly, knows completely, and judges accurately? Or people's—who only ever see part of the picture, who cannot judge the heart no matter how hard they try, and who bring all their own gunk and preconceptions to the table? What God sees matters. What I see matters—it determines how I behave. But what other people see? That's between them and God. It's not my problem.

On the day that Adam and Eve ate that piece of fruit Satan offered them, on the day that they disobeyed the one and only rule God placed before them, on that day corruption entered into this world. It infected the plants and the ground and the animals and, most of all, the people. Corruption spread until there was nothing on this earth that wasn't affected by it.[289]

But God...

"He has granted to us His precious and magnificent promises, so that by them you may become partakers of the divine nature, having escaped the corruption that is in the world."[290]

There are two meanings for the word *escape*. The first is that somehow I avoided the thing altogether. I got out of Dodge, evaded the roadblocks, and crossed the border into Mexico before the law caught up to me. The second is that, having been overtaken, caught and captured, imprisoned and locked up, now the door has been blasted open, I have fled my cell, and I march out of that prison having *escaped*.

I don't think it's difficult to guess which meaning is intended. After all, I remember all too well the prison I was in. Cold and shivering, alone and afraid, beaten down by guilt, tormented by shame, mired in hopelessness—I know I did not escape my rightful, lawful, legal fate. I was sentenced and condemned by it.

And then I wasn't. Awakened in my prison cell, eyes opened to the door unlocked by grace itself, led out by the hand of the Lamb of God who died for me, I now stand looking back at the corruption I have escaped, and I am no longer bound by it.

The nature of man has been a subject of interest, speculation, and debate for as long as humankind has lived upon this earth. The debate about nature vs. nurture has been going on for generations, and I seriously doubt society is approaching a satisfactory answer. But God's word offers one.

Originally, my nature was corrupt. Once upon a time, Adam and Eve did something horrible. They sinned, and that corrupted their nature so that every descendant of theirs, us included, inherited the sin nature. And this is that sin nature:

"For those who are according to the flesh set their minds on the things of the flesh. For the mind set on the flesh is death... because the mind set on the flesh is hostile toward God; for it does not subject itself to the law of God, for it is not even able to do so, and those who are in the flesh cannot please God."[291]

"Not even able to do so." That's what I was. By my very nature, I absolutely *could not* do the right thing to save my life. But I am something new now.

"However you are not in the flesh but in the Spirit. If Christ is in you, though the body is dead because of sin, yet the spirit is alive because of righteousness. For you have not received a spirit of slavery leading to fear again, but you have received the spirit of adoption as sons by which we cry out, 'Abba! Father!' The Spirit Himself testifies with our spirit that we are children of God, and if children, heirs also, heirs of God and fellow heirs with Christ."[292]

Once upon a time, Jesus did something marvelous. He lived a life of righteousness and died in our place so that every child of His, myself included, inherited the new nature.[293]

If I understand this correctly, when a person has leukemia, sometimes the only way to cure it is with a bone marrow transplant. Your blood, which is cancerous, is coming from your bone marrow, which only produces more cancerous blood. In order to correct this, you have to have matching bone marrow from a healthy donor, one whose marrow produces healthy blood, in order to make your own body produce, voilà, healthy blood. Otherwise, no matter what treatment you take, what chemicals you pump into your body, what measures you go to in order to combat the disease from the outside, there is no cure. As long as your very bones are producing the disease, you're lost.

You and I, at our very core, our very nature, were producing cancerous death that God calls sin. We couldn't help it. We couldn't stop it. It flowed through our very veins and our hearts were pumping that sin to every part of our lives. No matter what poison we pumped into our systems to kill it, it just kept coming, and there was no external cure. Our only hope was to have someone else's core, someone else's essence transplanted into us, so that at our core we would begin producing life-giving blood.

Enter Jesus, peeking into my hospital room, raising His hand to volunteer: "I understand someone in here needs a bone marrow transplant?" And, wouldn't you know it, since the Son of God chose to be born into the human race like I myself was, that makes us blood relatives and a perfect match.

Regardless of your stance on nature vs. nurture or your position on exactly what kind of nature humankind is born with, most agree on this: You can't change your nature. Quite true. You can't.

But Jesus can.

Jesus did.

"Therefore, if anyone is in Christ, he is a new creature; the old things passed away; behold, new things have come."[294]

You've heard the expression, "You can't teach an old dog new tricks." Whether that is actually true of dogs or not, that is how I saw salvation for years. I once was a dog with a bad master (sin), and I did what sin taught me to do. But then I got a new master (grace), and here I am, the same old dog, trying to learn new tricks.

But the Bible describes me as a totally different creature. A more apt analogy would be that of the caterpillar. The caterpillar's body is broken down, a process that is about as deathlike as a living creature can survive. It is turned into soup and remade from the ground up. The butterfly bears no resemblance to the original creature. In fact, it is a *new* creature. There are several boxes a bug must check off in order to qualify as an insect. You look at a caterpillar, and the checklist, and the answer is no, uh, no, uh, still no. But the butterfly checks every box. It is literally a new thing.

When you and I are saved by grace, we are not old dogs learning new tricks. We are broken down into soup, as dead as dead can be, and made into something totally new. Before, we missed the boxes. Nope, nope, nope. Can't please God to save our lives. After, we check every box—holy, blameless, righteous, check, check, check. Everything a child of God should be.

When I was a kid, my family's favorite place to go for family vacation was Branson, Missouri. And there was this place called the Butterfly Pavilion, and I hated it. The butterflies that were flying through the air? Wonderful. The butterflies in the trees? Great. The butterflies landing on flowers? Rock on, little butterfly. But I was always afraid I'd step on them. Because, despite the fact that their old selves were as dead as dead can be, and despite the fact they were totally new creatures, you'd be shocked how much time butterflies spend on the ground.

You and I are new creatures. We are made to be flying through the sky or landing on flowers, and instead we find ourselves on the ground. Why? Perhaps because that's where we spent so much time. Satan would love us to forget that we are new creatures so that he can keep us creeping along the sidewalk when we could be winging our way skyward.

Most games played on the internet nowadays seem to have the idea of a virtual avatar, an online persona with virtual characteristics, virtual possessions, and virtual strengths and weaknesses. Online, you can be a mage or an orc or a level ten sorcerer. And there's this term that gamers use to differentiate what happens in the game from what happens in the outside world: IRL (in real life).

I think somewhere along the way, we've taken the idea of virtual reality, imaginary identity, a make-it-up-and-that's-what-you-are mentality, and begun to think that way.

And so, when God says my sins are washed clean, that my record is not only expunged but exchanged, that I am dressed in Christ's righteousness and am a new creation, I imagine that He rewrote my online profile. Redesigned my avatar. And here I am still sitting here, little ole me, with my pale face and poor posture, eating Cheetos out straight from the bag with my mini blinds closed, lest I accidentally get exposed to sunlight, or, God forbid, an actual human person.

No. When God changes you, He changes you IRL. Maybe not your complexion, posture, or diet (or maybe all three), but the change is real. It is not my online profile that has been rewritten. Reality has been rewritten. It's an actual character change, a change in behavior, in motivation, in status and worth. I am someone new. For real.

I grew up on the idea that if it came from me, it was horrible. If it came from God, out there somewhere, it was good. But if it came from *me*, it was automatically bad. You'd compliment someone, and they'd reply, "Oh, if there was anything good in that, it was God, not me." Okay, but "me" is different now! And just because it comes from "me" doesn't make it evil. In fact, what comes out of this new nature is definitively good.

"Delight yourself in the Lord; and He will give you the desires of your heart."²⁹⁵

This can be taken two ways: first, that whatever my heart desires, God will give me when I delight in Him. That's how I took it for years. That if I wanted what I wanted, I first had to make God my delight. I don't know that that's actually wrong, but I do believe it's incomplete. The second way to take that verse is that when I delight myself in the Lord, God will start putting into me new desires.

This is what happens when God gives me a new nature. What I want changes. What I want to do changes.

Who I want to please changes. Before, I was incapable of pleasing God.[296] Now, God is at work in me to actually want to please Him.[297] Before, sin was all I could manage. Now, righteousness is my new nature, and sin is just an old habit that Jesus Christ in me has the power to break.

"For it is God who is at work in you, both to will and to work for His good pleasure."[298] If I want to do good, it is God at work in me. If I actually do the good, it is God at work in me. And *I have God at work in me.*

There's a Pixar movie called *Inside Out* where you get to see a little girl's life from the perspective of little people-shaped emotions who run the levers, switches, buttons, and knobs inside the control center that is her brain. There's Joy, Sadness, Anger, Fear, and Disgust, and each of them vies for control of the girl's actions, trying to do what each of them insists is best for her.

You and I have a control center in our brains—buttons and knobs and levers and switches, so to speak—and it used to be run by Selfishness and Pride and Fear and Whatever-Else-Used-to-Control-Me. And then a cataclysmic cartoon-style mushroom cloud vaporized everybody at the controls, leaving nothing but thin little smoke trails rising from innocuous piles of dust.

"I have been crucified with Christ; and it is no longer I who live, but Christ lives in me."[299] And it is now Jesus Christ who is at the controls.

When Joy was at the controls, the little girl was happy. When Fear was at the controls, she was scared. When Disgust had control, she was dramatic and complaining.

When Selfishness was at my controls, I was manipulative. When Pride was at the controls, I was intolerable. When Fear was at the controls, I was pitiable.

When Jesus is at the controls, I am incredible. It is no longer I who live, but Christ who lives in me.

The Jesus who walked this earth was moved with compassion for people who didn't deserve it. The Jesus who walked this earth forgave at the drop of a hat and was delighted to do it. The Jesus who walked this earth had no end of patience with people. The Jesus who walked this earth had the weight of the world on His shoulders and still took time to address the hurting.

He touched the untouchable, forgave the unforgivable, loved the unlovable, and befriended the friendless. He hurt His reputation by associating with the outcasts. He preached peace when His countrymen called for war. He prayed for forgiveness over the men who crucified Him.

This is the character of the Man who lives in me. This is the character that belongs to me. And when I live, it is this Person who drives me.

When I believe otherwise, I creep along the ground, hoping not to get stepped on. When I accept this as true, I soar.

LIVING THE TRUTH

What have I been carrying around on my record? What impact has that had on my life? How does that make me feel?

What have I done to try to fix/erase/outweigh my record? How's that been going for me? What would I give to have my record gone? How would my day-to-day life be different if I recognized that my record is already gone?

What would it look like if Jesus had lived my life? What choices would He have made differently, what mistakes would He have avoided, what good deeds would He have done in my shoes? If this was my record, how would I look at the past differently? If this was my record, how would I look at the future?

What little people-shaped motivations used to run the control center of my brain? What happened to them the day I died? What lies do they tell me to give their ghosts control of the levers again? What is the result? How would things be different if I refused them a voice or a hand at the wheel?

What is Jesus, the Person, like? If I was to describe Him, the Man who walked this earth, to a friend, how would I describe His character? (Make a list.) This is God's quite-accurate description of *my* nature. What would happen if I accepted this as true?

If my decisions started coming from my new nature instead of old habits, what would change? If my behavior started lining up with Jesus' character in me, what would change?

CHAPTER 6
Who Are You Wearing?

O nce upon a time, there was a tiny little shepherd boy named David, and a very tall king named Saul. And when Saul, the great and mighty, was too scared to face the giant Goliath, David offered to go in his place. Saul, wishing to be helpful, magnanimously offered David the use of his own armor. But it was too big, too heavy, and David couldn't for the life of him move in that stuff. So he went without it.[300]

Several chapters ago, we discussed how important it was to know our enemy. Though God designed us for a glorious purpose, we as the human race have gotten sidelined because we have an enemy attacking us. And in the same passage where we are warned about said enemy, we are given a suit of armor to wear.

Unfortunately, sometimes it feels like just putting it on and moving in it is half the battle.

"Stand firm, therefore, having girded your loins with truth, and having put on the breastplate of righteousness, and having shod our feet with the preparation of the gospel of peace; in addition to all, taking up the shield of faith with which you will be able to extinguish all the flaming arrows of the evil one. And take the helmet of salvation, and the sword of the Spirit, which is the word of God."[301]

But God would not have designed for us armor that we could not wear, a weapon that we could not wield, and a task that we could not do. So, let's look at our armor one piece at a time, what it is and how to put it on, so that "having done everything," we can "stand firm."[302]

WHY TRUTH IS A BELT

The armor of God starts with what we call "the belt of truth." Personally, when I'm getting dressed in the morning, the belt is the last thing I put on, not the first. It's underclothes, shirt, pants, socks, shoes, and *then* I look at my outfit and decide if it calls for a belt. Does it really *need* that particular accessory?

Clearly I've never put on a suit of armor. Truth is not an accessory. It's essential, and there's a reason it goes on first.

There are two massive mistakes Christians make when putting on the armor of God. The first mistake is that they do not start with truth.

If you take up the shield of faith but do not have it anchored in truth, your faith will be reliant on the wrong thing, a lesser thing, and it will fail. If you put on the breastplate of righteousness, but do not anchor it in the truth of who God is, of what Jesus has done for you, then you are only wearing self-generated righteousness, filthy rags, and these are not only useless against fiery darts, they're also flammable. If you prepare your feet with the gospel of peace, but do not know the truth, you are the blind leading the blind. And if you dare to wield the sword without an understanding of the truth, you will be wildly swinging a weapon you are ill-equipped to handle and causing injury to everyone in your path.

And if you don the helmet of salvation, certain that your salvation is secure, but that certainty has no basis in truth, then you are in for a nasty surprise when you meet your Maker for the first time and He says, "I never knew you; depart from Me."[303]

Because truth is so essential, Satan has been attacking it from day one—not only what the truth is, but where we can find it.

Lie #1: Truth is everywhere. You'll trip over it crossing the street if you're not careful. Truth is in all of us, and if it feels like truth to me, it is true for me. This is my truth, that is your truth. Live your truth. Truth is relative, all-inclusive, and up to me.

Lie #2: Truth is nowhere.

The truth is that God, the God of truth,[304] who cannot lie,[305] wishes to be known by His people. He wishes to communicate with His people. And, unable to simply blaze among us in all His glory lest we burn,[306] He has communicated truth to us in His word, the Bible. Not only was it perfect and flawless when it was written,[307] but God has been watching over it ever since, through all the kings and emperors who tried to destroy it, through all the time, age, spiders, and exposure to sea air, and through all the languages and translations, so that what you and I have today is what He wants us to have.[308] You want to know what God has to say? Look no further than the Bible.[309] And if we find God's word hard to understand at times, fear not. Jesus left us a personal tutor who will lovingly open our eyes to the truth a piece at a time.[310]

But Satan would attack God's word as the source of truth. He seeks to paint what is literal in God's word as figurative, what is historical in God's word as parable, what is commanded in God's word as mere proverb.[311] If you don't like it, ignore it. If it doesn't work for you, reinterpret it. If it doesn't help you, go find something else that does. If it doesn't say what you want, make it say something else. He would have us believe the Bible has no more power than the next self-help book, that it lost its relevance with the fall of the Roman Empire, and that if you want a transformed life, you'll have to look elsewhere, because God offers nothing more than outdated rules, false promises, and religious guilt. The devil would have us believe the Bible is less than the God-breathed source of life-changing truth that it is. And believing it to be less, we neglect to put on the truth, and go into battle unprotected.

But people also make a second mistake. They start with truth, and that's where they stop.

There is a limit to what the truth can do. The demons know the truth.[312] Fat lot of good it does them. Scripture is one of Satan's weapons of choice.[313] It's not setting him free anytime soon. The scribes and Pharisees entrusted with the written word of God on this earth were actually the furthest from the truth of any people Jesus encountered.[314] And I myself spend years reading, studying, and memorizing the word of God, but until the Holy Spirit opened my eyes, the most my study ever did was puff me up.[315]

If, when I get dressed in the morning, I put on a belt and nothing else, I walk out my front door essentially naked. If, when I put on my armor in the morning, I put on the truth and nothing else, I walk into battle undefended. This is because truth, in order to have an effect, must be lived.

"But prove yourselves doers of the word, and not merely hearers who delude themselves. For if anyone is a hearer of the word and not a doer, he is like a man who looks at his natural face in the mirror; for once he has looked at himself and gone away, he has immediately forgotten what kind of person he was. But one who looks intently at the perfect law, the law of liberty, and abides by it, not having become a forgetful hearer but an effectual doer, this man will be blessed in what he does."[316]

"Put on the full armor of God, so that you will be able to stand firm against the schemes of the devil. Therefore, take up the full armor of God, so that you will be able to resist in the evil day."[317] The partial armor of God isn't enough. Never does Paul claim I am ready for battle until I am dressed in the *full* armor of God. Though I put on truth, I am not ready yet. I am not yet prepared for battle, and I am not yet fortified against the evil one's attacks. Not yet.

So, first, put on the belt of truth. But don't you dare stop there.

WHY RIGHTEOUSNESS IS A BREASTPLATE

"Stand firm then, with the belt of truth buckled around your waist, with the breastplate of righteousness in place."[318]

Do you know why firefighters wear red suspenders? To hold up their pants (duh). The same reason the rest of us wear belts—to hold something else up. And as I understand it, a Roman soldier's belt did not actually afford him any protection.

What?! What's the point of wearing a piece of the armor of God if it doesn't actually protect? If the belt of truth offers no protection, and does no good by itself, then why does truth matter at all?

Because of what sits on it.

The belt was meant to secure something, hold something up. The breastplate of righteousness had to be affixed to it, attached to it. It's much like, I suppose, the stabilizing waist straps on a hiker's backpack that puts all the weight on your hips since they can handle the weight better than your back and shoulders can. The breastplate sat on the belt, and it was held up and kept in place by the truth.

Stupid question, maybe, but what *is* righteousness? I have an image of a prim little back row Baptist, polishing her shiny gold halo. An external standard, a bar I have to meet. A list of good works every good Christian should do. Daily exercises to be checked off in order to be good, to be holy, to be righteous.

Actually, the Bible describes that type of righteousness quite vividly. "All of us have become like one who is unclean, and all our righteous acts are like filthy rags; we all shrivel up like a leaf, and like the wind our sins sweep us away."[319]

"Filthy rags," believe it or not, is the kid-friendly term for what "our righteousness" is in the eyes of God.

Technically, according to the Isaiah 64:6 footnote, these are "rags stained by menstrual impurity." Yuck!

Back in the day, during "that time of the month," women were considered unclean, unable to enter the temple where God's presence was. And anything they sat on became unclean. And anyone who touched them became unclean. And... well, you get the picture.

My sin makes me unworthy to enter God's presence. It makes me unclean. It sullies everyone and everything I touch. All my good deeds are my attempt at sopping up the sin and cleaning myself up, but in reality, everything my sin touches becomes sinful, even my attempts at righteousness. Now I am only spreading the uncleanness. My righteousness is only making the problem worse and contaminating everything it touches as well.

God makes it very clear that any righteousness I could achieve just doesn't measure up. Any external standards I could meet just aren't good enough. But in the same breath that He stomps all over the ludicrous idea of *my* righteousness, God tells me where righteousness comes from—better yet, what righteousness is. "But by His doing you are in Christ Jesus, who became to us... righteousness."[320]

There's this weird question that interviewers ask at those red-carpet events on TV: "Who are you wearing?" Not "what" are you wearing—that would be pretty obvious. Can't you see I'm wearing a red dress? But "who?" Who designed that drop-dead gorgeous gown you are wearing? Who made you look like that? Who did the real work behind this? Who do we credit with this spectacular vision I'm looking at? Where can I get such clothes?

Righteousness is not a what. It's a who.

Eeeek (scratchy record sound). Let me repeat that.

Righteousness is not a what. It's a who. And it is Jesus Christ I am to put on every day.

"But put on the Lord Jesus Christ."[321] It is His heart of "compassion, kindness, humility, gentleness and patience" that should come out every time I act, every time I speak.[322] It is God who is love that should govern my behavior.[323] Remember, I am crucified with Christ. It's not even me living anymore.[324]

If I put on actions or even attitudes, I am picking up something outside of me, putting something onto me that is not intrinsically, naturally me. This is insufficient. It doesn't last. It is inevitable that no matter how many times I check the box, after a certain amount of time goes by, the checkmark fades and I have to do another "righteous" thing in order to be considered righteous.

But if I put on the Lord Jesus Christ, I am simply allowing the Person inside me to come out. After all, He's the One who always knows what to say, and also when to say nothing. He knows when to agree to do something, and when to say no. He knows the right thing to do in the most complicated situations and what I should do in every circumstance. When I put on the Lord Jesus Christ, I don't have to go looking for ways to serve. They are right in front of me. When I put on the Lord Jesus Christ, I don't have to constantly police my attitude because my old attitude is dead, and the attitude of humility that sent Jesus to the cross is what lives in me now.[325] When I put on the Lord Jesus Christ, every righteous word, thought, attitude, and action is the most natural thing in the world because it comes from the One who lives in me.

All of my most vital organs are protected by this one piece of armor, the breastplate. My heart, my breath, my very core. My identity. I may not be wearing a big white X over my chest like the British once did, but Satan knows exactly where to aim. How do I protect my heart? My *self*? How do I put on something that already lives in me?

Stop being a Martha and start being a Mary. Martha had a checklist of things she thought would make her a good host to Jesus Christ, who was staying in her house. Instead, she was busy, distracted, judgmental, and totally missing the point. All the stuff Mary was supposed to do just flew out of her head as she sat, enraptured, at Jesus' feet, soaking in everything He had to say, spending time getting to know her Jesus. When Martha complained, Jesus said that of all the myriad of things she wanted to get done, only one thing in the whole world was necessary, and Mary had it down.[326]

WHY THE GOSPEL GUARDS MY STEPS

"And having shod your feed with the preparation of the gospel of peace."[327]

Since I was a little girl, I always thought this was an odd thing to include. The list of things to put on in preparation for war include truth, righteousness, faith, salvation, and the word of God, all of which are grand, overarching things with many specific applications. And to me, "the preparation of the gospel of peace" is a very specific application. So why, in the grand scheme of what is necessary for you and me to stand firm against the schemes of the devil, does being prepared to share the gospel make the list?

Perhaps because the gospel is not one narrow, specific application of something greater. The gospel is everything.

Why do you think we were left here on this earth? Once upon a time, I was lost in the dark, dead in sin, and then one day, the sunrise from on high shined into my life, opened my eyes, brought me from death to life, and seated me with Him in the heavenly places, and that is the most glorious news—gospel—that I could possibly hear. Now, the question is, why am I still here?

Is it about truth? No. If the Christian life was about you and me knowing the truth, having our eyes opened to the truth of who God is and how He works and what He wants, then the very best way for that to happen is for God to take us home immediately. After all, our minds will be infinitely capable of understanding the truth in a way we will never be able to here on earth. There will be nothing clouding our eyes, nothing confusing our minds, nothing compromising our memories or inhibiting our ability to understand the infinitude that is God. "For we know in part... but when the perfect comes, the partial will be done away. For now we see in a mirror dimly, but then face to face; now I know in part, but then I will know fully."[328]

Is it righteousness? Again, I say, no. The moment you and I reach heaven, the last of our sin nature will be done away with. All our old habits will die for good and never rise again. The whispering voices of the ghosts of who we used to be will cease. The rattling chains that used to enslave us will be broken once and for all, and we will never again be subject to what held us down. We will be made perfect, finally and completely. We will be holy as He is holy and spend forever in that state. No, if being here on earth was about righteousness, we wouldn't be here on earth. We would be in heaven.

How about faith? I think that one could be argued. Faith will be done away with in heaven. It will have its end. It will no longer be necessary, as what we once believed without seeing, we will see in all its fullness.[329] And there is a blessing for those who do not see and yet believe.[330] Perhaps we are left here on earth because there is a blessing to faith that does not exist when faith is made sight, and God does not wish us to miss out on any blessing.

But I still think us remaining here on earth for the purpose of faith is a bit of a stretch. Faith is required because no one has seen God at any time,[331] because Jesus went back to heaven and has yet to return.[332] Faith is required because life is not ended. But life is not ended because faith is required. No. We are here for another purpose.

Might it be so that salvation may have its work? Salvation is a process that God begins before the foundation of the world, where He chose us in Him for adoption that He might forever shower us with kindness.[333] Salvation is a process that continues at the moment where He justifies us—trades our sin for His righteousness and makes us new. Salvation is continued as we are conformed more and more to the image of Christ. And salvation is complete when we are glorified in heaven.[334] If the Christian life were about completing the process of salvation, God would snap His fingers and end my life the moment He saved my soul.

And if it were about the word of God, can you imagine a moment when the word of God is more alive, more effective, more powerful than when we meet the living, breathing Word Made Flesh who ever stands to intercede for us?[335] No. If the Christian life were about any of these things, heaven would be now and life would be over.

And yet it isn't. Here I am on this earth, fighting this war, and battling this enemy here and now for a reason. And that reason is the gospel.

But I must ask: How many of you reading this feel your heart sink? How many of you are thinking, "Oh, what a shame if the gospel is the whole point, because I am not cut out to share the gospel"?

I think Satan has attacked how we are taught to share the gospel so that we don't do it. It's all about making us feel guilty. If you're not sharing the gospel, you're not a good Christian; if you're not sharing the gospel, the people around you are going to hell and it's your fault; if you're not sharing the gospel, are you even a believer in Jesus? Because if you were, it would be easy, it would be constant, and the people around you would be coming to Christ in droves.

Satan has made it all about what we *have* to do, what we're *supposed* to do, what we *should* do, and that robs the gospel of peace. It robs the gospel of joy. It robs the gospel of spontaneity and passion and sincerity and everything the gospel needs to be in order to draw people to it. The gospel becomes stilted, formulaic, preachy, judgmental, awkward, and pushy, and none of those things draw people to Jesus like the lighthouse in the dark storm that the gospel should be.

Sharing the gospel ought to be like breathing. Thinking about doing it should be energizing. It should get me out of bed in the morning. It should get me revved up like a cup of coffee and send me out into the world eager to find my opportunity to do it. Sharing the gospel should embolden me. It should awaken me. It should excite me. I should be on a high after doing it, regardless of the outcome, because the thing that fills my heart with passion has overflowed and spilled out of my mouth and I couldn't help it. Because I got to stand on a rooftop and proclaim good news to the people. The gospel should let me rest at night satisfied and content because today I have done what I am on this earth to do.

So why is it not that way?

Consider this: Sharing the gospel may employ a list of verses or a series of steps or whatever mnemonic device you may use, but the gospel *is* none of those things. This is the gospel:

The gospel is a full and satisfied beggar telling a starving one where to find food.

The gospel is a cancer survivor telling the terminal patient about the miracle cure.

The gospel is offering to share an umbrella in the freezing downpour.

The gospel is the adopted child sharing hope with the one still in foster care.

The gospel is pointing out the way to a warm bed to the homeless person after I myself have just gotten off the street.

The gospel is pulling the life ring off of me as I sit safe in the boat and throwing it back out for the person still drowning.

The gospel is sharing the story of my Prince Charming finally coming to rescue me with the person who is still alone and unloved as promise there is still hope.

The gospel is the CPR that restarts a dead heart, reinflates empty lungs, and brings the dead back to life, and I just passed my certification in a world full of people dropping right in front of me.

The gospel is everything. And I, who have been given everything, am too full of the goodness of the Lord not to overflow onto those who have yet to receive it.

There is no one right way to share the gospel any more than there is one type of Christian or one type of unbeliever who needs to hear it, and never was the good news shared the same way twice in Scripture.

Stephen gave an entire lecture on the history of the Jewish people in order to present to them their Messiah.[336] Paul quoted pagan philosophers to demonstrate that these people already *knew* they were missing something essential, which gave him the opportunity to tell them exactly Who they were missing.[337] Jesus shared the good news every time He opened His mouth, and no two times were the same, because no two audiences were the same.

When He spoke to fishermen, He said, "Follow Me, and I will make you fishers of men."[338] When He spoke to shepherds, He called Himself the Good Shepherd.[339] When He spoke to farmers, He described the Farmer sowing the seed, which is the word of God, and described the hearts and their condition to receive it.[340]

Who are you? And what does the good news sound like coming from your mouth?

For my mother, it spills out in natural conversation with complete strangers, who often have never even heard the name of Jesus or the radical idea that God loves them and are eager to hear more. My sister may go months without speaking the name of Jesus to a particular person, but, after she's shown love, compassion, understanding, and interest in that person's life, suddenly they will ask the most opportune question and there is no possible answer but the good news. For me, I don't go door to door giving out gospel tracts or do medical missions in some far-off land. I preach peace to those who are near.

As one who spent years sitting in the pews of a church, years teaching Bible clubs to small children, years helping lead worship with a microphone in my hand, I knew all the answers and never knew Jesus. I spoke for God and had never encountered Him. I could share the gospel a dozen different ways, but to me it was never good, and it was never news. I wrote college papers on the doctrine of grace, but grace never amazed.

So, when I speak the good news, I will tell you of who I was, of my destitution and blindness and bold arrogance to claim to speak for a God I did not know, and the lengths God went to in order to chase me down and show me the truth for the first time. And I will tell it to you though you are sitting in a pew like me, though you are serving the Lord as I did, though you could quote circles around me and know your Bible backward and forward. Because none of those things save, and I will never again imagine that all churchgoers are heaven bound. Because I wasn't.

My mission field has a steeple on top of it, but it is no less a mission field. I could feel bad that I don't have my mother's gift for conversing with strangers or my sister's gift for befriending her neighbors. I could bemoan the fact that I am not cut out to be a foreign missionary or a door-to-door salesman offering the only thing in the world that's absolutely free. Or I can rejoice in the fact that I have a story to tell and an audience who needs to hear it. And I can share the best news that I ever received because I can't help myself.

Why is it "the gospel of peace" that is meant to guard my steps? That is meant to get me out of my tent in the morning and prompt me forward on the battlefield? Why not faith or truth or righteousness? Ought not these things guard my steps, guide my path, urge me onward?

Why am I to march forward urged on by the gospel of all things? Perhaps it's because I far too often forget what I'm fighting for. There is a heaven, and there is a hell, and people that Jesus died to save are out there, headed for a fiery judgment day, and I, having been snatched from that place when my feet were inches from the fire, have good news on the tip of my tongue.

I may be gearing up for war, but I am to be clad in peace.[341] We do not march through this world for the purpose of making war. We make war for the purpose of spreading peace.

Our real enemy is not the people we encounter. Our enemy is not flesh and blood at all, but "the world forces of this darkness... the spiritual forces of wickedness in the heavenly places."[342] It's not about holding picket signs and delineating who I hate and what I disagree with. It's about the gospel of peace, the gospel that saves. And nobody's mind, heart, or identity is going to change unless they start at salvation. You don't change yourself to come to Christ. Christ comes to you when you are dead, and it is He who changes you. I am here to put God on display, to light up the way to salvation, but it is Jesus who does the soul-saving, life-changing work, beginning to end.

If I lose sight of what and whom I'm fighting for, then I will lose heart, stay at home, and languish in a field hospital with the certainty that I can't go back out there. If

I lose sight of the people I'm fighting for, I'm lost. God saved me. This is good news. God wants to save you. That's reason enough to lace up my sandals, step outside my tent, and march into a warzone.

WHY FAITH IS A SHIELD

If the movies are to be believed, Roman suits of armor were largely metal. The shields, on the other hand, were made of wood. Unfortunately, the Greeks were notoriously fond of dipping their arrows in tar and setting them on fire. Assault a Roman legion with a volley of flaming arrows, and you've got hundreds of soldiers shrieking like little girls, throwing away big hunks of flaming wood, and running and screaming for the hills.

Interestingly, Satan doesn't attack with sword strikes or cannonballs. He strikes with arrows. Flaming arrows. That means that the shield, which is usually an asset to any soldier in combat, could just as easily become a liability. Unlike truth or righteousness or the gospel of peace, faith is as likely to be a liability as it is to be an asset.

God advertises Himself as the hope that does not disappoint,[343] as the stronghold that cannot be shaken,[344] as the living water and bread of life that completely satisfy,[345] as the God who never fails.[346] And "he who believes in Him will not be disappointed."[347]

Satan wants us disappointed. He'd love us to have hope, to have faith, to have certainty, and to believe with all our heart in something that fails us. Because when faith fails, we toss away our flaming shield and refuse to pick up another one. We refuse to be fooled again. We refuse to again be naïve, and we either march back into battle unprotected by faith and isolated from those who believe with such child-like simplicity, or we refuse to march back into the battle at all. I imagine there is nothing more intoxicating to the devil than when he has built up someone's faith so that it is a huge, strong, wooden monstrosity that he can then light on fire and use to destroy us. The bigger they come, the harder they fall. And I imagine the stronger the faith, the worse you're burned when it finally catches on fire.

When Jesus walked this earth, He extolled the virtues of faith. But it was never the size of a person's faith that mattered. In fact, He claimed that faith so small you could lose it between your fingers could cast aside mountains and remake the terrain. "Truly I say to you, if you have faith the size of a mustard seed, you will say to this mountain, 'Move from here to there,' and it will move; and nothing will be impossible to you."[348] He does not claim that nothing "possible" will be impossible for you, or nothing "reasonable" will be impossible for you. No. He uses a description of the utterly impossible to describe what even a pinch of faith can do. So, it was never the size of faith that mattered.

It was also never the strength of a person's faith that mattered. One of my favorite expressions of faith in all of Scripture was when Jesus encountered a man whose son was sick, and he said, "'If You can do anything, take pity on us and help us!' And Jesus said to him, "'If You can?" All things are possible to him who believes.' Immediately the boy's father cried out and said, 'I do believe; help my unbelief.'"[349]

Don't you love that? I believe, but I don't. I'm filled with faith and fear, hope and doubt, certainty and confusion. I am faithful, and faithless. Help me.

Thank goodness, "if we are faithless, He remains faithful."[350] And Jesus healed the boy in spite of his father's unbelief.

On the other hand, there once were seven brothers who were going around, offering to cast demons out for people. Full of bluster and absolute certainty, they went up to a demon-possessed man and attempted to cast out the evil spirit "by Jesus whom Paul preaches."[351] The demon's response was absolutely hilarious: "I recognize Jesus, and I know about Paul, but who are you?"[352] And then he beat the guys senseless and left them crawling away a bloody mess.

So, if it is neither the size nor the strength of a person's faith that matters, what does?

"In addition to all, taking up the shield of faith with which you will be able to extinguish all the flaming arrows of the evil one."[353]

Long about the time Greeks started firing flaming arrows, Romans started soaking their shields before going into battle. That way, no matter what hit it, it would just sort of fizzle out.

Imagine that for a moment. Satan cackling with glee as he nocks a tar-dipped arrow, freshly dripping from a nearby bucket of tar, holds it up to a torch to ignite it, and then lets it fly straight at me. And then...

Ftzzzzz. Nothing but an innocent curl of smoke to signal something almost happened.

Do you want to render the devil totally impotent? Do you want his attacks to have no effect but to send a rippling chuckle through the ranks? It isn't about the size or strength of your faith. It's about what your faith is dipped in. What your faith is soaked in. What your faith is... *in*.

I want my faith to be in something not just fire-resistant or fire-retardant or even fireproof, but something fire-quenching. And only God Himself can render Satan's flaming attack a laughable failure.

Abraham is lauded as being a man of faith. "By faith Abraham, when he was called, obeyed by going out to a place which he was to receive for an inheritance; and he went out, not knowing where he was going. By faith he lived as an alien in the land of promise, as in a foreign land, dwelling in tents with Isaac and Jacob, fellow heirs of the same promise; for he was looking for the city which has foundations, whose architect and builder is God."[354]

And then, the big one. "By faith Abraham, when he was tested, offered up Isaac... his only begotten son."[355]

It's tempting to put our faith in ourselves—in what *we* can do. Abraham learned that one the hard way. Promised a son, told he would be the father of a great nation, promised that the entire world would be blessed through his lineage, Abraham became confident that he could, in fact, do as God had promised. He took for himself a younger woman who was still of childbearing age and gave himself a son. We all know how that turned out.[356] There's still a great, big flaming shield in the Middle East where that one got discarded.

And had Abraham put his faith in himself when God told him to sacrifice the son of promise, Abraham would have simply refused, designated it his own job to protect what God had entrusted to him, and never made that trek of faith up that mountain.

It's tempting to put our faith in an outcome—in what we expect God to *do*. But that kind of faith is equally flammable. Abraham had his guess about the outcome: "He considered that God is able to raise people even from the dead."[357] And had Abraham put his faith in that, he would not have been listening for the voice of God to stay his hand and would have instead killed his son anyway.

Instead, Abraham put his faith in who God *is*. God is a God who keeps His promises, and God never fails. Knowing that, certain of that, and trusting nothing else, Abraham walked up that mountain willing to sacrifice his son, and his hand was stayed, and Isaac was spared. Abraham acted in faith—in faith of who God is—and was not disappointed.

It is also interesting to note that the shield is the only piece of armor that can reasonably be used to defend someone other than me. Knowing the Greeks' propensity for flaming arrows, and, perhaps, the dumping of flaming oil on people who ventured a little too close to their walls, the Romans developed a formation of soldiers, all with shields locked together, held over their heads and down to the ground on the sides so that they could creep along like a giant turtle, completely invulnerable to enemy attacks. If you are one soldier alone, all your enemy needs is a bit of an angle on you and they can get around your shield and hit you in the side. They can get under your shield and hit you in the shins. They can go over the top of your shield and get you in the head. But if the soldiers were locked together and moving in formation, there was no place an enemy could get an arrow through, and there was nowhere the army could not go.

Faith is always better, stronger, and more effective when locked together as a unit. When it is combined with the faith of my brothers and sisters on either side. When my faith defends you and yours defends me. When we are all locked together, moving in a single direction, with a single goal, side by side and step by step—that's impossible to break.

If I am planning a campaign today and I expect the enemy to be equipped with tar and torches, bows and arrows, then I am a fool if I do not begin by soaking my faith deep in who God is before I leave camp. If my faith is in the outcome of the battle, in the ground I hope to gain or the hill I hope to take, then I march carrying kindling through a battlefield hot with embers and choking on ash. If my faith is in myself, I leave myself open on all sides to an attack that I will not see coming.

I want to laugh at the devil as his best and most pointed attacks amount to nothing but a curl of smoke. I want to sing praises to the God of all creation as I march side by side with others who know the God I know, who praise the God I praise, who trust the God I trust, and who have story after story of His unfailing mercies. I want to carry faith soaked in God Himself and find myself never disappointed.

WHY SALVATION IS A HELMET

There's a French term for the very last thing to put on before you move out, the icing on the cake, the cherry on the sundae. It's a term I can't pronounce, let alone hope to spell, but perhaps this story will illustrate the term.

My cousin (older now and better with words than he used to be), was gearing up to go skiing. To ski properly, you must be attired in many layers of warm and protective gear. The proper kind of socks. Warm pants. A sweater, perhaps. Ski bibs over that. The fancy kind of jacket that is both warm and breathable lest you start to sweat, soak your clothing, and end up freezing.

And then, the very last thing you put on before you hit the slopes, in the words of my cousin: "the piece of resistance."

Having geared up with all the defensive-wear that we own, the very last piece of armor is what the Apostle Paul called "the helmet of salvation"[358] and what my cousin called the "piece of resistance." With this, the armor is complete. You are battle-ready. It is now safe to walk out among the fiery arrows at will.

When I was a teenager, I was taught how to present salvation to children, and it was done with what was called the "wordless book," a little construction paper booklet of five colors, each representing something a child needed to understand in order to receive salvation.

Perhaps because that's how salvation looked to me for so long, I imagined it to be an elementary topic. Something you learn in kindergarten, like tying your shoes or sharing your crayons. Something so basic you never really revisit it. It's simply the foundation for the more complex things that you learn, study, work at, practice, and use on a daily basis. All the while salvation is lying underneath it all, essential, but essentially dusty and forgotten.

Yes, tying your shoes may be something you learn in kindergarten. Still, it is something you cannot leave the house without doing.

Salvation is not child's play. It is not an elementary topic that we leave behind when we get older and wiser. It is something we must intentionally and determinedly remind ourselves of every day before leaving the house. Without this, I am not battle-ready. Without this, I am not safe to leave the house. Without this, forget war. I can't ski. Or visit a construction site. Or ride a tricycle. Put on the helmet of salvation or don't even consider leaving the house.

What's interesting to me is that you cannot take off salvation. It cannot be forgotten, misplaced, left behind in the tent as I go about my day. I couldn't get rid of the thing if I tried.

Salvation is a process God started before time began, and "those whom He foreknew, He predestined to become conformed to the image of His Son... And these whom He predestined, He also called, and these whom He called, He also justified, and these whom He justified, He also glorified."[359] So this process, which God began, God will finish. After all, "if God is for us, who is against us?"[360] We have been placed in His hand, and once in that place, we are immovable: "I give eternal life to them, and they will never perish; and no one will snatch them out of My hand."[361] Be assured, "He who began a good work in you will carry it on to completion."[362]

I've heard parents say to their children, "You'd forget your head if it wasn't attached." The truth is, we'd forget our salvation if it wasn't attached. And regardless of the fact that we can't actually lose it, we can absolutely live as if it is not there.

That's one of Satan's imaginary and temporary victories that he revels in along the way to his doom. Hell (the actual place) is where sin is punished, God is absent, and hope is lost. Robbed of the chance to actually drag me there, Satan will spend an exorbitant amount of energy and quite a few of those fire-tipped arrows trying to plunge me into a living hell.

Satan tells me that my past sins must be dealt with, must be atoned for, must be balanced out with the appropriate measure of penitence or good works. He tells me that I cannot rise to the heights of heart-soaring forgiveness until I have beaten the old sin out of me, until I have suffered long enough, until I have spent long enough in God's doghouse that I have finally earned the right to slink up to the big house again.

This is a lie. This is hell.

Satan tells me that with one sin too many, God will abandon me. That with the commission of the same sin one too many times, God will give up on me. That there is a depth so deep He can no longer reach me. That there is a place so far that He can no longer retrieve me. That there is a place so bad that He will not come for me. That there is a state so ugly that He will refuse to hear me, or one so far removed from me that He cannot hear, though He might wish to. Satan tells me that if my prayers are unanswered, it is because I have done something wrong. And if God's work is invisible, His voice inaudible, His will unknowable, then He isn't there—my fault, I'm sure.

Satan tells me that my old nature is ever and always who I will be—broken, lost, and ugly, unable to do the right thing. He tells me that I will never break the cycle, never escape the past, never learn my lesson. He tells me that I will never change. He puts pictures of old me over all the mirrors so that no matter what I do, I cannot see myself as anything more than the worst version of myself. He paints a bleak future, obscures the path, blocks the truth, and tells me lies, and I buy it.

And here I am, still on planet earth, freed from the condemnation that could ever send me to the true and actual hell, and yet I am living in a place where sin is punished, God may as well be absent, and hope is lost. I am plunged into a living hell when I should be experiencing heaven on earth.

Salvation is the thing that takes hell off the table for me. "Therefore there is now no condemnation for those who are in Christ Jesus."[363]

I would understand, "there is not condemnation," but *no* condemnation? Does that mean there is more than one kind? You bet there is. And not a single one of them still applies to me.

There is the condemnation of hell, which was made null and void the day Jesus saved my soul. And there is the condemnation of my own mind, trapping me in a living hell when I accept Satan's lies as fact. And that condemnation has lost its grip on me as well. How? The same way the first did: salvation. The helmet that defends my very vulnerable mind.

If accepting condemnation with my mind condemns me to a living hell, then accepting salvation with my mind saves me to live in heaven on earth.

I leave the chains of the past behind because I have been set free.[364] I leave my old self buried in the graveyard because I now walk in newness of life.[365] I walk unencumbered because the record of my sins was nailed to the cross.[366] I move fearlessly because there is nowhere I can go where God is not present, active, and in control.[367] I am delighted as I see Jesus' character replace my own, for I died and He now lives in me.[368] I represent heaven wherever I go because I am its citizen.[369] My eyes are forward, not backward, because I have a glorious future that nothing can prevent.[370]

My mind is susceptible to attacks, my eyes can play tricks, and my thoughts can be captured on the battlefield if I am not careful. And so I will not leave the house without filling my mind with salvation thoughts, setting my eyes and my mind on heavenly things where my Jesus is,[371] and guarding what is easily tricked and led astray with this most foundational truth: No one can snatch me out of His hand.[372]

WHY THE WORD OF GOD IS A SWORD

My dad is a woodworker, and one thing he insists on is having the right tool for the job. Even if it's a job he'll only be doing once, it's better to rent the right tool for the day than to try to make do with something else. You'll only spend five times longer to do a job half as well.

When I walk into my heavenly armory, I am going to find five pieces of armor—belt, breastplate, whatever piece of armor a person wears on their feet, shield, and helmet—and only one weapon. The "sword of the Spirit, which is the word of God."[373] But may I remind you what the enemy is equipped with? Flaming arrows.

If Satan is attacking from a distance, why aren't I equipped with a bow? A catapult? A cannon? A stealth bomber? Satan is sitting up there, smug in his high ground, perhaps ensconced comfortably on a nice wall, sitting back and picking me off with flaming arrows, and I am equipped with a sword that reaches as long as my arm.

Has God failed to provide me the right tool for the job?

In the words of the Apostle Paul, "May it never be."

May I suggest that if my enemy is literally out of reach of the only weapon in my arsenal, then perhaps the job of destroying him does not belong to me.

"The battle is not yours, but God's."[374] "For the battle is the LORD's."[375] "For the LORD your God is the one who goes with you, to fight for you against your enemies, to save you."[376] "You need not fight in this battle; station yourselves, stand and see the salvation of the LORD on your behalf."[377] "Victory belongs to the LORD."[378]

If I go into battle thinking it is mine to win and mine to lose, lo and behold, I open myself up to the possibility of losing and the probability of taking the credit for whatever win I eek out (see Moses and the water-from-the-rock debacle[379]). But if the battle is the Lord's, and He fights my battles for me, and it is Him I send ahead of me when I march into battle, then I am assured of victory, and the glory is His.

So, why do I have a sword? Is it merely decorative? Symbolic? Honorary? And what am I actually supposed to be *doing* while I'm out here on the battlefield? After all, I got all dressed up to be out here in the first place, and arrows are flying.

If the enemy is literally out of reach of my sword, what *can* I reach?

God doesn't send me to fight His battles for Him. And it is God Himself who will defeat Satan and cast him into hell. He sends me into battle for this purpose:

"The Spirit of the Lord God is upon me, because the Lord has anointed me to bring good news to the afflicted; He has sent me to bind up the brokenhearted, to proclaim liberty to captives and freedom to prisoners; to proclaim the favorable year of the Lord and the day of vengeance of our God; to comfort all who mourn, to grant those who mourn in Zion, giving them a garland instead of ashes, the oil of gladness instead of mourning, the mantle of praise instead of a spirit of fainting. So they will be called oaks of righteousness, the planting of the Lord, that He may be glorified."[380]

This is why I'm here. This is why we're all here. To bring good news to the afflicted. To bind up the brokenhearted. To proclaim liberty to captives and freedom to prisoners.

As I march across this battlefield, I am going to come across people who have been imprisoned by lies, crippled by shame, destroyed by fear, broken by sin. And I have a sword. Not to use on them—these people are not my enemy. "For our struggle is not against flesh and blood, but against the rulers, against the world forces of this darkness, against the spiritual forces of wickedness in the heavenly places."[381] But this sword cuts through the strongest chains, exposes the deepest lies, opens the oldest doors long rusted shut, and frees the prisoners.

But, oddly, to a world of people imprisoned in chains, seeing me coming with a sword on my hip is not the sign of impending rescue. Too often, people see the sword I carry and flee the very help I offer. Why?

Because I am not supposed to be recognized by my proficiency at wielding the word of God. The very most recognizable thing about me, the thing that signals me as a follower of Jesus Christ, a rescuer, here to help, is this:

Love.[382]

Love should stand out first when I crest the hill and they see me through the smoke. Love should sound the loudest when, through the shelling and shouting, they hear me approach. Love should shine the brightest when it's so dark you can barely make me out. Love should lead.

God's word is everything. Truth is powerful. And it is necessary to save. But what's recognizable about me should be love.

I imagine it's the difference between hearing the sirens of a police car and the sirens of an ambulance. Both are emergency services. Both are essential to the safety of the people. Both are good and beneficial and necessary. But when you hear the one coming, you know somebody's about to be in trouble and tense up, lest you get in trouble as well. When you hear the other coming, you know that someone's already in trouble and relax, because help is on the way. Lead with love, and truth can do its work.

The sword is a short-range weapon. You have to be face to face and eye to eye with someone before engaging. Perhaps this is why I am not equipped with a catapult or a bazooka. Because without ever locking eyes with the person I am here to help, I would indiscriminately blow up enemy strongholds and outposts without giving a second thought to the people trapped inside. Equipped only with a sword, I am forced to see the pain in the faces

I encounter, able to see the need in close-up detail, and wield the sword with delicacy and intention, cutting only into imprisoning iron, not imprisoned flesh.

A sword is meant to sit at your hip, right where your hand can rest on it and grab it up at a moment's notice, so that it's always at your disposal, so that it almost becomes a part of you, an extension of your arm, so they say.

When I march into battle, the last thing I want is to come across someone who's tangled in chains that are the lies of the devil, call to that person that I can help, run over to them, and reach for my scabbard, only to find I've left the one thing that could help me back in my tent.

I want the word of God to be always in my heart, ever in the back of my mind, always on the tip of my tongue. I want it reachable, available, nearby and usable whenever I come across someone in chains.

But the second-to-last thing I want to do is hurry over to that same person, intending to help, and find myself awkwardly wielding the thing as the person is flinching and fending me off with a bit lip and obvious concern, because I don't know what I'm doing and am trying to consult the sword manual with one hand while I poke uselessly at the chains.

It takes little to no practice to wear a suit of armor proficiently. Putting a helmet on your head takes no great skill or talent. Picking up a shield is not particularly difficult. Neither is strapping on a sword. But *using* it, that takes great skill, and that can only come from practice.

I can study the word of God. I can memorize the word of God. I can consume the word of God with painstaking regularity. And that helps. It is the same as sitting at the edge of a practice field and watching the swordsmen doing their thing. It is the same as studying the blocking and parrying moves in a book.

But the years of practice with the sword master that allows me to leave the castle confident of the tool in my hand? That is when I actually handle the sword with my own hands and use it as it is meant to be used. On me.

I must be careful how and where I wield that sword. It can cut flesh as easily as chains. And the word of God used against people frees no one. And so I wish to practice before I ever leave the castle, using the word of God on my own chains, wielding it against my own sin, carving the log out of my own eye before I dare approach the speck in someone else's.[383] And having become proficient with the use of the sword on my own life, I can walk out onto the battlefield certain that whatever the situation, no matter what I must cut through, I am equipped—both by sword and by experience—to deal with it.

"Finally, be strong in the Lord and in the strength of His might. Put on the full armor of God, so that you will be able to stand firm against the schemes of the devil. For our struggle is not against flesh and blood, but against the rulers, against the powers, against the world forces of this darkness, against the spiritual forces of wickedness in the heavenly places. Therefore, take up the full armor of God, so that you will be able to resist in the evil day, and having done everything, to stand firm."[384]

All this equipment has one thing in common.

We are to put on truth, and Jesus claims not only to be the bringer of truth, but to *be* that truth, and there is no other. "I am the way, and the truth, and the life; no one comes to the Father but through Me."[385]

We are to put on righteousness. And Jesus Christ died to become that very thing. "But by His doing you are in Christ Jesus, who became to us wisdom from God, and righteousness and sanctification, and redemption."[386]

We are to take every step in the gospel of peace. "For

He Himself is our peace."[387] His coming, His death, and His resurrection—everything that Jesus is—that is the good news we share. "Behold, on the mountains the feet of him who brings good news, who announces peace!"[388]

We are to defend ourselves using a shield that is soaked in the character of Jesus Himself. That's why the psalmist says, "The LORD is my strength and my shield; my heart trusts in Him, and I am helped."[389]

We are to wear a helmet of salvation: "The LORD is my strength and my song, and He has become my salvation; this is my God, and I will praise Him; my father's God, and I will extol Him."[390]

We are to wield the word of God. "And the Word became flesh, and dwelt among us, and we saw His glory, glory as of the only begotten from the Father, full of grace and truth."[391]

I say again, "Who are you wearing?" Identity may be the target, but it is also the armor, and the weapon. If it is Jesus' image I bear, His nature I act from, His character I exhibit, then it is that which I fight back with. He is the Truth I put on, the Righteousness I wear, the Salvation I am protected by, what my Shield is soaked in, the Word I fight with, and every step I take beats out the message: Jesus saves. When my identity is attacked, I attack back with Jesus.

And if Jesus is every piece of armor I put on and the sword I wield, then the time I spend in my tent, putting it all on, comes down to this: Know Jesus. Sit at His feet. Soak Him in. Never want to leave. That is how I can "be strong in the LORD and in the strength of His might." That is how I "put on the full armor of God." That is how I am wise to the devil's schemes, how I struggle against the "world forces of this darkness." And this is how I can "resist in the evil day," "having done everything, to stand firm."[392]

"God is our refuge and strength, a very present help in trouble. Therefore we will not fear, though the earth should change and though the mountains slip into the heart of the sea. The nations made an uproar, the kingdoms tottered; He raised His voice, the earth melted. The LORD of hosts is with us; the God of Jacob is our stronghold. Come, behold the works of the LORD. He makes wars to cease, He breaks the bow and cuts the spear in two; He burns the chariots with fire. Be still, and know that I am God."[393]

God does not randomly remind us to be still and know He is God in the middle of a description of His great power in battle. He reminds us to be still and know that He is God because in the middle of a great battle, that is how I put on my armor.

Standing at the edge of the sea, the Egyptians on one side and an impassible stretch of water on the other, the Israelites cried out in fear. This is what Moses said: "Do not fear! Stand by and see the salvation of the LORD which He will accomplish for you today; for the Egyptians whom you have seen today, you will never see them again forever. The LORD will fight for you while you keep silent."[394]

"While you keep silent." While you hold your peace. While you be quiet. While you rest. While you speak not a word. While you hold your tongue. While you be still.[395]

"Be still and know that I am God"—this is how we put our armor on.

"Be still and watch as God fights your battles for you"—this is how the battle is won.

Never forget who fights your battles for you, and who guards you as you go. "For the battle is the LORD's,"[396] and "he who believes in Him will not be disappointed."[397]

LIVING THE TRUTH

How much truth do I have a firm grasp of? What kind of belt would that make (for instance, a flimsy, thread-thin tie or a ridiculous boxing–champion–sized belt)? Am I satisfied with that? How best do I take in and retain information in order to put it to use? Given that, what would be the best way for me to continuously put on the belt of truth?

What do my efforts at generating and putting on my own righteousness look like in my life? In what ways does this "righteousness" leave me vulnerable to enemy attacks? What are the "many things," Martha-style, that I concern myself with? What proportion of time do I devote to those things versus the amount of time I spend doing the one necessary thing (Luke 10:38–42)?

How does the idea of sharing the gospel make me feel? What way was I taught to share the gospel, and how might that be contributing to my attitude toward it? Who are the people I'm made to reach? When it comes to the gospel, who am *I*? What does the good news sound like spilling out of *my* mouth?

How would I describe faith? When I "have faith," what is it I'm counting on? Do I know the character of God well enough to know what I can count on? What practical step can I take to ensure my faith is being bolstered from all sides by others who share it?

In what ways is my mind attacked? In what ways does salvation protect my mind? What practical thing can I do to "put on the helmet of salvation"?

How much of God's word do I have in my scabbard (easily accessible, usable, there when I need it)? In what way do I normally use the word of God? Is that what it's meant for? What specks do I routinely see in the eyes of others? What logs might I be ignoring in my own eye that need cutting out first?

CHAPTER 7

The Best Nose You Can Be

For the sake of argument, let's say for a moment that time travel was possible. Let's say you could jump into a hot tub or a DeLorean or a blue police box that's bigger on the inside than the outside and travel backward to a single time in history. Who, of all the course-changing people in human history would you like to meet? What, of all the history-making events in earth's history would you like to witness? What, of all the great moments, would you like to visit, live in, be a part of?

Whether you're a Christian or not, it is arguable that all of human history turns on a single event, a single life, that of Jesus Christ. No matter what abbreviations you use (BC and AD, or BCE and CE), time is still measured forward and backward from Him. Whether because He was the Son of God or because He was a really impressive fraud, His message changed the world, whether anyone wants to admit it or not. You can dispute that He was born of a virgin, and you can dispute that He rose from the dead, but you can't dispute that He lived, and that He changed everything. So, for a lot of Christians, if they had an Infinity Stone that controlled time, they'd travel back to the time of Jesus, see some of His miracles, hear His teaching, witness the resurrection.

Yeah, that'd be hard to top.

And yet, crazy as it sounds, Jesus did not treat His thirty-three years on this earth as the golden age of Christendom, to forever go downhill from there. When Jesus returned to heaven, He did so as if the work was just getting started. As if it was just about to explode exponentially. As if the earth shattering had just begun.

At a certain point, when my brother, sister, and I were old enough, our parents had a conversation with us about what would happen if something happened to them. *"Kids, if something happens to your mom or me, you'll go live with Uncle Russ."* Years later, they had another conversation, one about life insurance. *"Now, listen up, kids, I have a life insurance policy so you'll be okay after we're gone."* Neither was a pleasant conversation, mostly because both were just offering us consolation prizes, the next best thing after the best, most wonderful thing we could have is taken from us.

When Jesus was on His way to the cross—literally, while He was eating His final meal—He had a similar conversation with His disciples. Makes sense. He knew He was about to die, and soon after that, to leave this earth entirely. They were (it is assumed) a bunch of teenagers here, about to be apparently abandoned, thrown into confusion, and left presumably alone, and they needed to know that Jesus had made provision for them when He was gone.

"I will not leave you as orphans. I will ask the Father, and He will give you another Helper, that He may be with you forever."[398]

But Jesus did not leave His people with a consolation prize, with the next best thing, given that He Himself couldn't be with them always. What Jesus left behind, He claims, is even better than Himself. "But I tell you the truth, it is to your advantage that I go away; for if I do not go away, the Helper will not come to you; but if I go, I will send Him to you."[399] And "truly, truly, I say to you, he who believes in Me, the works that I do, he will do also;

and greater works than these he will do; because I go to the Father."[400]

Jesus, murdered, resurrected, and then taken from this world, leaving His disciples staring up at the sky, dumbstruck—this is better than had He simply remained on this earth, walking among us for two thousand years. Jesus, healing the sick, feeding the hungry, preaching peace—those He left behind would do even greater, bigger, farther-reaching things than that.

God, sitting up in heaven, looking down on Jesus and His ministry, on the tiny little spark that was the good news of salvation and the life-transforming message that was meant to change the world, had to make a decision. A critical decision. *How am I going to get this message out?*

Do you realize what options God had at His disposal? Forget hiring a skywriter. He could have etched the good news across the sky in clouds, in lightning bolts, in sunset red every evening. Forget a verse-a-day in your inbox. God could have thundered a verse from the heavens with His heavenly megaphone every morning. Forget evangelists handing out gospel tracks on street corners. He could have stationed actual angels at every crossroads in every city, capturing the attention, awe, and hearts of every passerby.

He could have left Jesus Himself, patrolling the cities, cape flapping like a superhero. Every iPhone could suddenly fritz in the middle of cat videos and Angry Birds and instead broadcast the good news. Gracious, He could simply snap His fingers and download into every brain the full word of God pre-translated into the language of the mind hearing it.

If any of those options would have been best, God would have done them. He is not limited by the resources available to Him. He doesn't have to wait for His power to recharge. He is limited by nothing. And yet, when He could have chosen absolutely *anything* to reach a dying world, He chose... the church.

Perhaps you're thinking, with a bit of awe and wonder, "Whoa, that's special." More likely you're thinking, "Bluck! *Why?*"

Sometimes the church isn't a very welcoming place. Sometimes it seems the church hurts more people than it helps. Frankly, if you're reading a book on identity, it's likely you've been hurt by people at some point in your life. And it's a pretty decent bet that some of that hurt occurred in the so-called safe space that is the church.

Uh, what were you expecting? Some of the folks attending church will be like I was for so many years:

totally lost but not knowing it. And so, even though I advertised by my T-shirts, my speech, and my activities that I was a child of God, I, in fact, knew nothing about Him and knew even less about acting like Him. A lost sinner masquerading as a believer. And the way I treated people while wearing my disguise gave them all a really bad taste in their mouths about Christians. After all, they assumed I was one.

On the other hand, the rest of the church is still made up of people who were born corrupted, lived for years in the habit of corruption, and still have a hard time breaking those habits. Selfishness, pride, and judgment still run rampant, and, as we are all still works in progress, that is not likely to change. Hopefully we are individually maturing, changing, becoming more like Christ. But collectively, the church will always be made up of people at every stage of the journey, and therefore, the church, collectively, will make mistakes, burn people, and leave a lost world less than enthused about joining up.

But here's the good news. We are not here to advertise us: Come, join the church; all your problems will be solved! We are here to advertise God. Come, all you who are weary, and He will give you rest.[401]

Allow me to make a critical distinction before we go much further. We have *church*, lowercase *c*, which refers to any given building with a steeple on top, that qualifies for tax exemption, or that considers itself a religious organization. That's not what we're talking about here. The *Church*, capital *C*, is not a building. It's a people. A group of people who are related by blood (Jesus'),[402] united by citizenship (in heaven),[403] and called to the same purpose (to put God on display).[404]

I could spend pages discussing all the ways the Church fails to do what it's supposed to do, but that sounds like guilt, not grace, and I'm not a big fan of guilt. So, assuming we all know what it looks like when the Church does church wrong, let's discuss what can happen when the Church does church right.

"Therefore I [the Apostle Paul], the prisoner of the Lord, implore you to walk in a manner worthy of the calling with which you have been called, with all humility and gentleness, with patience, showing tolerance for one another in love, being diligent to preserve the unity of the spirit in the bond of peace.

"There is one body and one Spirit [the Helper Jesus promised], just as also you were called in one hope of your calling; one Lord, one faith, one baptism, one God and Father of all who is over all and through all and in all.

"But to each one of us grace was given according to the measure of Christ's gift... for the equipping of the saints for the work of service, to the building up of the body of Christ; until we all attain to the unity of the faith, and of the knowledge of the Son of God, to a mature man, to the measure of the stature which belongs to the fullness of Christ.

"As a result, we are no longer to be children, tossed here and there by waves and carried about by every wind of doctrine, by the trickery of men, by craftiness in deceitful scheming; but speaking the truth in love, we are to grow up in all aspects into Him who is the head, even Christ, from whom the whole body, being fitted and held together by what every joint supplies, according to the proper working of each individual part, causes the growth of the body for the building up of itself in love."[405]

This is the version of the Church that had people complaining that Christians have "turned the world upside down."[406] This is the version of the Church that was investigated by the government to see if they posed a real threat, and the conclusion was, "Behold, how they love one another!"[407] This was the version of the Church whose faith was so powerful that killing them off became counterproductive, as those who witnessed their deaths were coming to Christ faster than they could be killed off.[408]

Imagine if we could be this version of the Church again.

Imagine if people stopped us on the street to find out why on earth we were so calm in the middle of trouble. Why we are so kind when people are treating us terribly. Why we bother to care for the people no one else cares for. Why we're "afflicted in every way, but not crushed; perplexed, but not despairing; persecuted, but not forsaken; struck down, but not destroyed."[409] Why we "love [our] enemies, do good to those who hate [us], bless those who curse [us], pray for those who mistreat [us]."[410] Why we do "not grieve as do the rest who have no hope."[411] Why we have "the peace of God, which surpasses comprehension."[412]

Why we are patient, kind, not jealous or bragging or arrogant or self-seeking. Why we don't keep score when we're wronged, why we don't gloat when something bad happens but are happy for others. Why we don't give up on people. Why we believe the best. Why we hope. Why we persevere. Why love never fails with us.[413]

That would turn the world upside down.

The discussion of identity, whether by secular folks or Christians, tends to be an individual thing—Who are *you* specifically, uniquely, individually? And yet we are not meant to live our lives in a vacuum, independent from everyone and everything, untouched and untouchable. We are not built to do this life alone. In a world that prizes independence and individuality, being your own role model and needing no one, we've got to remember that we are not built that way. God made us to need each other. We are meant to live as, function as, and fit together as part of a bigger whole.

"Two are better than one because they have a good return for their labor. For if either of them falls, the one will lift up his companion. But woe to the one who falls when there is not another to lift him up. Furthermore, if two lie down together they keep warm, but how can one be warm alone? And if one can overpower him who is alone, two can resist him. A cord of three strands is not quickly torn apart."[414]

Frankly, there are things that the Church can do that people (individual and alone) just can't. One person cannot be every place. And yet we are commanded to "go therefore and make disciples of all the nations, baptizing them in the name of the Father and the Son and the Holy Spirit, teaching them to observe all that I commanded you."[415] And "you will receive power when the Holy Spirit has come upon you; and you shall be My witnesses both in Jerusalem, and in all Judea and Samaria, and even to the remotest part of the earth."[416]

No one person can possibly do that. There aren't enough airline miles in the world, not enough hours in the day, not enough bandwidth in the Amazon (the jungle, not the website) to livestream yourself to the remotest parts of the earth in the limited space of a lifetime. But with a whole Church taking up this cause, the Bedouins in the desert and the Eskimos in the Arctic and the Pygmies in the jungle and the gamer in his mother's basement are all within reach of somebody who knows the good news.

One person cannot reach every heart. When Stephen preached the gospel in Acts 7, he spoke through the entire history of the Jewish people in order to demonstrate that Jesus was the Christ. But this would have meant nothing to the Gentiles Paul was preaching to. It wasn't their history. It wasn't their promises. And though Jesus was their Savior, too, they had no context for a Messiah that would have made sense. But the message of Jesus can't be squashed into a box. So, Paul, speaking to Gentiles, used their own philosophers' sayings to make the same point. He started with something they understood and were familiar with and agreed with and then made the case for Jesus from there.[417]

My church (lowercase c), the building I attend and by extension the portion of the Church (people) who attend with me, includes a couple who are part of a motorcycle club. They look the part, they dress the part, they talk the talk and walk the walk (or, I suppose, ride the ride). And they live, sleep, and breathe Jesus Christ. So the people who look, dress, talk, walk, and ride like they do have a high level of respect for this couple, and therefore, also, for everything they say about Jesus.

Also in my church is a couple who spent decades south of the border as missionaries, and though they are semi-retired, they reach out to the Spanish-speaking community in our little town, people who literally do not speak the same language as me. But because these retired missionaries speak their language, spent years immersed in their culture, and understand the ups and downs and particulars of their lives here, they have an in to speak to people who would never listen to me.

Also in my church are nurses and administrators who work at a pregnancy support center. They offer free ultrasounds, family services, parenting classes, and so on. And those young men and women who go there needing help also get the help they didn't know they needed—the good news of Jesus—from people who have the credibility to offer it, because they didn't just preach and send people away, but backed up their words with down-to-earth, practical help.[418]

The Apostle Paul says, "To the Jews I became as a Jew, so that I might win Jews; to those who are under the Law, as under the Law though not being myself under the Law, so that I might win those under the Law; to those who are without law, as without law, though not being without the law of God but under the law of Christ, so that I might win those who are without law. To the weak I became weak, that I might win the weak; I have become all things to all men, so that I may by all means save some."[419]

Without crossing the line into sin or into religious slavery, Paul found ways to associate with, live among, and become like those he tried to reach so that he was in a position to reach the hearts of those around him. Even though *I* have no way to reach any of these folks, that's okay. There aren't enough hours in the day to learn every language, soak in every culture, join every group, or volunteer in every ministry. But while I personally cannot be all things to all people, the Church can be. And I can see my church doing its part all around me.

No one person can use every method. God has made us different from one another, and no one person is meant to do everything. We are meant to do *our* thing. "Since we have gifts that differ according to the grace given to us, each of us is to exercise them accordingly: if prophecy, according to the proportion of his faith; if service, in his serving; or he who teaches, in his teaching; or he who exhorts, in his exhortation, or he who gives, with liberality; he who leads, with diligence; he who shows mercy, with cheerfulness."[420]

Maybe I have time, but not money. Rather than despair that I cannot give with liberality, I will devote my time to service. Maybe I have love, but not words. Rather despair that I cannot exhort fervently, I can sit and hug and hold and gladly show the mercy I'm made for. All I can do is what *I* can do. And that's all that's asked of me.

We are not meant to be cookie-cutter Christians, all out of the same mold, exactly the same shape, for the exact same specific purpose. If this were so, we would all have the same amount of money so we could give equally. We would all have the same skill with people so we could all lead perfectly. We would all have the same facility with words so we could exhort identically.

There is no single mold for Christians. There isn't a certain number of molds for Christians, either. We're not supposed to fit into molds. This wonderful biblical list of giftings I quoted a few paragraphs ago? You can't fit the whole of Christendom into those, because this list is only one of several, and each one has different things on it.[421]

God's people do not fit into boxes, categories, lists, or graphs. And we're not supposed to. This is not a flaw. This is by design. Because when it comes to reaching a lost world, God leaves no avenue untapped, no method untried. Some people are reached because the message was preached to them by someone with the skill to rightly handle the word of God.[422] Some people are reached because their physical needs were met by someone who delights to serve.[423] Some people are reached because in their deepest pain, someone oozing with mercy sat down beside them and wept with them.[424] And most people need all of the above, and more besides. But no one person is equipped to send God's love down every single avenue. No one person is everything another person needs. If they were, they'd be, well, Jesus.

Jesus Christ, walking around on this earth, was the image of the invisible God.[425] The fullness of the Deity in bodily form.[426] This is what God would look like if He were walking around on earth, because, well, He *was* God walking around on this earth. But only God Himself can contain God Himself. Do you have any idea how huge He is?

God's history had no beginning. There was no day when God began thinking, speaking, acting, doing. It's been going on literally forever. If someone had the capability to write at infinite speed every aspect of the life of God, the biography would never be finished, because there was never a moment when it started. It just is and always has been.

God's character has no conflict. He can be both just and merciful, both hater of sin and lover of sinners. He can be both an expert at war and the God of peace. He can be both holy and longsuffering. He can both know the future and forget past sins.[427] He can both be totally sovereign and allow choice. He can be God and Man, dead and alive again, in heaven and universally present. With the strength to crush the enemy and the gentleness not to crush me.

God's goodness has no limit. He is its definition and standard. You hold a thing up to God to see how close it is to His likeness to know the level of goodness it is. If it is good, God did it.[428] If it is a good gift, God gave it.[429] If it is a good act, it was orchestrated by God.[430]

How do you advertise a God this size on a single billboard? How do you display a God this size on a single canvas? In a single gallery? On a single internet?

You can't.

Instead of a billboard, instead of a single masterpiece hanging in a gallery, imagine a photo mosaic. Over here, you have a photo of a yellow tulip. Over there, one of a red barn. A few photos down is a kid holding a puppy. You get the idea. A thousand tiny photos, and when you're up close, all you see is a bunch of random pictures—flowers, people, buildings, and so on. But if you step back far enough, you start to see another picture, one made up of all the tiny ones. And every single photo contributes to that one jumbo image.

That is what the Church is to God. None of the individual photos is by any means the fullness of God. It's impossible. And none of the photos look like each other. Sometimes, they're so varied you can't imagine how they're actually part of the same image. But if you step back and see the Church as a whole, you'd see the multifaceted image of God on full display.

God is too big to be accurately portrayed by anyone but Jesus. No one person can put the entirety of God on display. But, created in His image to be one small photo in the mosaic, I get to put a piece of Him on display. And when I stand alongside every other photo on the wall, God is seen.

Jesus, the whole God walking around on this earth, is described as the prototype from which every subsequent child of God is patterned.[431] And all of us, each of us, individually, is meant to look like Christ.

But we are *not* meant to look like each other.

Imagine mixing every beautiful, unique, and vibrant color of paint on the palette into one blob. You end up with a colorless brown/grey/purple that has none of the beauty of the individual colors and is useless for painting anything. You can't paint with a single color. You need all of them to paint God. We have to be separate to be useful.

As a fiction writer, I have to create characters, and the temptation is to make a character I love be good at everything—have every skill, every good quality, be made for every situation. If you've ever read the Nancy Drew mysteries, she sometimes came across like that. A new situation would come up, and lo and behold, she'd have the skill needed. She'd be an expert in the field. All by herself, she could solve any mystery, no matter the context, because she was a genius at everything.

As a Christian, I have the same temptation to try to be good at everything. To accumulate every skill, cultivate every good quality, hit upon every good work like a game of Whac-A-Mole—*Ooh, there's one! Get it!* I want to be involved in every ministry, an expert for every situation, able to save any soul all by myself, no matter the context, because I am Jesus at everything.

But that's not realistic, not for a character and not for a Christian. No person is equipped for every situation. No person is an expert in every field. And Christians aren't supposed to be. Believe it or not, when we try to be good at everything, we fail at the one thing we're supposed to do.

Imagine again the photo mosaic, each photo a masterwork of color—each photo the exact *same* masterwork. Step back from the wall, and all you'd have is a brown/grey/purple blob that shows you nothing. We have to be different from one another, separate and unique, for God to be seen. Obscuring who we are made to be in order to be like someone else only obscures the image of God.

This is the Church's identity. All of us tiny photos standing together to somehow form a billboard big enough to put the infinite God on display. But to truly know *my* identity, I need to know my place on that billboard. What tiny photo am I, and how do I fit into the larger picture?

If there were a crash course in everything you could possibly need to know about functioning as one part of a larger whole, this is it. It was first taught by the Apostle Paul two thousand-ish years ago. His first students were the Corinthians, but the crash course was captured for us in 1 Corinthians 12 so that, two thousand-ish years later, we could sit in on the lessons, too.

Lesson #1 We are made to be different.

"Now there are varieties of gifts, but the same Spirit. And there are varieties of ministries, and the same Lord. There are varieties of effects, but the same God who works all things in all persons. But to each one is given the manifestation of the Spirit for the common good."[432]

Lesson #2 "Different" does not have to divide us.

"For even as the body is one and yet has many members, and all the members of the body, though they are many, are one body, so also is Christ. For by one Spirit we were all baptized into one body, whether Jews or Greeks, whether slaves or free, and we were all made to drink of one Spirit. For the body is not one member, but many."[433]

Lesson #3 Your faith doesn't have to look like my faith. My faith doesn't have to look like anyone else's.

"If the foot says, 'Because I am not a hand, I am not a part of the body,' it is not for this reason any less a part of the body. And if the ear says, 'Because I am not an eye, I am not a part of the body,' it is not for this reason any less a part of the body."[434]

Lesson #4 I am exactly what I'm supposed to be. To be anything else is to be something less.

"If the whole body were an eye, where would the hearing be? If the whole were hearing, where would the sense of smell be? But now God has placed the members, each one of them, in the body, just as He desired. If they were all one member, where would the body be?"[435]

Lesson #5 I am essential and irreplaceable.

"But now there are many members, but one body. And the eye cannot say to the hand, 'I have no need of you'; or again the head to the feet, 'I have no need of you.' On the contrary, it is much truer that the members of the body which seem to be weaker are necessary; and those members of the body which we deem less honorable, on these we bestow more abundant honor, and our less presentable members become much more presentable, whereas our more presentable members have no need of it."[436]

Lesson #6 We rise or fall together; when we work together, we rise.

"But God has so composed the body, giving more abundant honor to that member which lacked, so that there may be no division in the body, but that the members may have the same care for one another. And if one member suffers, all the members suffer with it; if one member is honored, all the members rejoice with it."[437]

It is tempting to look at others and wish I were like them. To look at me and think I should be different. To look at God and say, "Why did You make me like this?" But if I had to sum up the entire passage, it would be with this: Don't let the eyes look down their nose at you. You be the best nose you can be.

God created the Church for unity. There is no excuse to get out of it and no way around it. We are meant to be one body, all looking like Christ. But God also created the Church for individuality. There is no excuse to get out of it and no way around it, either. We are meant to be individual members of that body, and we are not meant to look like each other.

Still, "I'm not made that way" or "Hey, that's just not me" can easily become excuses, and I want to make sure we're not using our individuality as an excuse to fall back into old habits.[438]

Individuality is not an excuse to sin. Remember, sin hurts us. Sin is not good for any person or in any dosage, and God never designs anyone for sin. Different from each other yes, but all in His image, to be increasingly like Jesus, and there's nothing sinful in Jesus' nature. So, no matter how I'm made, I am meant to be throwing off the old stuff, the bad stuff, the stuff that hurts me and keeps me from being the masterpiece I'm supposed to be.

"In reference to your former manner of life... lay aside the old self, which is being corrupted in accordance with the lusts of deceit."[439]

"And put on the new self, which in the likeness of God has been created in righteousness and holiness and the truth."[440]

Individuality is not a way to avoid obedience to God's word. If God calls a thing righteous and holy and true, then that's what I want to embrace. Because that's my nature, whether I've figured it out or not. Whether I'm used to it or not. Whether it comes easily yet or not. It's a divine nature we've all inherited,[441] and righteousness *is* what's natural to us now. So, while we are all beautifully different from one another, I wouldn't be surprised if, given our common heritage, you might notice a bit of a family resemblance.

And individuality is not a reason to sit complacently by and never change. I am clearly *not* supposed to change from the unique person that God made me to be into some assembly-line Christian who looks just like everybody else. But I am *absolutely* supposed to change from the corrupted, gunk-covered, habit-ridden person I have been living like into the masterpiece that God designed me to be.

And so, I want to know who I am. Not just the basics, the generalities, the way I am the same as every other believer, but also the ways I am different, so I can put God on display exactly as intended. So, yes, of course, we are all meant to put God on display. But *how* is where things get interesting.

It's also where I run into a major problem. The intent of this book is that by the end of it, you will know who you are. Great. You get to the end of chapter 1 and know that you are created in God's image, formed by His hand, a particular masterpiece of highest value. Whoopie. You get to the end of chapter 4 and know that you are designed to put God on display by living out His character, starting with love. Yay.

But if the point of this chapter is to tell you that you are not meant to be like everyone else, then you'll end up at the end of this chapter still not knowing who *you* are, because I can't possibly cover all the possible, individual permutations of all the wonderful qualities God designs into His people.

The best I can do is give you a filter that you can run things through, to separate the gunk from the good stuff, to strain out all the things that are not you, so that what's left in the end is what is so definitely you. The work of actually sifting? That, you'll have to do yourself.

FILTER #1: If guilt tells you to do it, it's gunk.

I used to believe that guilt was a function of grace. That when the Helper, the Holy Spirit, wanted to get my attention and point something out to me that I should be doing, He'd use guilt. I'd feel that heat, that pressure, that pit in my stomach, and when I'd act on that feeling, it would finally ease. (Actually, I think they diagnose that as the anxiety disorder OCD, but that's neither here nor there.) The point is, guilt is Satan's tool. If it comes from guilt, it doesn't come from God. If guilt tells you to do it, don't do it.[442]

"But the wisdom from above is first pure, then peaceable, gentle, reasonable, full of mercy and good fruits, unwavering, without hypocrisy."[443]

Now, I ask you, does guilt feel like any of that? Does any of that feel like guilt? In fact, they are mutually exclusive, and if anything is mixed with guilt, the whole impulse needs to be thrown out, because the wisdom from above is pure.

Satan would love to have us wasting our time on every activity under the sun to the exclusion of the very things that we are, in fact, called to do. Get us tangled up in a thousand and one "good" things that we are not meant for, and we will have no time or energy left for the beautiful, masterpiece works we are designed for.

FILTER #2: If you do it "to be a good Christian," it's gunk.

It is a terrible and persistent habit within the Church throughout the centuries to teach human traditions as if they were doctrines from God.[444] To label more things "sin" than even God does. To make a longer list of things to make oneself righteous than God does. To require more of a person to be saved than the only thing God requires: the blood of Jesus Christ.

And so, even in grace-preaching, Bible-believing, freedom-spouting churches, there is an intentional or perhaps unintentional image of what constitutes a "good

Christian." Common restrictions on a "good Christian" are what we're supposed to wear or not wear, do or not do, words we do or don't use. How often we read our Bibles. How constant our church attendance is. Whether we attend an appropriate amount of Bible studies. How much we serve in church. Whether we jump to make a casserole or volunteer to serve in the church nursery when there's a need.

The problem is that every person and every church is going to have a different picture of that "good Christian," and it's impossible to please everyone. Worse, to try to serve two masters. If one of those masters is someone else's opinion of what you should be, you will cease to serve God. "For am I now seeking the favor of men, or of God? Or am I striving to please men? If I were still trying to please men, I would not be a bond-servant of Christ."[445]

If you do manage to meet someone else's standard, you will fill yourself with pride. If you fail to, you will fill yourself with insecurity. Neither is God-honoring. And neither makes you the person you're meant to be. Don't let outward people-pleasing stop you from honoring God from the heart.[446]

FILTER #3: If you do it to be like someone else, it's gunk.

A common downfall of people of passion is that when I get all fired up about a certain ministry, when my heart is broken over a particular need, when I am consumed with passion over a particular issue, I can easily put that on you, too. If you loved God as much as I do, you'd be just as concerned about this as me. If you cared about heavenly things as much as I do, you'd make this your priority, too. If you had your eyes on Jesus as much as me, you'd... be like me. After all, clearly, this is the most important thing a child of God can be doing.

My childhood pastor is all fired up about the word of God. It is life and breath to him. Where most people would love to say they'd read the Bible through in a year, he aspires to read it through one more time this year than the number of times he read it last year. Where most of us would love to say we read our Bibles every day, he reads twice a day. For pleasure. And spends the rest of the day reading it for work.

It's easy to make a case that Scripture reading and memorization should be every believer's top priority. And I'm sure my childhood pastor could easily list a hundred verses describing the value and benefits of God's word. He could give you example after example of "good Christians" who devoted themselves to the word of God as he does.

But reading God's word doesn't make a Christian good. Jesus does. And while there is no dispute as to the value and benefit of God's word, nowhere in that venerated word of God are we commanded to daily Bible reading, yearly all-the-way-through reading, or a specific amount of memorizing. To make any of those specifics *my* priority just to be like him would be to neglect whatever priority God has called me to.

A friend of mine has started a ministry of mentorship and discipleship for fatherless boys. He eats, sleeps, and breathes it. His heart breaks over these boys, over their need for Jesus, for role models, for someone to come alongside and show them what it means to be a man, let alone a man of God. He believes that single moms and their kids are the widows and orphans of today, and according to God, "Pure and undefiled religion in the sight of our God and Father is this: to visit orphans and widows in their distress."[447]

How easy it would be to say that this should be every believer's priority! That the only religion God actually likes consists of this, and everything else is busywork. How easy it would be to question: If my heart doesn't break for these boys like his does, am I even a believer? After all, love is from God, and he who does not love does not know God.[448]

And yet I am not him. God hasn't burdened my heart for this but for an entirely different thing, and if I give my heart and soul and time and energy away to what is not *mine* to do, I neglect something equally important.

But when I hear these men speak of what God is doing in their ministries and all they are doing for God, it is easy for me to feel inadequate, small, pathetic. Like I'm never doing enough.

You too? Solution: Find *your* passion. Again, don't let the eyes look down their nose at you. You be the best nose you can be.

FILTER #4: If you're good at it, it's the good stuff.

"For we are His workmanship, created in Christ Jesus for good works, which God prepared beforehand so that we would walk in them."[449]

Not only was I designed with the intent that I would perform good works, my design is also specific, so that I am capable, equipped, and adequate for those specific good works. I have literally been made *for* those good works.

When my brother and I were little, he enjoyed playing the Nintendo game *Donkey Kong* (not the arcade game but the one from the nineties). Since I had zero hand-eye coordination and abysmal reflexes, I was the Keeper of the Cheater's Manual. Each level was a maze of jungle or desert or factory or whatever, and it was easy to get lost. The best way to conquer the level was simply to follow the banana trails laid out for you, but there was so much to look at, so much to distract a person, and if my brother got off the path, that's what I was there for.

Unfortunately, God does not provide us with a cheater's manual to life, the God's-eye view for every stage of our lives, full-color depictions of where the pitfalls will be, where the prizes are, and directions on how to achieve each one. What He does give us is a banana trail. "Good works, which God prepared beforehand that we would walk in them."[450]

Just like in the game, not every banana is meant for every person. Donkey Kong was only to pick up the yellow bananas. Not the green ones or the red ones or the purple ones. If he tried, he was just wandering through semi-transparent bananas he could never actually touch or collect.

See, each of the five Kongs you were allowed to be had different strengths. Chunky Kong was big and strong enough to break boulders. Diddy Kong was fast enough to outrun a ticking clock. Tiny Kong was small enough to fit through tight spaces. And if you tried to follow the wrong banana trails, you ended up facing a task you were not equipped for.

It was frustrating. Because here you were, sitting there with a banana in sight, and instead you had to leave it for someone else. But the truth was, you weren't leaving those bananas ungathered. You were just leaving them for someone else to get. And together, all five Kongs collected every banana on the level.

Trying to do someone else's good works leaves my own works undone and leaves me frustrated, worn out, feeling like a failure. No wonder. Those works weren't set up for me, and I was not set up by God to succeed at them. But *my* pathway of good works was uniquely designed just for me. And me for them.

Since last I checked, God has not actually color-coded all the opportunities for good works out there, so I need to start with what I am good at and go from there. If I am big and strong, find a boulder. If I am tiny, find a tight space. If I am fast, find a race and run it.

If you're reading this thinking, "I have no idea what I'm good at" or perhaps, "I'm really not good at anything," then it may take some process of elimination to discover your own particular banana trails.

When I was fourteen, I joined Child Evangelism Fellowship, and learned how to teach five-day Bible clubs to little kids. I did this all summer for three summers, and once a week during the school year after school. And I learned two things:

I am really not made for kids. They're sticky. And noisy. And hyper. And I have no idea what to say to them. Where the other teenagers were high-fiving kids and playing games and blowing up balloons and having a grand time, I was trying not to step on anybody or hyperventilate. All I wanted to do was get out of there.

But I learned a second thing. I am really made to teach. Where the others were struggling to piece together a coherent Bible lesson, the process made perfect sense to me. Where the others would get stuck and forget their place and skip points accidentally, I was hitting every point. Where the others struggled to fill twenty minutes, I was struggling to hold it to thirty. Where the others were failing their evals and having to redo them, I was passing with flying colors.

And I would not have known either thing about myself without giving it a try. So, having put in the time and discovered both something that is *so* not me and something that is definitely me, I can have confidence when opportunities come up. Serving in the church nursery? Assisting with Awana? Helping in VBS? Those are bananas of someone else's color. I don't need to grasp at transparent bananas I'll only be frustrated in trying to collect.

But leading a ladies' Bible study? Speaking at a women's retreat? Why, yes! I'd be glad to. Because that's what God's made me good at. And rather than feel guilty about what I say no to, I will trust that some other Kong is made precisely for those things and will take care of it. And together, we'll get every banana out there.

FILTER #5: If it comes easy, it's the good stuff.

No one ever said life was easy. In fact, God specifically promises that it won't be. "In this world you will have trouble."[451] Pretty much a universal constant. Life gets burdensome and hard, and sometimes just getting out of bed is a challenge. We have work and responsibilities and bills and all of these things weigh heavy on us, yes.

But Jesus doesn't.

"Come to Me, all who are weary and heavy-laden, and I will give you rest. Take My yoke upon you and learn from Me, for I am gentle and humble in heart, and you will find rest for your souls. For my yoke is easy and My burden is light."[452]

When I was a kid, we visited historic Williamsburg on a vacation/homeschool field trip, and they had old-timey tools and we could see what life was like back in ye olden days. One such tool was a yoke. It was child-sized and meant to have two buckets of water hanging from either side so that a little colonial kid could haul water from the well. They even let us try it. But I couldn't even lift the yoke, much less whatever I was supposed to haul with it.

I don't believe that's the yoke Jesus was talking about. I believe what He was referring to was the tandem yoke you put on a pair of oxen. That yoke didn't actually bear any weight; it just kept the oxen together, headed in the same direction. In fact, I imagine the only time such a yoke would chafe and weigh heavy on an ox would be if it was trying to veer away from its partner.

I believe that's what Jesus' yoke is supposed to do. Not put the weight of the world on my shoulders, not put the pressure of revealing the character of God to a lost and dying world on me as if they live or die on my testimony. Rather, it's to keep me in step with Jesus, going in the same direction.

So, if walking in step with Jesus makes the burden light, then perhaps when I start to feel a burdensome heaviness on the good works before me, it's because I'm veering off in the wrong direction.

They say if you love what you do, you don't work a day in your life. It's the same with the Christian life. If you're doing what you're made to do, it doesn't feel like work. Find something that doesn't feel like work, and work at it.

I am in the terrible habit of discounting my gifts, and one of the reasons is because it comes easy. I sing backup at my church, and it comes almost as easily as breathing to me. It is not a constraint on my time, it doesn't weigh on my mind, and it costs me virtually nothing to show up and sing. And I get quite a bit of enjoyment out of it. So, if someone compliments me, I feel like throwing the compliment away, discounting what I did because it was easy.

How silly! If a burden being light is part of how I know I'm made for something, then what am I doing stomping all over it when someone sees my good works and glorifies my Father who is in heaven? That's the whole point![453] If I discount a gift because it comes naturally, I have completely missed the point of those gifts.

Warning: When you find what you're made for, the devil does not like it. And he allocates resources based on who is the biggest threat. So, if you are trudging along, minding your own business, making no trouble, he'll largely leave you alone. If you are discovering your worth, your value, your purpose, your individuality as God designed it and begin to follow the path of good works God laid out for you, watch out. The easy things don't always stay easy. Opposition begins, and you have to decide whether you will keep following God's path for you, easy or not, or whether you will go back to living under a bushel. The choice is yours.

Recently, singing—one of the easiest things in the world to me—became hard. It filled me with anxiety, made me want to crawl under a rock, and I was seized with an overwhelming desire to quit. This thing that God made me for, and I wanted to throw in the towel. But if Satan has limited resources and puts them where he thinks they'll be most useful, then I will sing on, and eventually he'll get the idea that I'm a waste of time and go bother someone else for a while. He is not stealing this from me.

FILTER #6: If it makes you happy, it's the good stuff.

I have a T-shirt I've worn for so long that the words are all but rubbed off. It currently reads, "oc... la... Pr... wa..." (you get the idea). It used to say, "Chocolate: Proof God wants us to be happy."

I wear the shirt because I love chocolate and it makes me smile. But it brings up an interesting question. *Does* God want us to be happy?

I know God wants us to be holy.[454] I know He wants us to be righteous. I know He wants us to be changed from the corrupted person we used to be. But happy?

Jesus died to start that work of change in our hearts. And (as previously mentioned) when He left this earth, He left us something even better than if we still had Jesus Himself living among us. When you have the Helper that

Jesus promised, the Holy Spirit, in your life, everything changes. Starting on the inside, He starts to change you. And here is where it starts:

"But the fruit of the Spirit is love..."

Okay, if there was a dead horse, we'd still be beating on that one. Yes, we got it, thank you.

"But the fruit of the Spirit is love, joy..."[455]

Some would argue there's a difference between "joy," some deep Jesus-thing that bears no resemblance to happiness, and "happiness," that frivolous, superficial emotion that comes from circumstances. Frankly, folks, there is one Greek word that gets translated as both "joy" and "happiness," and since God doesn't bother making a distinction, neither will I. Joy = happiness, for the purpose of this discussion.

Not only would God, who loves His children, really like for us to be happy, it is one of the fundamental, transformational things that happens to us when we have the Holy Spirit, second only to love, which is second to none.

Jesus came "that they may have life, and have it abundantly."[456] And as He was on His way to the cross, everything Jesus said to His disciples was "so that My joy may be in you, and that your joy may be full."[457]

So, yes, God wants us to be happy. I also believe it's one of the tools He uses to point us in the right direction.

About a hundred years ago, Eric Liddell was the son of missionaries. His parents were missionaries, his sister was a missionary, and it was presumed that as soon as he finished college back in England, he'd return to the mission field. After all, he was a gifted preacher. And yet, as he told his sister in the movie *Chariots of Fire,* "God made me fast. When I run, I feel God's pleasure."

It would be easy to say that, obviously, preaching the good news in China was a better use of his life than running in the Olympics. But Eric Liddell knew something about himself, about how God made him, and he was not going to throw away any good gift that God gave him just because it didn't seem as honorable as some of the others (don't let the eyes look down their nose at you. You be the best nose you can be). And so he chose to run in the Olympics.

The trouble came when the qualifying heat for his chosen race fell on a Sunday. Eric Liddell had the personal conviction that he shouldn't run on Sundays, and had he gone back on his conviction, he would have been dishonoring God.[458] So he stood up for what he believed, against the pressure from his countrymen, from his king, from his own desire to win the race, and he honored God. And God honored him, allowing a fellow runner to give up his spot in a different race so that he could run and win the gold.

You don't have to be in ministry to minister. The impact Eric Liddell made on his society at the time was huge. Every paper carried the story, everyone was talking about the runner who wouldn't run on a Sunday. And it forced everyone to ask the question, "What do I believe, and what would I give up for it?" One hundred years later, people still know of the man who stood up for his faith and ran for God. And afterward, he did return to China, and preached there until he died, because, again, he would not leave any gift God gave him unused.

I feel God's pleasure when I write. It's an easy argument to make that writing a Christian book to be used in Bible studies or adult Sunday schools or for the personal growth of Christians is obviously God-honoring. Well, duh, right?

But do you know what I get more pleasure from? Writing science fiction.

If God gave me an imagination, creativity, and a love of building a fictional world from scratch, if God puts heart-bursting, face-splitting joy in my heart when I write science fiction, then who am I to say, "No, God. I'll just wear grey and do 'godly' things instead"? No! This *is* godly because it comes from God! If love comes from the Holy Spirit and joy comes from the Holy Spirit and peace comes from the Holy Spirit, then when joy starts bursting the pipes and spilling out, I can know, absolutely, that a work of the Holy Spirit is being done here, and no work of God is ever wrong or wasted or frivolous. And I will leave no gift of God unused.

Opportunities abound. Everywhere I look, there will be a way to serve God, to serve the Church, to love people. And any and all of them may be good. But they're not all mine. And so I will run every opportunity through the filter. What is gunk and what is the good stuff *for me*? Trusting that God has someone else working on the things I say no to, knowing that no one can do what I am called to say yes to nearly so well as I can, I will stick to the pathway of good works laid out for me, and in that way, I will do exactly what I, as a masterpiece, am made to do.

Individuality is not a footnote, an aside, an "oh, by the way..." It is essential. If I want to live every ounce of salvation fully, if I want to enjoy every gift of God to the extreme, if I want to be effective in this world, happy in this life, satisfied with who God made me, I have got to know who God made me to be. And I've got to live it, so that I can put God on display exactly and specifically as intended, every day of my life.

LIVING THE TRUTH

If I was God, how would I have chosen to get the word out about salvation? In what way is the Church better than that?

What has been my experience with the church/Church (good and bad)? How do I account for that? In what ways have I contributed to the good? In what ways have I contributed to the bad? How might that change?

Who do I tend to judge for being different from me? Who tends to judge me for being different from them? In what ways might our differences actually be a better way to put God on display than if we were the same? (Be specific.) How can I make an effort toward unity with these people?

What things do I do in my Christian life out of guilt? (Make a list.) What do I do solely because that's what "good Christians" are supposed to do? (Add these to the list.) What things do I do just to be like someone else? (Add these to the list.) Now, rip up the list. Or set it on fire.

What am I good at? (Make a list.) What comes as easily as breathing to me? (Add to the list.) Fill in the blank: When I _____, I feel God's pleasure. (Add to the list.) Are there any things on this list I'm leaving undone or unused?

Are there things on the above list I discount? Why? When I imagine doing the things on the above list, what reason or excuse comes into my head that makes me change my mind? What assumptions, beliefs, or choices are getting in the way of being the best nose I can be?

CHAPTER 8
Three Hundred Broken Pots

W ho are you?

I mean it. Go ahead. Describe yourself to me in a hundred words or less. If you and I met in an elevator, and you had thirty seconds to convey you to me, so that I would walk away with a pretty decent idea of who you are, what would you say?

By the time I'm even old enough to think such complex thoughts as what my own identity should be, I've already been told who I am. Dozens of times. Hundreds of times. In a myriad of ways. I've probably been told directly, by my parents, by my grandparents, by my teachers—whoever might be so inclined as to comment on me as a person, as a daughter, as a student, or what have you. It's been implied who I am by grades, by friendships or lack of them, by where or if I'm invited to go somewhere, by whether I'm picked first or last for a team. It's been shown to me who I should be, what I should look like and act like, on every television show, movie, commercial, and social media post. By the time I'm old enough to realize how impactful my opinion of me is, I've already formed one based on every other person's opinion around me.

If I, Courtney Weir, were to form an opinion of me based on what society's opinion would be, I would see a college dropout, a lazy mooch who lives off her parents' generosity, whose fanciful writing hobby costs more to maintain than it brings in, who has no real friends and couldn't attract a guy to save her life. A girl who couldn't even take care of a dog.

That's me, in a nutshell. Not very flattering.

So perhaps I realize that stuffing myself into someone else's box is not healthy or wise and I decide to do an honest self-appraisal—no second opinions, no outside influences. Just me looking at me and measuring myself honestly. Maybe then I could come up with a more accurate image of myself to hold on to.

I'd see a published author who serves at her church, who writes, sings, and posts music online, and who occasionally has the opportunity to speak on her books' topics to women in her community.

Better, yes?

But there's still a problem.

Every measure society or I can measure myself by is going to be, by necessity, external. We might think of ourselves in terms of where we're from, where we work, the grades we make, the awards we win, the achievements we've accomplished. Often, we measure ourselves by how much money we make, what title we hold, what car we drive, what we wear, what size we wear it in, or how much we can lift. How about how much we get done in a day, or by the number of things we're involved in, or how many people notice us doing them? What about the number of friends we have, how many comments we get, or how many likes we receive? But all of these fail to tell us who we are for one very important reason.

The outside doesn't define the inside. The inside determines the outside.

When Jesus walked this earth, He encountered the very same fallacy. God had handed down to humankind a list of ways to put Him on display, ways to show Him off to a watching world, and as those laws got handed down through the centuries, a group of law-keepers came about. They held the law, copied the law, taught the law, and enforced the law. They were called Pharisees.

This is what Jesus said to them: "Woe to you, scribes and Pharisees, hypocrites! For you clean the outside of the cup and of the dish, but inside they are full of robbery and self-indulgence. You blind Pharisee, first clean the inside of the cup and of the dish, so that the outside of it may become clean also. Woe to you, scribes and Pharisees, hypocrites! For you are like whitewashed tombs which on the outside appear beautiful, but inside they are full of dead men's bones and all uncleanness. So you, too, appear righteous to men, but inwardly you are full of hypocrisy and lawlessness."[459]

The Greek word *hypocrite* literally means "to speak through a mask." It was the word for a stage actor. I presume (as this was long before the days of hi-def) that it was difficult for the precise facial expressions of an actor on stage to be seen by the poor folks in the cheap seats, so they'd hold up an exaggerated smiley or frowny or angry or whatever-face mask in front of their face and speak their lines through that.

This is what Jesus warns against. You are not the mask. You are not the outside of the cup and dish. You are not the lovely coat of whitewash. *You are what's inside.* No matter what the outside looks like. "For as [a man] thinks in his heart, so is he."[460] "It is not what enters into the mouth that defiles a man, but what proceeds out of the mouth, this defiles a man."[461] What your life produces—actions and words—is entirely dependent on the source: who you are on the inside.[462]

What I am on the inside will come out. There's no hiding it. There's no stopping it. It doesn't matter how often you whitewash the tomb. If it's rotten inside, the rot will keep eating through to the surface and it will be seen. But if you first clean the inside of the cup and dish, the outside will become clean also. "Does a fountain send out from the same opening both fresh and bitter water? Does a fig tree, my brethren, produce olives, or a vine produce figs? Nor does salt water produce fresh."[463]

Every external measure, every visible attribute, every word, every action, every attitude and impression I could make, these come from the person I am on the inside.

But it's common to not really know who I am. It's equally common to have a faulty impression of who I am.

Why? Because there is only one person on the planet who can actually see inside of me. And no, it's not me.

Once upon a time, the nation Israel started looking around at all the nations around them, and noticed that they all had kings, and, wishing to downgrade from God to king, Israel asked for one.

The first guy God chose for them was the epitome of what a king should be, head and shoulders taller than anyone. But that went badly pretty quick, so God set out to replace him, and He sent the prophet Samuel to go pick out one of Jesse's sons for the job. Jesse paraded his sons before Samuel, and "when they entered, he looked at Eliab and thought, 'Surely the LORD's anointed is before Him.' But the LORD said to Samuel, 'Do not look at his appearance or at the height of his stature, because I have rejected him; for God sees not as man sees, for man looks at the outward appearance, but the LORD looks at the heart.'"[464]

Samuel, attempting to follow this advice, checks out all the other sons, and still doesn't see whatever invisible thing God is looking for. When he turns to Jesse and asks, surely apologetically glancing at all the confused rejects, *ahem*, "you got any other sons?" Jesse admits there's one last one tending the sheep, but really, you don't want him. David was scrawny and short and, perhaps reading between the lines a bit, too young to grow proper stubble and might be mistaken for a nice-looking girl in the wrong light. Really, not king material.

But God, looking at the heart, saw a heart after His own, God's kind of guy.[465] And because what you are on the inside you are, and because there's nothing more "king material" than total devotion to God Almighty, this scrawny little sheepherder became the giant-slaying, army-leading, nation-conquering King David of lore and legend.

Jesus, and only Jesus, knows the hearts of all men.[466] Every word that will come out of me is known before it does.[467] Everything about me is known before I was born.[468] Every possibility, every future, and every action, word, or thought all comes from a heart that God created and knows better than anyone ever will or ever could.

"The heart is more deceitful than all else; who can understand it? I, the LORD, search the heart, I test the mind."[469]

Who can understand the heart? Well, God can. Not my mother, my friends, or my society. I can't even know my own heart. But God can. And, generally speaking, we don't ask God what He thinks nearly enough.

Let's review. God knit this heart together while I was still in my mother's womb. Not a single bit of me was unknown to Him.[470] And He crafted me, individually and particularly, in His image, formed with His own hands, to be a masterpiece.[471] God saved this heart, purchased with the blood of His Son, conferring on me the value of priceless and beginning the lifelong transformation process of making me like Jesus. God designed this heart for a purpose—to put Him on display, and to do so in a special way that is unique to me.[472]

Try introducing yourself that way in an elevator sometime. It'll probably go over like a lead balloon, people scooching away inch by inch and jabbing surreptitiously at the button for their floor with a bit more urgency than they had before, but regardless of how it goes over, this is a more accurate description of you than you'll ever give listing externals.

And I believe this. This glorious description of who I am, I believe it... when I can see it reflected on the outside. When I'm writing five days a week, regularly posting music, and working to get my latest book published, yes, I feel pretty great about me. I can see God working. I can see God displayed in my life. I even smile on occasion.

But what about the other times? When I check my last post and see I haven't written any new songs in eighteen months? When I'm tracking not how many pages I've written this month, but how many seasons of how many television shows I've plowed through? When I'm barely able to sing at my church, much less speak there?

If Jesus Christ inside of me is meant to change me from the inside out, and that change is meant to be reflected on the outside, then what happens when the outside isn't going so good? When all the things I'd like to do fall by the wayside? When I start losing ground in all the places I'd like to be improving? When all the goals I've made continue to not get done? When I am not at all where I thought I would be at this point in my life? When all I see is failure, mistake, useless?

Why can't I get it together? What's wrong with me?

What then?

Once upon a time, God saved the nation Israel from slavery in Egypt. And this, God says, is a picture of salvation. He then led Israel from Egypt to the Promised Land (not unlike our journey to the Promised Land that is heaven). And in between, there was a whole lot of very dusty walking.

Forty years of dusty walking.

It does not take forty years to walk from Egypt to Israel. Even taking into account a bunch of sheep and oxen and children and carts and such, even taking into account the elderly and the need to rest, even taking into account the somewhat circuitous route to hit all the great watering holes and avoid all the roving bands of Moabites and what have you, it would only take a matter of months to get from Point A to Point B. And yet, it didn't.

Israel built a portable tabernacle to carry with them, and God's presence—His glory, a physical display of Him that looked like a cloud during the daytime and a pillar of fire at night—came to rest on top of the tabernacle. And these were Israel's marching instructions:

"Whenever the cloud was lifted from over the tent, afterward the sons of Israel would then set out; and in the place where the cloud settled down, there the sons of Israel would camp. At the command of the Lord the sons of Israel would set out, and at the command of the Lord they would camp; as long as the cloud settled over the tabernacle, they remained camped. Even when the cloud lingered over the tabernacle for many days, the sons of Israel would keep the Lord's charge and not set out. If sometimes the cloud remained a few days over the tabernacle, according to the command of the LORD they remained camped. Then according to the command of the LORD they set out. If sometimes the cloud remained from evening until morning, when the cloud was lifted in the morning, they would move out; or if it remained in the daytime and at night, whenever the cloud was lifted, they would set out. Whether it was two days or a month or a year that the cloud lingered over the tabernacle, staying above it, the sons of Israel remained camped and did not set out; but when it was lifted, they did set out. At the command of the LORD they camped, and at the command of the LORD they set out; they kept the LORD's charge, according to the command of the LORD through Moses."[473]

Here God seems to beat a dead horse communicating all this. He could have said, "Follow the cloud, people. When it stops you stop, when it goes, you go." But I think He knows our tendency toward impatience. And he has to remind us that whether it's two days or a month or a year, you stay in camp while the cloud is in camp. And it was just as much a matter of obedience to wait as it was to move forward.

This command was given before Israel chickened out at the border and a whole generation missed out on the

Promised Land.[474] Before there was any discernible reason to linger, God had them sitting at that mountain for a full year.[475] The point?

Sometimes God has us sitting still for a reason.

The truth is, whether the cloud is moving forward, my bags are packed, and my cart is trundling forward, or whether the cloud is in camp and I'm sitting at the flap of my tent idly slapping at flies, God is at work, doing His thing. God is working on me whether I see it or not, and there is a very great danger in expecting to see it. In fact, that expectation is an indication of a very deadly fallacy that strikes at the heart of identity.

But I'm getting ahead of myself.

Another circumstance that comes along and changes my opinion of me is when hard times come. Financial troubles, family issues, health problems, losing a loved one, mental health episodes... honestly, I could spend pages and never list everything, but you know what hard times look like. Feel free to fill in the blank with yours.

When hard times come, it is common to wonder if God is punishing me. If He has removed His grace and favor and affection from me. If He no longer has a good plan for me. If His attention is elsewhere.

Every single bit of this affects who I am. I am supposed to be a beloved child of God. Why then is He treating me like this? Am I even His? And suddenly, an external circumstance has me doubting the very core of my identity.

When hard times come, it is common to blame myself. To think I've brought this on me, that I've done something to deserve this, that if I were a better Christian, I'd at the very least be handling this better. I immediately go digging through my actions, thoughts, and behavior, looking for the culprit. Failing to find it or seizing upon any little thing that it could be, I begin beating myself down for the hardship I've brought on myself.

And again, who I am becomes a casualty of circumstance.

When hard times come, they tend to be all-consuming. They monopolize more time, more energy, more money, more emotional expense than I have to spare, and I start seeing all the good, external things I had been doing fall away. I can no longer serve like I wanted. I can no longer give like I used to. I can no longer help others like I prefer to. And all those great labels that used to apply to me when I was behaving as a "good Christian"? Those no longer apply.

Am I still who God made me to be, or just a failure at all of the above?

Are you starting to see the fallacy yet? Whether it's other people's opinions of me, the comparison to an ideal society or the Church holds up, or a simple self-evaluation, I'm making the same faulty assumption every time.

That identity is based on what I do.

Hold up now. Did we not just get through saying that who I am on the inside *will* inevitably work its way to the outside? And if Jesus lives in me, everything that is Jesus will eventually live itself out in my life?

Yes. But that doesn't always look like what *I* think.

Before there were comic book superheroes, before there were Greek demigods, there was Samson, a real-life superhero who was given literal super-strength by God Himself in a time when the nation of Israel was being oppressed by the ever-oppressing Philistines.[476] He liked to taunt the enemy with riddles[477] and sing songs about himself doing great feats of strength:

"With the jawbone of a donkey, heaps upon heaps,

With the jawbone of a donkey I have killed a thousand men."[478]

Eh... a poet he was not. Perhaps it rhymed better in Hebrew.

But when he wasn't boasting, he was setting fields on fire, ripping gates off their hinges, and allowing himself to be captured just to spare the people who were supposed to hand him over—*it's okay, little people. I got this.*[479]

But as is the trend of super-powered people everywhere, he got overconfident, cocky, and accidentally monologued his secret source of strength to a hired femme fatale who betrayed him to his enemies.[480] Yes, this is a true story. But not the only one of its kind.

As previously mentioned, Israel's first king had it all—the looks, the stature, the respect of his people.[481] When God put him on the throne, he became unstoppable. Riches, armies, land, and a people who followed him around making up songs about his mighty deeds.[482]

Also, as previously mentioned, this went badly. At a certain point, King Saul no longer saw himself as the unknown son of a donkey rancher and began to see himself as the king God made him to be, and rather than following God's battle strategy, he decided to circumvent God's orders for the sake of greater riches.[483] In one fell swoop, that decision cost him the throne and left alive a line of Israel-haters who attempted genocide against God's people centuries later.[484]

Solomon, who followed along two kings behind Saul, was the wisest man who ever lived.[485] He applied his wisdom to every earthly pursuit and failed at nothing. He had a wise and considered opinion on just about every topic there was, and people came from all over just to hear him do his thinking out loud.[486]

On top of that, Israel was never richer, bigger, stronger, or more successful than under Solomon's rule. He had so much gold that silver was relegated to the level of asphalt—eh, just pave the roads with that.[487] He was the richest king of his time,[488] and if you add up his net worth and account for inflation, nobody in all of history ever comes close to amassing the fortune that Solomon did. And his principles of wise business practices are literally the bestselling books of their kind, translated into more languages than any other.[489]

The point? This, too, fell apart. Relying on his wisdom instead of God's, he married seven hundred women and had three hundred mistresses (wisdom he had. Common sense he had not). He let all their idols and gods into the house (I don't care how big his house was. Letting one thousand women try to put their individual stamp on the place was a train wreck waiting to happen). And all this drew his heart away from the God who gave him the wisdom in the first place.[490] And as is the tragic trend with really great businessmen (or in this case, kings), his son ran the whole empire into the ground.[491]

Do you see the trend? Outwardly strong, rich, wise. Reliant on their strength, riches, wisdom. Forgetting the source of all three, they forgot God.

This comes as no surprise to God. One of the first things He said when He pulled His people out of Egypt, before the long, dusty walk, before the judges, before the kings, He said, "Then it shall come about when the LORD your God brings you into the land which He swore to your fathers, Abraham, Isaac and Jacob, to give you, great and splendid cities which you did not build, and houses full of all good things which you did not fill, and hewn cisterns which you did not dig, vineyards and olive trees which you did not plant, and you eat and are satisfied, then watch yourself, that you do not forget the LORD who brought you out of Egypt, out of the house of slavery."[492]

Centuries later, God is looking back at the history He'd just watched unfold, and He sums it up this way:

"Yet I have been the LORD your God since the land of Egypt. I cared for you in the wilderness, in the land of drought. As they had their pasture, they became satisfied, and being satisfied, their heart became proud; therefore they forgot Me."[493]

When times are good, I forget. When I look in the mirror and see something to be proud of, it's all too easy to puff myself up with self-praise instead of directing that praise to God. When the surface stuff, the external stuff, is admirable, then I am in great danger of forgetting the God who made me that way. And as much as I'd love to believe that having Jesus Christ inside me should make me strong or wise or rich beyond measure, it is often those very things that draw eyes—mine included—away from God.

It's almost a catch-22. An impossibility. When Jesus is in me, He will begin to change me from the inside out into something that is in some way beautiful. And yet, when I look into the mirror and see what I want to see, it is likely I will forget who made me this way. What then am I supposed to do?

"Let your light shine in such a way that they may see your good works and glorify your Father who is in heaven."[494] Somehow, someway, people will be able to see the externals, the good works that they can see with their own eyes, hear of with their own ears, experience for themselves, and aim all the praise at God.

How? What is "such a way"? So that my lovely exterior doesn't draw gasps and stares and admiration of the lovely exterior, but rather glorifies *God*. After all, He is the Giver of that loveliness. He is the One who made me this way. How do I live "in such a way" that God is put on full display, with no doubt that it is His glory people are seeing?

Jeremiah starts by telling us what is *not* the way so that we can see what is. "Thus says the LORD, 'Let not a wise man boast of his wisdom, and let not the mighty man boast of his might, let not a rich man boast of his riches; but let him who boasts boast of this, that he understands and knows Me, that I am the LORD who exercises lovingkindness, justice and righteousness on the earth; for I delight in these things,' declares the LORD."[495]

Solomon had the wisdom. Samson had the might. Saul had the riches of his country at his disposal. All these things were given by God. All of these were good gifts, not to be sneezed at or ignored.[496]

But none of these things were ever meant to be "boasted in."

"To boast" is a really interesting word. In the KJV, it was translated "glory." To celebrate, to throw a party for, to shine a light on. To put on display. So maybe making up songs of one's own greatness was *not* the way to go? This is, after all, where all three went wrong. They boasted in, shone a light on, and put on display external things. Yes, they were given by God. Yes, they were good gifts. But when you boast in all of that *and forget God*, you set yourself up to fail.

And God prefers to set His children up to succeed.

"For consider your calling, brethren, that there were not many wise according to the flesh, not many mighty, not many noble; but God has chosen the foolish things of the world to shame the wise, and God has chosen the weak things of the world to shame the things which are strong, and the base things of the world and the despised God has chosen, the things that are not so that He may nullify the things that are, so that no man may boast before God. But by His doing you are in Christ Jesus, who became to us wisdom from God, and righteousness and sanctification, and redemption, so that, just as it is written, 'Let him who boasts, boast in the Lord.'"[497]

God likes to take the foolish and put the wise to shame. He chooses the weak and fearful and makes armies flee. He takes the things the world despises and He raises them up to do mighty things.

Paul's best example of this crazy God-phenomenon is Jesus Himself. Into a world of intellectuals, searching for wisdom and signs, Jesus came, the least likely-looking Savior in history. He put on weakness when He could have come in strength. He did a foolish thing by dying when He could have done the smart thing by conquering. He could have come as God. He came as man.[498]

When God uses the weak, there's no doubt who did it. When God uses the small, pride is humbled and all eyes turn to Him. No one needs to see me out there, great all by myself. They need to see me small and weak and my great God standing behind me, going before me, lifting me up.

There are two things in Scripture that we are supposed to "boast" in. Two things we are to celebrate, throw a party for, shine a light on, and put on display. 1) God (duh), and 2) our weaknesses.

"And He has said to me, 'My grace is sufficient for you, for power is perfected in weakness.' Most gladly, therefore, I will rather boast about my weaknesses, so that the power of Christ may dwell in me. Therefore, I am well content with weaknesses, with insults, with distresses, with persecutions, with difficulties, for Christ's sake; for when I am weak, then I am strong."[499]

There's a movie called *Knight and Day* with Tom Cruise and Cameron Diaz, and, fair warning, I'm going to spoil this entire movie. So plug your ears, hum loudly, and skim this next part quickly if you care.

Tom Cruise and Cameron Diaz meet on an airplane, and, as people in movies are prone to do, fall in love in the amount of time it takes for the plane to reach cruising altitude. About this point, bad guys attack since, obviously, Tom Cruise is a spy. He, of course, takes out all the bad guys and keeps her safe, all the while she's in the bathroom, oblivious.

The plane then is crashing, and he, of course, crash-lands the plane and keeps her safe, completely without her help.

Then the bad guys come for her and there's a car chase scene, in which he shoots away all the bad guys and keeps her safe, all while she is being worse than useless.

Then the bad guys capture them and she's being so over-the-top whiney about it that he knocks her out so he can rescue them both, all while she's practically unconscious.

Then the bad guys think she's some kind of ally of his, so he sets her up to betray him so she will be written off and sent home, all without her realizing that's what he's doing.

About this time, she realizes she really likes this guy, but now she can't find him. What's a girl to do? This is about the time that she gets herself in serious, tied-to-a-chair trouble with the bad guys, but instead of being terrified, she's smug. She's actually quite delighted to be incapable, in over her head, surrounded by bad guys, because those are precisely the situations where *he* keeps showing up. Where trouble is, he can't be far behind.

This is what it means to boast in my weaknesses. It's not that my frailties or insecurities or insufficiencies or broken places are anything to boast about in themselves. But because they absolutely necessitate *Him* showing up. How delightful it is to find myself totally incapable, in over my head, bad guys circling. Because that is when God shows up. There is no better platform for God's power than my weakness. And when I am weak, *then* I am strong.

Sometime after Israel got settled into their Promised Land and sometime before David fired a rock at a giant's head, the Midianites, unhappy about Israel moving onto their turf, attacked the nation. And because Israel wasn't particularly paying attention to their God at the time, they were unprepared to fight back and ended up enslaved, right there in their homeland. Again.

But God, being God, wasn't through with them, and so He decided to take pity on them and get them out of this mess.

"Then the angel of the LORD came and sat under the oak that was in Ophrah, which belonged to Joash the Abiezrite as his son Gideon was beating out wheat in the wine press in order to save it from the Midianites. The LORD looked at him and said, 'Go in this your strength and deliver Israel from the hand of Midian. Have I not sent you?' He said to Him, 'O LORD, how shall I deliver Israel? Behold, my family is the least in Manasseh, and I am the youngest in my father's house.' But the LORD said to him, 'Surely I will be with you, and you shall defeat Midian as one man.'"[500]

So Gideon, on the Lord's orders, assembles an army and gets ready to do as God says, but God stops him short and says, "The people who are with you are too many for Me to give Midian into their hands"—hold up. Surely this is a typo, yes? Surely God meant to say, "The people who are with you are too *few* for Me to give Midian into their hands." But no. Sorry, folks, this army's just too big for Me to work with. "For Israel would become boastful, saying, 'My own power has delivered me.'"[501]

Therefore God has Gideon assemble the army and announce that anyone who's knee-knocking scared might as well go on home. Twenty-two thousand of them moseyed on back to their fields and vineyards, leaving ten thousand still with Gideon. God gives the army a once-over, shakes His head, and declares there's still just too many. He sends them down to the river to take a drink and culls out the ones who knelt down to drink from the river and sent them on home, leaving the ones who scooped the water up with their hands and slurped it like a dog. And when all was said and done, Gideon's mighty-ish army of thirty-two thousand men was down to a mere three hundred.

Then Gideon "divided the 300 men into three companies, and he put trumpets and empty pitchers into the hands of all of them, with torches inside the pitchers. So

Gideon and the hundred men who were with him came to the outskirts of the camp at the beginning of the middle watch; and they blew the trumpets and broke the pitchers, and cried, 'A sword for the LORD and for Gideon!' And all the army ran, crying out as they fled."[502]

When the Midianites woke up in the dead of night, they saw lights all around them and imagined an army much bigger than the one that surrounded them. Although, if you want to be technical, they saw the true size of the army, for the army was led by God, and there is no bigger force to come up against than God when He is on the side of His people.[503]

But if the trumpets had blown and the Midianites looked up and saw three hundred men holding three hundred pots, they would not have been scared, because the true size and strength of that army was still concealed inside the pots.

You and I are described as pots turned on God's wheel, and within us, inside us, is Jesus Christ, the Light of the World.[504] And sometimes, for the world to see the true size and strength of God's power, we, the pot, must break.

God is not limited by weaknesses, by insufficiencies, by inadequacies, by frailties, by failures, by brokenness, tears, or pain. God is not limited by any external measure I fail to live up to. In fact, He prefers working with broken things. These are, in fact, the very things that put Him on display. It may be an odd thing to say in a book entitled *Identity and Where It Comes From*, but... *it's not about me.*

A beautiful, brilliant, strong, whole, and healthy pot—no cracks, no brokenness—is merely concealment for the glory of God that lies within. Our purpose is not to sit on a shelf, our perfectness on display, boasting in our strength, beauty, or wisdom. Our purpose is to break, to display instead the light of Jesus Christ. That is what makes whole armies flee.

Some seasons of life are marked more by waiting in camp than by moving forward. Some seasons of life are marked more by brokenness than by strength. But the God who made me is still the God who made me. Christ who lives in me is still in me. Nothing of me has changed but the outside, and as long as God is still at work—and He is[505]—nothing will return empty.[506]

If you were crafted by the Potter, you are a masterpiece. And if you were broken by the Potter, there is no better way for Christ to shine than as you are now. Who you are is determined by what's inside the pot, and no matter what your pot looks like or what state it's in, it is meant for one purpose: to put the glory of God that is inside you on full display. Nothing could be more beautiful than that.

If I let people—who can only see the outside—determine my identity, it will change with every season of my life. If I let *me*—who sees sin long killed, hears the lies of guilt and slavery, and (let's face it) still puts way too much emphasis on the outside—determine my identity, it will change with every sunrise.

But if I let God—who crafted me in His image, sees the heart He brought to life, the soul He redeemed, and the purpose He intended—determine my identity, then no matter what I feel, think, or see, and no matter what season of life I'm currently going through, I will always be the masterpiece I was designed to be. Whether I am strong and beautiful and accomplishing visibly great things, or whether I am broken and beautiful and Jesus is shining out brighter than ever, I am where I am meant to be, doing what I am meant to be doing, and I am still exactly who I'm supposed to be: a vessel of mercy, putting God on display.

For years, my mother suffered from an undiagnosed condition that had not yet been recognized by the medical community, one that caused debilitating bone and muscle pain. This left her in a wheelchair for years, and on many days, she was unable to raise her head. During those years, she had to pull back from serving at the church and was often unable to do for her husband and children all the things a "good" wife and mother would like to do. And while I praise God for the eventual diagnosis (Aromatase-induced arthralgia) and the solution (a mountain climate and regular acupuncture), I also thank God for that season in my mother's life. I would never have learned the sufficiency of God's grace otherwise. This poem is for her.

The wisdom of man may seem so great, may rise to the
    highest towers.
But as the heavens are higher than all of the earth, so is
    God's wisdom higher than ours.
We try by our strength, our power, our health to bring
    glory to God if we can,
But, lo and behold, "by our strength" is nowhere in
    God's plan.
Had He wanted an army, Midian was large, like locusts
    that cover the field.
Had He wanted a warrior, He could have it as well, but

God wanted a man who would yield.

Though Gideon was least in his father's house and least in all Israel besides,

God saw in him weakness and turned it to strength to prove that His hand decides.

32,000, though not nearly enough to battle the enemy host,

Was too great a number for God to use, for in their strength they would boast.

10,000, courageous, and yet not enough, but God weeded them down to a few.

For then when the world saw 300, they would marvel at what God could do.

Trumpets, a torch, and a pitcher. No shield, no arrows, no sword.

They marched in the weakness of themselves and in the strength of Jehovah their Lord.

The enemy camp before them, the darkness all around,

Their lights engulfed in pitchers, and not making a single sound.

And on God's mark, the pitchers broke, the lights began to shine,

And enemy forces began to see the army God calls "Mine"

With terror and confusion, the troops of darkness fall,

While the saints of God began to blow the trumpets heard
*   by all.*
Millennia later, a trumpet sounded, a curtain ripped in two.
And God Almighty, Christ the Lord, our Light, came shining
*   through.*
The enemy lies vanquished, God again destroyed our Foe.
Now all that's left to do is break for our Saving Christ
*   to show.*
If we have beauty, strength, and health, they'll look and see
*   our pot.*
But when we choose to break for God, they'll see what we
*   are not.*
They'll see the fullness of God's grace a perfect pot would
*   hide.*
They'll get a glimpse of perfect peace that they have been
*   denied,*
The power of weakness turned to strength that strength
*   alone can't show,*
And the goodness of a loving God that they so yearn
*   to know.*
If 10,000 troops is still too much to shower God with praise
Then let us break 300 pots and shout His name always.

On God's mark, your pot has cracked. He shines for all to see.
Now blow that trumpet good and loud. You stand in victory.

—For Mom
When the brokenness brings tears,
let God's mercies bring still more
(and your family will bring the tissues).

4-16-2012

LIVING THE TRUTH

If I were to describe myself in thirty seconds, what would I say? How much of this is external? How much do these externals determine my opinion of myself? How would I describe myself starting on the inside? Does that change my opinion of the outside at all?

What periods of my life would I qualify as waiting periods? How did I respond in those moments? What does the cloud remaining in camp look like in my life, and how do I recognize it? If I saw this as just as much a command as the command to move forward, how might my response be different?

What hard times have I gone through (or am I going through) in my life? What questions or doubts come up for me when I'm going through hard times? What about myself don't I like during these times? What does God say He is doing to the person that is me during these times (1 Peter 1:6–7; James 1:2–4)? What questions or doubts does that put to rest?

In what ways am I outwardly strong/smart/impressive? In what ways can these things become liabilities? In what ways am I outwardly weak/small/pitiful? In what ways have these qualities actually worked out to my benefit?

When I have something to celebrate, what do I usually do? How do I celebrate? Have I ever done that for a weakness? What would it look like if I did? Find somebody and "boast" about a weakness to them. (Blame the book if you need to.)

What in my life do I imagine limits God? What if I saw these things as God whittling down my army to three hundred? If God asks me to go into battle, outnumbered and unarmed, will I still go? What does that look like in my life?

CHAPTER 9

The Real Epidemic and the False Cure

At the time I'm writing this book, we are facing a worldwide problem. Everyone on earth is affected by that problem one way or another. And everyone has an opinion on what to do about it. That problem is COVID-19. Whether you're an ICU nurse who deals with it daily, whether you're convinced the whole thing is just a hoax, or whether you're forced to change every policy of your business just to keep the doors open, everyone is being affected by it.

At the time I'm writing this book, we are facing another worldwide problem. Everyone on earth is affected by that problem one way or another, and everyone seems to have an opinion on what to do about it. And this problem is just as epidemic.

Those hit hardest are children who are abandoned by both parents, high schoolers who are cyber-bullied on social media, and those who don't match society's ideals for one reason or another, but no one is immune.

The symptoms vary. It can present as arrogance and the constant need to put others down. It can show up as shyness and constant putting oneself down. It can exhibit itself as pulling away from other people or as a desperate need to surround oneself with people. It can look like never giving a second thought to a person besides oneself. And it can present as being so busy taking care of others that the patient completely neglects his or her own well-being. In serious cases, one is prone to self-sabotage, self-destruction, and even self-harm. And in extreme cases, it results in suicide.

There is no known medical cure. There is no blood test. It doesn't show up on an MRI. And the only way to know you have it is by its symptoms.

Typically, whoever discovers a disease gets to name it. Or it's named after the most well-known person who had it. I certainly didn't discover it, nor am I the most well-known person to have it, but if you don't mind, I'm going to take the liberty of giving it a name.

Funhouse Mirror Syndrome. You look into a mirror and see something distorted, something that is not you.

The first symptom of Funhouse Mirror Syndrome is called pride. The Bible tells us that pride is a sin. Pride was Satan's sin,[507] and it was the first thing he tempted Adam and Eve with.[508] It is pride that goes before destruction, a haughty spirit before a fall.[509] God is opposed to the proud, but gives grace to the humble.[510] And on the list of things that God hates—things that are an abomination to Him, that He cannot stand—sex sins don't even specifically make the list. Pride, on the other hand, is at the very top.[511]

Pride is an artificial elevation of self. In the words of Romans 12:3, pride is for someone "to think more highly of himself than he ought to think." When Satan did this, he imagined that he could be like God. He wanted to raise himself above the other angels, and in his words, "I will make myself like the Most High."[512] At least Satan was smart enough not to imagine he could top the Most High. We humans aren't quite so modest.

I wish I could tell you that I sat down and academically studied the topic of pride throughout Scripture, that I studied the people who committed that sin and evaluated what actions and attitudes they had that got them labeled as prideful. I wish I could tell you I looked up every time the word *pride* was used in Scripture and came up with a good description of the disease based on that. But no. I'm describing the disease of pride based on my own symptoms. All the years I myself have spent infected with the stuff.

Pride is when I look at God's wisdom, His advice, His word, and opt for my own opinion instead. When I decide that His thoughts don't apply, don't work, or don't serve my agenda. This is me imagining that my thoughts and my ways are higher than God's. The opposite is true.[513]

Pride is when I look at Christ's goodness, His righteousness, His holy blamelessness on my behalf and decide to stand on my own good works instead. *Why should You let me into heaven, God? Look at all the fabulous things I've done.* According to Jesus, this is the height of folly.[514]

Pride is when I look at God's strength, His power, His ability and decide to plow ahead in my strength, certain I can reach perfection if I try hard enough, work long enough, apply myself well enough. And pride is being dissatisfied with my insufficiencies, as if God has not the power to make up for them.

Pride is when I look at God's timing and prefer my own. Pride is when I look at what God has provided and wish I had something better. Pride is when I look at God's plan and think I could have come up with a better one. Pride is when I look at the pot that is me and say, "God, why did You make me like this?"

Pride is when I compare something of mine to something of God's and choose mine over His.

If pride is an artificial elevation of self, then it is just as likely to come out with people as it is with God. Pride absolutely has to compare itself to others. And when it does, my needs, my desires, my agenda, my schedule, and my priorities will always trump yours. My opinions will always be right. What I have to say will always be more important than what you have to say; my time will always be more valuable. When I judge myself against you, the tally always comes out in my favor, and I will find you to be deficient compared to me. I will treat others as less important, less valuable, as... less.

Maybe I do this out loud and in your face. Maybe I do this in my heart and my words and demeanor are all sweet flattery and self-deprecation in order to fish for compliments. Maybe I try to smother this attitude with a pillow because it's not exactly an attractive quality, but if you're like me, you'll be secretly pleased that this is your sin instead of one of the uglier, more public ones. After all, pride happens when you're better than everyone else. Can I help it if I just... am?

Here's what I did. Being the Bible-reading, Scripture-memorizing, Sunday-school-attending girl that I was, I knew pride was bad, and I knew I had it. And despite my secret little pleasure at being saddled with such a minor, socially acceptable, barely-sinful-at-all sin, I did want to smother it with a pillow. So, I searched Scripture and found my pillow.

I came up with a list of verses that speak of the ugliness of human nature and how far short of God's glory I, as a member of the human race, fall, and I pounded those into my head. Romans 3, where I'm called a useless open grave who speaks with nothing but snake venom, among other lovely things.[515] Jeremiah 17:9, where the human heart is called desperately wicked. Psalm 51, where David comes face to face with his sin and is broken up about it, a prayer than any sinner could easily claim as their own.

And then, of course, there's the list of verses that describe what a believer in Jesus should look like, the list of commands that I should be following—Galatians 5:22–23, Colossians 3:12–17, etc. etc. etc. You make yourself a list of all the things you *should* be doing and you compare that to all the things you're *actually* doing, and surely that will puncture the inflated sense of self. That will bring the artificially elevated self-image down to its proper level. Right?

Didn't work.

For centuries there has been the assumption that to defeat pride, I must destroy self. That somehow self-denial and hardship and pain equal godliness. The prophets of Baal in Elijah's day believed that doing themselves serious, bloody harm by cutting themselves would give extra power to their prayers so that Baal would hear them. (Didn't work.)[516] For centuries, monks would take vows of poverty as if there was something inherently more godly about being poor than being rich. (There's not.)[517] Similarly, those same folks would deny themselves tasty food and families and other good things God created, thinking that refusing themselves good things would somehow make them better Christians. (It didn't.)[518] The churches Peter wrote to had to be warned against imagining that suffering in itself equals spiritual brownie points. (It doesn't).[519] And many people throughout history have even gone so far as to flog themselves, as if that would free them of sin. (Epic fail.)

"'Do not handle, do not taste, do not touch!' These are matters which have, to be sure, the appearance of wisdom in self-made religion and self-abasement and severe treatment of the body, but are of no value against fleshly indulgence."[520]

Self-abasement is one of those terms that means exactly what it sounds like. Dare I say, "taking oneself to the basement"? Bringing oneself low. That's what we're trying to do, isn't it? Take myself down off the high horse, bring myself down from the falsely elevated place I've put myself, and come down to a nice little properly humble level?

And yet, according to this verse, beating yourself up—literally or figuratively—doesn't work. Sounds like it would, doesn't it? But it only results in more pride. Look how far I go to be godly. Look what I've given up. Look how little I own, how much I suffer, how deep my scars. It is the Pharisee tooting his own horn as he comes into the temple so that all the people may see how self-sacrificing he is.[521]

This does not achieve humility. It might, however, get me to insecurity.

There's this song I sing at church, and somehow I got saddled with the guy's part, and I have to hit a note even lower than my male worship pastor and hold it out for ages. Whenever we sing this song, I half-hope that I'll get sick the morning of. Not to get out of it, but because it enables my voice to hit lower notes with ease. Yes, the sickness makes me feel crummy. But it also allows me to do the thing I need to do. So it's better to be sick, right?

If insecurity is the second symptom of Funhouse Mirror Syndrome, I have to wonder: Is it *really* a sin? Is it truly harmful to me? Yes, it makes me feel crummy, but perhaps it's actually keeping me humble, and allowing me to do what I need to do. Right?

In truth, my secret refusal to give up insecurity is just as stupid and self-defeating as my secret pleasure at pride. Both are a sickness, and both need to go.

Again, I speak not as a scholar but as an expert, as a patient of this very illness. And from my years of experience, I suggest that insecurity is made up of three things:

An attempt to please everyone. 2) Fear. 3) Self-hatred.

They say you can't please everybody. Jesus Himself said it a full two thousand years ago. "No one can serve two masters."[522] And yet we still try. It's impossible because

A) it's exhausting trying to think what every single person around you is wanting, expecting, even needing from you, but also because B) two people are going to demand two mutually exclusive things from you. With one action, I will have people on both sides telling me I did it wrong—one because I went too far, and one because I didn't go far enough. It is quite literally impossible to please everyone.

But it gets worse. By its very nature, the attempt to please everyone prevents me from pleasing the one Person I am designed to serve. "For am I now seeking the favor of men, or of God? Or am I striving to please men? If I were still trying to please men, I would not be a bond-servant of Christ."[523] Either being a bond-servant of Christ is offensive to so many that any attempt to please people will have me shutting up about Jesus, avoiding the subject, and missing out on opportunities to put Him on display, or my many, many efforts to please people are going to take up all my time and energy, leaving me unable to pursue what really matters in life. Either way, you can't do both.

If insecurity is the pursuit of pleasing people, then insecurity prevents me from pleasing Christ. That is point-blank the definition of sin—"for all have sinned and fall short of the glory of God."[524] Sin: I aim to put God on display and miss the mark. Insecurity, by its nature, misses the mark every time.

Insecurity is also fear. Fear of people's opinion, fear of making mistakes, fear of failure. It is fear left, right, and center, and that fear both consumes and directs me. It is my motivation forward and what drags me backward. And just as in the case of serving lesser masters, the fear of anything less keeps me from the fear of God.

Fear is a healthy respect for the power a thing has over me. If I fear cancer, it is because I recognize that cancer can radically change my lifestyle, hurt my body, shorten my life expectancy, control my schedule, and dominate my time for however long it takes to eradicate.

So, what does it say when I fear people's opinion of me? That I recognize that those opinions control how many friends I have, what social events I'm invited to, even what job I may or may not get? How about whether I'm worthwhile, valuable, deserving of the space I take up and the air I breathe?

And yet this is *not so.* Having a healthy respect for the power a thing has over me essentially *gives* that thing power over me. And here's the truth:

Nothing in this world has power over me that God does not give it.

Jesus stood before Pontius Pilate, a man with real authority and a rather Roman-arena-like thumbs-up/ thumbs-down power to decide whether Jesus lived or died. And when Jesus seemed less than impressed with this power, Pilate said, "Do you not know that I have authority to release You, and I have authority to crucify You?" And Jesus replied, "You would have no authority over Me, unless it had been given you from above."[525]

Pilate imagined that he had the authority to execute Jesus or to set Him free. Authority that came from the Roman Empire, the greatest empire on earth. And yet not a single ounce of that power belonged to Pilate. It belonged to God, and it was merely on loan. If God determined that Jesus would die that day, He would die. If God determined He would live, no army or any number of armies, no empire, and no king could possibly make it otherwise.

If to fear is to acknowledge the power something has over you, then no wonder I cannot fear God and fear anything less at the same time. When I grant power to something less, I take it out of the hands of God. And while no power on this earth—me included—can wrest control or power from God Himself, what I ascribe that power to with my mind is essential; it impacts my life drastically.

If I fear, my comfort zone is tiny or nonexistent. If I fear God, there is no spot on this planet outside my comfort zone. If I fear, then I refuse, I quit, I shy away, I fail. If I fear God, I act, I move, I conquer, I achieve, and nothing I do can possibly be considered a failure, for God was behind it. If I fear, I continue to live in the spirit of slavery Jesus died to take from me.[526] If I fear God, this is only the beginning, and a life lived on the fear of God is a life lived well.[527]

The fear of God demolishes the fear of everything else. God holds the leash on every fearful thing. Neither cancer nor scary cancer treatment can steal a single thing from my life that God does not chose to take. *He* numbers my days. *He* chooses what those days consist of. *He* decides when and why and for how long I hurt and for what good reason.[528] People's opinions don't determine what my life looks like or whether it's worth living. God does. If I am possessed by the fear of God, then I would have no fear of man or cancer or any other force, because not a single one of them holds the power that God does. If God is God, then every fearful thing in this world amounts to no more than impotent little Pontius Pilate, whining that Jesus wasn't properly scared enough.

Finally, insecurity is self-hatred. Jesus said, "If anyone comes to Me, and does not hate his own father and mother and wife and children and brothers and sisters, yes, even his own life, he cannot be My disciple."[529]

Perhaps from this verse or perhaps from elsewhere, there is almost an implication in Christian circles that to love God, I must hate me. That to love others, I must despise myself. That to be a good Christian, I must be down in the dust with the worms.

The word *hate* has three meanings in the Strong's Greek Dictionary. "To hate," "to despise," or "to love less by comparison." Oddly, no one imagines we are to hate our parents. After all, we are commanded to show our parents obedience when we are children and to respect them no matter what age we are.[530] No one imagines we are to despise our own wives and children. After all, we are commanded to love them with the same love Jesus did.[531] Remember, love is our primary way of putting God on display, our primary proof to the world that we are His, our primary command to follow, and if we obey this, we've got the whole Law and the Prophets covered, yes?[532]

And yet, here I am imagining that to be a good disciple, I must hate me.

If I love me more than I love God, I will have falsely elevated myself to a laughable level, and that is pride. If I love my family more than I love God, I will have falsely elevated them, and that is idolatry. So I must love myself less by comparison—and my family less by comparison—when I look at the awesomeness of the God I serve.[533] Duh. But if I grind myself into the dust on the faulty assumption that self-hatred is some sort of worship, it is not. And I am falsely devaluing that which God has valued most priceless.

Perhaps I imagine that self-hatred is called for because nowhere in Scripture do I ever see the command to love myself. After all, self-love is a trap if ever there was one. And yet, what Scripture does do is make the assumption that people, by their nature, love themselves—"For no one ever hated his own flesh, but nourishes it and cherishes it"[534]—and that, because this is basic human nature, we are then to love others in relation to how we love ourselves.[535]

With the same care you apply to your own needs, with the attention you pay to your own life and livelihood, with the strength of your own hopes and dreams, care about others. I have to wonder how many of us struggle to love our neighbor because we never learned to show that level of kindness to ourselves. When I am asked to look to the interests of others, it is in addition to looking after my own, not instead of.[536] Dare I say, if I fail to look after my own interests, I will have nothing, financially, physically, or emotionally to give to others. If how I treat others is relative to how I treat myself, then when I devalue myself, I bring those others down with me.

"I have been crucified with Christ; and it is no longer I who live, but Christ lives in me."[537] Therefore, if I aim hatred inward at the person I am, the personality I exhibit, and the choices I make, I am in fact aiming hatred at a place where I no longer live. I aim hatred at the Person who lives in me now. And when, in my hatred of self, I feel the need to apologize for any passionate conviction I express, or to shut up whenever I feel the urge to speak, or to resign and go home so as not to bother anybody when I am asked to speak or to serve, then who is it I am squelching? Who is it I am trampling underfoot? Who is it I am hating?

"Do nothing from selfishness or empty conceit, but with humility of mind regard one another as more important than yourselves; do not merely look out for your own personal interests, but also for the interests of others. Your attitude should be the same as that of Christ Jesus: who, being in very nature God, did not consider equality with God a thing to be grasped, but made Himself nothing, taking the very nature of a servant, being made in human likeness. And being found in appearance as a man, he humbled himself and became obedient to death—even death on a cross! Therefore God exalted Him to the highest place and gave him the name that is above every name, that at the name of Jesus every knee should bow, in heaven and on earth and under the earth, and every tongue confess that Jesus Christ is Lord, to the glory of God the Father."[538]

Selfishness, out. Conceit, out. Others, I am to value as more important than myself. I am called to have the same attitude at Jesus—He emptied Himself, He became nothing, He became a servant, He sacrificed His very life.

But if I am to take on Jesus' attitude, I must also take on His motivation. Jesus did not sit in heaven, bemoaning how unworthy He was to share the title of God with His Father. Jesus did not survey all the creating and sustaining work He'd done on the earth up to that point and shake His head at the smallness of it and think He really needed to be doing more to measure up. He did not take a good hard look in the mirror and hate what He saw. (He saw God. There is only one response to that.)

Jesus gave up His immortality, omnipresence, and invincibility, not out of hatred for Himself, but out of love for me. Jesus sacrificed His very life on the cross, not because He valued Himself so little, but because He valued me so much. Jesus girded Himself with a towel and did the job of a servant, not because He was fit only to wash feet, but because my feet were dirty.[539] Jesus did not empty Himself to be filled with self-loathing. He emptied Himself so He could be full of love. He did not become nothing because He was nothing. He became nothing because nothing short of that would reach me.

And so, I will consider others as more important than me, not because I look in the mirror and see someone unworthy of consideration, whose needs do not count and whose character is flawed, but because I look at you and see someone who needs me, who needs help, who needs love, who needs encouragement, and that is the attitude of Christ in me to offer it to you. I will look after the interests of others, not because my own life and future amount to nothing, but because I see someone God loves in need, and the love of Christ within me can't help but come out. I will become obedient to God in sacrifice, in suffering, even in death if that's what it takes. Not because I don't deserve to be happy or deserve to live happily ever after, but because the happiest ever after is a life that puts God on display, followed by heaven where nothing will block my view ever again.

I am called to humility and to love, but never to self-hate. To hate what God loves is a travesty. And to mistreat one of God's children is evil—even when that child is me. God rides upon the wings of the storm, fire blasting from His nostrils in anger when someone messes with one of His kids.[540] Do I expect any less when it is I who attacks this child of His?

The earliest discipline any beloved child experiences is not when he or she does something evil or when he or she harms another person but when he or she sticks a chubby little finger in a light socket, tries to climb over the rail of a very high crib, or attempts to swallow that which is not food—it is when they do something to harm themselves. And I submit that God's *every* discipline of

His children, from the earliest moment to the last lessons we will ever learn on this earth, is in service of protecting us from doing something that will harm us. After all, sin is definitively that which will harm us. This is why God stops us so soundly when we sin, so that we do not hurt ourselves.

Self-hatred *is* harm that I do to myself. God prohibits sin because it will inevitably cause me harm. Will He be any less emphatic when I inflict self-harm directly?

All this to say, insecurity is not a nice little cold that gets me out of work and gives me a pleasantly deep voice for a day. Insecurity is a cancer, and it's eating me alive.

Don't worry. Turn on the television to any channel and you will see the cure for insecurity advertised. They call it building self-esteem. This cure for false understanding of self is a bit newer than the self-flagellation that has been done for centuries, and this one's actually doctor approved. Therapists recommend it. Very often, I am encouraged to actually look myself in the mirror when I do this, and to speak with feeling.

I am important. I am beautiful. I am smart. I am... all the things I wish I was or perhaps would like to be.

Once again, I tried it. But it didn't work, doesn't work. Never has. Because at the very most, I am treating symptoms. Treating insecurity—a falsely devalued view of myself—by falsely inflating my view of myself. And that, if you recall, is pride.

Pride and insecurity are not opposites. They are two sides of the same coin. Two manifestations of the same disease, and one is not the cure for the other. Insecurity does not cure me of pride, and pride does not cure me of insecurity. Because they are the same disease.

People speak from arrogance, insist on the last word, the attention, and putting others down all in order to bolster their own self-confidence because they are, in fact, insecure. People shy away in insecurity, fail to act with boldness, and judge themselves with self-hatred because they imagine that the worth they so desperately crave is on their own shoulders to earn. How is that anything less than pride?

Satan has engineered the greatest conspiracy of all times, and in order to pull it off, he wears three hats. Wearing a ski mask and gloves so as not to leave fingerprints, he pours the poison of a distorted self-image into the water supply, causing the population to start to show symptoms. Then, mugging a CDC worker for his hazmat suit, Satan goes on TV posing as an expert, using guilt and shame to make me, the scared public, oh so painfully aware of Funhouse Mirror Syndrome. Then he tosses aside the hazmat suit and dresses up as a pharmacist, false mustache Scotch-taped to his upper lip, passing out pill bottles labeled as the cure when all they actually do is mitigate symptoms while Funhouse Mirror Syndrome runs its course unchecked.

Here's what's really heinous. Most drugs that are heavy-duty enough to require a prescription are also heavy-duty enough to cause unrelated side effects. It'll fix your headache but make you nauseous. It'll fix nausea but make you constipated. It'll fix constipation but make you dizzy. And around and around it goes. Pick your poison.

Satan would have us believe that he offers the cure when he doesn't. He touts the age-old miracle cure for pride, labeled *self-deprecation*, and if you read the list of ingredients, it'll list several Bible verses. But Satan uses Scripture to tempt,[541] and just because it uses Scripture doesn't make it a godly practice. All Satan needs is to mix in a little bit of poison with the good stuff and voilà, a "miracle drug" that addresses all the symptoms of pride and leaves you dying of insecurity.

He touts the brand-new miracle drug *self-esteem* as a cure for insecurity, and I'm sure there's some pretty harmless ingredients in there too. But at best, they mask symptoms while failing to address the disease, and at worse, they simply trade one poison for another, insecurity for pride. None of this is the cure. And all across the board, Satan is making a fortune in prescription sales and the population is largely oblivious to it.

(To be clear, this is a metaphor. I do not have a moral issue with prescription drugs or those who take them. If medication works for you, more power to you. Just don't buy what Satan's selling and think it's the cure.)

To continue the metaphor, there are, of course, members of the population who are paranoid about doctors in general and refuse to put anything in their body they can't pronounce and are left with the option to simply ignore the problem. Stop thinking highly of myself. Stop thinking low of myself. Just... stop thinking of myself at all.

Here's the problem: There are lots of things I can get through life without having an opinion on. I personally have no opinion about sports teams—not about which one is best, whether a particular defense is being coached effectively, or who should be drafted first next year (that is a thing, right?). And unless I marry a die-hard sports fan, I can probably make it till the day I die without forming any such opinion and be just fine. I also have no opinion on whether chess should be an Olympic sport or whether it was right that Pluto got downgraded from being classified as a planet.

But there is no way to make it to the end of life without forming an opinion of self. And there is no way to live a single day of this life unaffected by my own opinion of myself.

I can stop every thought about myself in its tracks as it starts to drift across my mind. I can distract myself from myself by consuming every moment with others-focused activity. I can grab my Bible and rip it open and read voraciously every time I'm tempted to consider me. But the poison is in the water supply, and whether I stop every self-thought from floating through my head or not, my opinion of myself is having an effect.

Who I am matters. Who I think I am matters too. And I still need a real cure.

There is a final choice, and while it may not have the flashy advertising of the others, Jesus Insurance pays for it completely, no cost to me. And that cure is called humility.

Humility is not to fall on my knees, nose to the floor in face of my own depravity. Humility is to fall to my knees, nose to the floor in the face of God's majesty. Humility is not being bowled over by how small I am. Humility is being bowled over by how great God is. Humility is not shame. Humility is worship. And if there are tears, they are tears of incredulous delight that this God of awesome power, divine holiness, and infinite magnitude *loves me.*

When Job made the rather prideful error of believing he understood the infinite God, God did not show Job a catalogue of his mistakes, a history of his failures, or a perfectly to-scale picture of himself. God described... God. And Job's response was humility: "I have heard of You by the hearing of the ear; but now my eye sees You; therefore I repent in dust and ashes."[542]

When Nebuchadnezzar surveyed his great and mighty kingdom that God delivered into his hand and said, "Is this not Babylon the great, which I myself have built as a royal residence by the might of my power and the glory of my majesty?" God interrupted him to rip his kingdom out of his hands and make him live in the wilderness and eat grass for seven years. And I imagine that during that time Nebuchadnezzar got a very good look at himself. And yet, here's where everything changed: "At the end of that period, I, Nebuchadnezzar, raised my eyes toward heaven and my reason returned to me." His reason returned when his eyes went up, because God "is able to humble those who walk in pride."[543]

When Isaiah, spokesperson for the nation Israel at a time when pride was king and God was not, was whisked up to heaven, he saw God in His glory. Humility happens when God is on display, for when Isaiah saw God, his automatic response was, "Woe is me, for I am ruined! Because I am a man of unclean lips, and I live among a people of unclean lips; for my eyes have seen the King, the LORD of hosts."[544]

Do you think it is coincidence that the humblest man on earth (Moses) was the only person God ever claimed to speak with face to face? The only one who actually saw the form of God and heard His words plainly?[545]

The biggest mistake I can make in trying to correct a faulty view of myself is to glare harder into the mirror, hoping to get a more accurate view of myself. Because who I am does not come from me. It comes from God. If I want an accurate view of me, I must stop hearing about Him by distant rumor and actually see Him. I must lift my eyes to heaven. I must see Him on His throne, lofty and exalted. If I want an accurate view of me, it comes from staring at the awesome God. Humility is simply the natural response.

When Naaman, a leper, came to Elisha for a cure, Elisha told him all he had to do was dip in the Jordan River seven times and he'd be healed. Naaman's response? He stalked away in a huff because surely it couldn't be that simple.[546]

Is that my response to this offered cure? No. Can't be that easy. All these years I've been trying to beat myself down to no result? All these years I've been trying to build myself up, and nothing? And you're saying all I have to do is... look at God? That's dumb. Too easy. It can't be that simple.

Maybe that's precisely why so many people miss it.

And while the solution is simple, it is not particularly easy. Oftentimes, the symptoms get worse before they get better.

A sneeze is meant to rid your body of the germs that have made you sick. A fever is meant to burn out infection. Pain tells you something is wrong. And when I come face to face with God Almighty, humility may make the fever worse to burn out the pride. I may sneeze to get rid of the insecurity. James 4:9 says humility often involves being miserable, mourning, and weeping. But the result is glorious.

God "gives grace to the humble. Submit therefore to God. Draw near to God and He will draw near to you. Humble yourselves in the presence of the Lord, and He will exalt you."[547] Humility is simply placing myself where I have the best view of God. And it is then that He puts me in my proper and rightful place.

Romans calls this "sound judgment." It is the perfect, proper middle between pride and insecurity. It is neither fever nor chills, neither narcolepsy nor insomnia, neither weight gain nor weight loss; it is the perfect freedom from symptoms.

"I say to everyone among you not to think more highly of himself than he ought to think; but to think so as to have sound judgment."[548]

Humility is a proper view of God, and hits the disease at its source. And from this comes sound judgment, a proper view of me, which knocks out the symptoms. And I would suggest that sound judgment is going to consist of three things.

Knowing where you come from

Knowing where you're going

Knowing where you are now

Know where you come from. Know the God who made you, His character and intention, and what kind of nature and value that confers on you. Know what He made you for, the purpose you have been instilled with. If you are one of those crazy people who watches a sequel before the original and somehow started this book at chapter 9, then go back and read chapter 1. Read chapter 4. Or, you know, just read the Bible. If you don't want to start at the very beginning, the book of Romans functions as a pretty good CliffsNotes for the entire thing.

Know where you're going. I don't just mean the place, which, I hope for every person who reads this, is heaven. I also mean the condition you will be in when you get there. From the day you were saved, you have been making progress from the dead-in-sin person that you were, and God is constantly at work, doing His thing, making you more and more like Jesus Christ who lives in you. And when He's finished, you will be glorious.[549] You will be holy. You will be blameless. You will be dressed in spotless white as if for a wedding, because you are the bride of Christ. "That He might present to Himself the church in all her glory, having no spot or wrinkle or any such thing; but that she would be holy and blameless."[550]

Know where you are now. We are all in the middle of that process, in the middle of that journey. We are each at some point between beginning and end, between dead, helpless, corrupt, and holy, blameless, perfect. And knowing where I am right now, what God has already done and what He has yet to do, is wise and sound and a clear-eyed view of who I am today. Loved at every step along the journey. Purposeful regardless of what moment I'm in. And hopefully closer today than yesterday, tomorrow than today.

When I am gripped with the humility of seeing God clearly, I will be possessed of sound judgment, the ability to see myself clearly.

How, then, *should* I feel about what I see?

When I see the corruption of God's design still affecting me, I will *not* feel

- Surprised. I will be affected by sin until the day I die. If I expect otherwise, I am foolish, and will constantly be beating myself up for failing to measure up. "If we say that we have no sin, we are deceiving ourselves and the truth is not in us. If we confess our sins, He is faithful and just to forgive us our sins and to cleanse us from all unrighteousness."[551]

- Complacent. Sin is not okay. Not at any point or in any amount, and seeing it calls for a response. "Or do you think lightly of the riches of His kindness and tolerance and patience, not knowing that the kindness of God leads you to repentance?"[552]

When I see the corruption of God's design still affecting me, I *will* feel

- Grieved. Not guilty, for that was paid for at the cross, but grieved, because sin hurts me, and I know it. "Cleanse your hands, you sinners; and purify your hearts, you double-minded. Be miserable and mourn and weep; let your laughter be turned into mourning and your joy to gloom. Humble yourselves in the presence of the Lord, and He will exalt you."[553]

- Patient. Don't worry. The grace is in the mail. "The Lord is not slow about His promise, as some count slowness, but is patient toward you..."[554] "For I am confident of this very thing, that He who began a good work in you will perfect it until the day of Christ Jesus."[555]

- Grateful. Because pain is the first sign of change.

When you're dying of hypothermia, you begin to feel warm and toasty and numb to the pain. A nice feeling, but deadly, because not only are you dying, you're also oblivious to it and clearly not doing anything about it. Or worse, you're taking off your gloves and coat because you're warm enough without them.

If I see the corruption that is in me, how it is still affecting me, then I will be grateful. Because the fact that I can see and feel it for the first time is proof that God is already warming me up from the hypothermia. And when God begins the process of warming me up from the cold death I was on my way to, things actually go from nice to bad. There's pain as feeling comes back into my extremities. I start to feel cold again—which is actually a step in the right direction, toward actually *being* warm. The same with sin. I am blissfully unaware until God shows it to me. There's cold, as I see how I've been living, and pain as I grieve over what I've done, and all the while I'm actually warming up, getting moving again. Healing. Thank you, God.

Nowhere in this is room for guilt. Guilt is Satan's tool, and it does not lead to repentance but to spiraling back into sin again. Jesus took sin *and* guilt with Him to the cross, and both are dead and paid for.[556] God's tool is grace.[557]

Here are just a few benefits of a daily dose of humility. They say that some people are born extroverts and some are born introverts, and the difference is not how socially competent you are or even how much you enjoy crowds but whether interaction with people energizes you or drains you of that energy. I don't believe you are drained or filled by people based on whether you're a born introvert or extrovert but rather by how many concerns you're consumed with when you're with people.

If I'm constantly concerned with what opinions are being formed of me, how people are judging me, whether I'm making a positive impression, whether I'm saying the right thing, whether I'm behaving the right way, whether my jokes are landing, or whether I'm talking too much or not enough—that will be draining no matter what personality I was born with.

But if I am free of such concerns and am simply being me, that is freedom. That is natural. Being who I was made to be is no more difficult in a crowd of thousands or a conversation of one than it is sitting on my couch in my PJs watching Netflix.

If I have a daily dose of humility, no longer will I have to walk into every situation, fragile ego in my outstretched hands, striking preemptively in order to protect my undefended pride. No longer will I walk out of every situation licking my wounds or beating myself up for every stupid thing I said or didn't say or the timing with which I said it. Because other people's opinions *will not matter.*

To be clear, how people *feel* matters. If I have offended someone, whether intentionally or unintentionally, then, yes, I want to make that right and apologize for my part in the offense. But what people *think,* this is not my job to correct, and it has no bearing on who I am. If I care about what people feel, I am compassionate. If I do *not* care what people think, I am confident. And I wish to be both.

With a daily dose of humility, my mind will be no longer consumed with calculations of every person's opinion of me as I walk, sit, stand, speak, and act. My mind will instead be free to consider how someone else might be feeling or what someone else might be needing or what someone else might be going through in the moment. My mind will be free to think of someone else.

With a daily dose of humility, my heart will no longer be raw and overly sensitive to the touch. My heart will be fortified, safe, and eager to reach out and touch someone else, invest in their welfare. My heart will be free to love others.

With a daily dose of humility, my actions will no longer be calculated to my desperate benefit and consumed by constant concern about being left wanting or hurting. My actions will be free to serve someone else. All without costing me anything.

Love is the only commodity I know of where my supply of it increases as I give it away. Therefore, instead of being depleted by every encounter, I am filled up every time, and I go home satisfied and ready to rest, as if after a big meal.

What kind of seismic ripples will this send through our world if believers in Jesus started walking around this way? Comfortable with who we are and therefore having no need to tear down the people we're with. Kind, encouraging, and easygoing in a world of needy, arrogant, insecure, uptight people. And though we don't care what people think, they are almost certain to think positively about us, because nothing is more attractive than someone who walks around humble, confident, with a right view of God and self.

The reason Christians are called a light in a dark world is because light stands out as what is so severely lacking to the rest of the world. In a world that is infected with a faulty view of self, a world sick with pride and insecurity, and sick *of* both, nothing stands out more than a person who is glowing with health. Such a thing makes us a walking advertisement: Talk to your doctor about humility, an all-natural drug with no harmful side effects. Symptoms may initially worsen before improving. Take with food.[558]

A person with a right view of God and self is unmistakable. This attitude draws curious, desperate eyes in our direction, and when they look, they will see what our cracked pots cannot hide: God on full display.

And when I see it? I will feel

- Delighted. Because any work of God is delightful, especially when He's working in and on me. "For You, O Lord, have made me glad by what You have done, I will sing for joy at the works of Your hands."[559]

- Excited. He has only just started, and I cannot wait to see what He does next. "Yet those who wait for the Lord will gain new strength; they will mount up on wings like eagles."[560]

- Worshipful. To see what God has done and acknowledge it as His good work is worship. Downplaying God's masterful work in me only denies Him the honor due Him. "Then all men will fear, and they will declare the work of God, and will consider what He has done. The righteous man will be glad in the Lord and will take refuge in Him; and all the upright in heart will glory."[561]

- Celebratory. I want others to see what God has done. I am overjoyed when they do. Because when God does His thing, it is something to celebrate, and it's no fun celebrating alone.[562] "Some boast in chariots and some in horses, but we will boast in the name of the Lord, our God."[563]

"To boast" is, among other things, to be deliriously happy, to rave foolishly, to celebrate unreservedly. There is no room for boasting in myself because when I see God's work in me, there is no question who has done it. And I will not deny Him praise simply because the work I see Him doing is in me. I will not deny Him boasting just because the work I see Him doing is on me. I will shout to the mountaintops what He has done in me just as loudly as I shout about what He has done for me, because my God will not be denied His praise, and the masterpiece underneath, that which is me and not corrupted gunk, is God's good work and every work of God is meant to be acknowledged.

"Come and hear, all who fear God, and I will tell of what He has done for my soul."[564]

One of the weirdest penalties you can get in football (American football, not soccer) is one for "excessive celebrating." When you come from behind, it looks like all is lost, and by some miracle you manage to catch an interception and run it all the way back for a touchdown, if you were to jump up and down a little too enthusiastically, dance a little too wildly, or holler a bit too loudly, they dock you for "excessive celebrating."

No, I don't think the winners should shove it in the faces of the opponents that they are losers, nor make anyone feel bad for losing. But that's "unsportsmanlike conduct." Excessive celebrating is a different thing.

Since the days the Puritans arrived in the New World, there's been a bit of a solemn, quiet, subdued pall cast over Christianity. There is an implication that we should not be too exuberant about our salvation, that we'd better not take full advantage of all the riches of grace, that we cannot boast about what we've been given, lest it be prideful or seen as such. That too wide a grin is not reverent, and that if we were to, God forbid, *dance* in joy over our salvation, there's a very real question of whether we even have that salvation in the first place.

It's almost like we're afraid of getting docked for excessive celebrating.

No, I do not want to rub it in the faces of those who have not experienced salvation that I have something they don't have... or do I? Were the Gentiles not brought into the family of God expressly to make the Jews jealous so that they too would come to Christ?[565] Am I not supposed to exhibit something so attractive, so desirable, so incredible to the world that they desperately want what I have and ask me about it?[566]

We are supposed to boast. Not in ourselves, but in who God is, in knowing Him, in having Him for ourselves.[567] We are supposed to rejoice in what we have. Always.[568] And if someone were to stop us in the street for dancing and call it undignified, God might just strike them barren in response.[569] Because if God's people are silent, the rocks will cry out.[570]

I have come from behind, all was lost, and by some miracle, I have been snatched from the jaws of hell—what else would be my response but to celebrate excessively? After all, that's what the angels in heaven do as soon as they hear of it.[571] When my sins are gone, is there such a thing as being too exuberant? When heaven is mine, is there such a thing as shouting too loudly? When Jesus has saved my soul, is there such a thing as dancing too wildly? Is there such a thing as excessive when the thing I'm celebrating is Jesus?

So, no, it's not about me. And how I feel about myself is not the point. But it is a happy side effect of a daily dose of humility. When God is glorified, put on display in my life, and I see it, how I feel about me is going to change. And it is going to change for the better.

What of mine do I substitute for God's? My wisdom for His? My timing for His? My plans for His? My wishes for His? In what way is this pride? What would a proper view of God tell me? How would this change my attitude?

What do I normally do when I recognize pride in myself? What have been the results? What do I normally do when I recognize insecurity in myself? What have been the results?

Who do I find myself trying to please? If I solely cared about pleasing God, would I do anything differently? How much weight do I give people's opinions? How much do their opinions affect my decisions? Think of the last time someone's opinion weighed heavily on me. If I cared how they felt but not what they thought, how would I have navigated that situation?

What do I fear? (Make a list.) In what way do these things have power over me? In each of these ways, how is God ultimately in control? (Consider finding verses that say as much.) In what ways am I giving my fears power over me that they should not have? How would my life change in these areas if I traded in my fear of something less for the fear of the Lord?

What kind of view of God do I currently have? How might I improve my view? How might that alter my view of me?

CHAPTER 10
The Most Pointless War in History

T he day that time started was a good day. God created light and separated it from the darkness, and
declared it to be good. The day after that was pretty good
too. Oceans and sky—all good. Day three was wonderful.
Dry land appeared, and God invented the most incredible
plants and flowers to go on it.[572]

But a few days in, God created something that should
have been glorious, incredible, the most worship-offering,
awe-inspiring, God-honoring thing He made: angels.

But there was one particular angel who wasn't
pleased with the role God designed for him, that of
reflecting glory back at God Himself. This angel wished
instead to receive the glory. To be like God. And not long
after he was created, the angel Lucifer, now known as
Satan or the devil, declared war on God Himself.

Big mistake.

When God goes to war, the hearts of the nations melt, knees knock together, and people wet their pants in fear of His coming. Without God lifting a finger or raising an army, His enemies go blind, go crazy, turn on one another, and flee. Without speaking a word, His power is known, remembered, feared, and His enemies come running to Him to fall to their knees, begging for mercy. Without firing a shot, God is victorious.[573]

When God goes to war, nature itself bends to His will. Water defies gravity, the sun stands still in the sky, donkeys speak, plagues spread, fields die, water turns to blood, and mountains crumble into the heart of the sea.[574]

When God goes to war, five men put a thousand to flight,[575] cars without mufflers turn into tanks and drive off the enemy sight unseen, weakness is turned to strength, strength to weakness, foolishness to wisdom, and wisdom to folly.

When God goes to war, who can stand?

The Old Testament describes the God of war, of despair, destruction, depression, and doom. To the untrained eye, He appears to be sitting on the edge of His seat, thunder and lightning in hand, eager to smite down

His people, scowling the whole time. When He judges, He judges completely, and even the memory of His enemies is wiped out. When He sends forth His wrath, it is complete, a consuming fire that leaves nothing in its wake. In the words of Joel, what the gnawing locust has left, the swarming locust has eaten; and what the swarming locust has left, the creeping locust has eaten; and what the creeping locust has left, the stripping locust has eaten.[576]

This is our God. This has always been our God. The One who sent His enemies to punish Israel and then sent their enemies to punish them, whose wrath can never be used up or turned aside, this is our God.

Many believe the New Testament God of compassion and forgiveness has mellowed some. Changed His plan, altered His approach, and decided to try love instead of wrath to get ahold of His people, but here's the thing: To believe our present-day God of love to be anything less than righteous, holy, wrathful, and warlike is folly. And to believe the burning, destroying Ancient of Days to be anything less than absolute love and longsuffering is tragic.

This picture of what it looks like when God goes to war—this is what it looks like when God holds back.

When Adam and Eve ate of the forbidden fruit, God sent them outside the garden, supposedly for their punishment. I think perhaps it was just as much for their protection. They were revealed and naked before Him, and He was unmasked and unhidden from them, walking beside them, talking to them face to face. How long are flammable, sinful, corrupted people going to last in the presence of this God? When Moses wished to see God's face, He obliged by covering poor little flammable Moses with His hand so Moses wouldn't spontaneously combust.[577]

The curtain in the temple, the sacrifices, the feasts, the laws—all that stuff described in mind-bending detail in Leviticus—it was all a firebreak, something to protect God's people from the raging fire that was His wrath. In the midst of a camp full of lovable gasoline, the Holy Fire had to hide away, pulling farther and farther back from His people until He withdrew to heaven entirely, leaving them in darkness for four hundred years, but at least they were alive.

For thousands of years, God kept holding in the thunder and lightning, the wrath and anger. He kept letting out the line, backing off from the ignition, holding in everything His justice demanded to let loose. Here is the hiding of His power, Habakkuk says.[578]

Enter Jesus.

Jesus was everything God loves. Perfect and holy, fireproof and glorious, beloved and adored. Imagine the bumper stickers God could have slapped on the back of the storm clouds He rides. This is Jesus to Him, everything wonderful and God and good in human form—what humankind was meant to look like, the uncorrupted form of the corrupted.

But about this time, God's wrath was about to overflow. Having held back for millennia, the sin of humanity was coming to a critical mass. There was nowhere to go, no further to get, and humankind was going to combust. When the time was right,[579] Jesus took up the robe of sinfulness of all of humanity and wore it like it was His and opened His arms and His life to the wrath of God.

I imagine there's no cap on the emotions God felt. Grief, sorrow, and howling anger at having to destroy His own Son. But He was also pleased to crush Him, to put Him to grief, because it is by His stripes that we are healed.[580]

God was blissfully relieved to have an outlet for His justice that was not me. To have an opportunity to let it loose without destroying utterly those He loves. And by the time Jesus breathed His last breath, God was satisfied. I always think of "satisfied" as being full, like after a good meal. But I think in this case it means empty. God had finally emptied Himself of all the pent-up wrath He'd held back for centuries, glad to release it onto the resurrectable Jesus so He could save the condemnable me.

This is the God of war, and when He does a thing, He does it utterly. Nothing left, not a brick left upon another, not a sin left struggling to crawl out of the crater. Total devastation. This is the magnitude and power with which He does what He hates, what He holds back, what He avoids and puts off as long as possible. Imagine the perfection with which He does what He longs to do.

God is described as waiting, longing to show mercy.[581] On the edge of His seat, mercy in hand, itching to rain it down on me and grinning the whole time. He can't wait. He delights to do this.[582] It is His favorite expression of His character.

God never changes. It is not in His nature to change, not in His wisdom to change His mind. And the God who created the world and watched it fall does not make mistakes. Jesus was not Plan B. He was the from-the-foundation-of-the-world plan to reconcile God's justice with His mercy, His truth and His love, His wrath and His compassion. Jesus was always Plan A.

God never changes. But Jesus changes everything. Starting with me.

When God went to war, He went to war against me. Somewhere along the line, I decided that God's way was not my way, that His plan was not my plan, that His offer was not what I wanted, and I went to war against a God I could never hope to match. And I strapped on my armor made entirely of bloody, filthy rags, lifted my sword of self-righteousness, and charged full steam ahead against a consuming fire that could not be stopped.

The day I realized who I was fighting was a dark day indeed. I was terrified, horrified, frightened beyond belief because it was too late to change sides. I couldn't defect because I had nothing to offer. I couldn't run because I was already crippled and pinned down in that foxhole, cannonballs whistling over my head. I couldn't hide because He was too close, about to step right on me, and I was already in the deepest hole I could dig. I was lost.

And then Jesus jumped into the foxhole beside me, ripped a corner off His robes of righteousness, and handed me a white flag. I didn't even have enough clean on me to make my own surrender flag.

So, terrified and with the Holy Fire approaching, I lifted that little square of humility handed to me by Christ, and, half expecting—no, fully expecting—that God would blast my hand off, I raised it to heaven and waited for His judgment.

And God peeked over the edge of my foxhole and judged me to be His. He picked me up in His arms, carried me home, cleaned me up, bandaged my wounds, healed my broken places, stripped off me the worthless rags I thought would stop a bullet, and gave me robes of white. "My Son's clothes," he says. "I bet they'll fit you."

God is either the biggest, most all-consuming enemy out there, or He is the biggest enemy-consumer I could have. Against God, I don't stand a chance. With God, my enemies don't.

I do not believe that salvation is a one-time experience. It is a life, a whole life, an eternal life, and it starts the moment God declared peace with me. And it is a life that is protected by the God who is still and ever going to war. But, this time, for me.

When God goes to war, I have a confidence not my own, a courage beyond my circumstances, and a peace that passes understanding.[583] My enemies melt with fear before me and every fear I've ever felt pales in comparison to the fear of the Lord, present tense, when God is fighting my battles for me.

When God goes to war, nature itself bends to His will. Mountains move by the power of faith, water holds my weight,[584] the sun shines through storm and night and rain and clouds, walls fall,[585] and giants topple.[586]

When God goes to war, He does it completely. Victory is assured, total, inevitable, and imminent. The God of war has made peace with me, and that war is over.

And this is what Satan's up against.

You'd think that Satan, being a semi-intelligent guy,[587] would have sat back, taken stock, and calculated whether he really wanted to pick a fight with this God. Whether he really stood a chance against God and His people.

"Or what king, when he sets out to meet another king in battle, will not first sit down and consider whether he is strong enough with ten thousand men to encounter the one coming against him with twenty thousand?"[588] The answer is, Satan did.

Without stopping to consider how all this was going to end, or perhaps like the scorpion stinging the frog half-way across the river because he just couldn't help himself, Satan rebelled against God, fell from heaven, and hit the ground hard. God is infinite. Satan is limited. God is eternal. Satan is created. God is in control. Satan is just a tool in His belt.

What then is a devil supposed to do?

No matter who's winning, no matter who's going to win, no matter how foregone the conclusion or how predetermined the outcome, propaganda is a powerful tool.

There's an episode of the television series *Leverage* where a team of thieves sets out to steal a country. Technically, all they really wanted were the results of an election. Knowing that five people cannot reasonably rig an entire country's election and get away with it, they instead decided to run a fake campaign and then announce the morning of the election that their candidate had won. There were parties in the streets, news stations repeating the news, and the incumbent leader stewing in his castle, wondering what on earth happened. The answer: nothing happened. But once the people believed the lie, it was going to be far too much trouble for the real winner to reassert the truth, so the guy just forfeited.

Satan can't win, so he claims he's winning. That evil has a stronger grip on this world than God does. That there are more places where God has lost control over world events than there are places where God still reigns supreme. That God is losing His grip, His footing, His planet, His people, and it's only a matter of time before Satan tugs it all from His grasp entirely.

Imagine a propaganda poster. Here's Satan, horns and pitchfork, forked tongue and yellow eyes, holding one end of a tug-of-war rope, while God, white beard, sandals, and long robe, is holding the other end. In the middle, where the flag or knot should be, is planet earth, haplessly inching back and forth between good and evil with neither claiming the clear advantage. This would be the caption: *Look at the world around you. Who do you think is winning?*

Satan would have us believe that he and God—the supreme evil versus the supreme good—are equal and opposite forces in this universe. Light and dark, dividing the world down the middle like in those nice photos of our planet from space. Good and evil, a perfect little scale waiting to measure a person's actions, balanced until something is set on it.

Opposite, they may be. Equal, they are not.

Knowing he's going to lose and that he'll spend eternity in the prison that God designed especially for him—hell—Satan would like as much company as possible. People God created to spend forever with Him instead spending eternity keeping misery company.

And yes, regrettably, grievously, heartbreakingly, people are headed for hell. But there is a moment when God peeks over the foxhole, sees the person His Son died to save, sees the white flag of surrender provided by His Son, and judges that person to be His. In that moment, God picks that person up, carries him home, and calls him his child. In that moment, the person goes from darkness to light, out of the kingdom of Satan, into the kingdom of God.[589] And from that moment, that person is untouchable. Jesus says, "I give eternal life to them, and they will never perish; and no one will snatch them out of My hand."[590] Take that, Satan.

So, if Satan's pointless war is already lost, if believers are beyond his reach, then what on earth is he fighting for?

Unable to defeat God, unable to damn me, Satan clings to the only thing he can truly destroy. Can you guess what it is?

Our world, our country, is in turmoil over quite a few issues, but in recent years they seem to boil down to identity—when life starts, sexual orientation, whether gender exists, euthanasia, even racism. It's about who we are, what we're worth, and how we treat others and ourselves based on those things.

The last thing in the world that I want to do is use this book as a soapbox to stand on to address a thousand and one controversial issues. Yuck. That just leads to confusion, anger, and division, and none of those things reflect the character of God. But I think there's a reason that when addressing my identity, who I am, I keep bumping into a thousand and one controversial topics. Satan is on the warpath, and this is his current chosen area to attack.

Why? Why am I so important? Why is attacking *me* his plan? Why is attacking my identity his strategy? This may not be new, but it bears repeating:

1. An attack on my identity is an attack on the character of God.

Satan can't do God any damage. God's shining armor can't be scratched, His glory can't be dimmed, His power can't be diminished, and His plans can't be thwarted. But God resides in heaven, acts invisibly, and speaks inaudibly. And the only way this world knows God is through a book that must be understood by fallible people, by languages that fall short of capturing His infinite character, through creation cursed and corrupted by the fall, and by us. Through people who *can* be tarnished, scratched, battered and beaten up, whose reputation can be ruined, and whose ability to reflect God can become compromised. If Satan can corrupt those who bear the image of God, then he can obscure God.

When Jesus came to earth, He came to save. He also came to be the visible, audible, touchable, literal down-to-earth God in human flesh. "He is the image of the invisible God."[591]

This is what God would say if He was face to face with you. This is what God would do if He was walking next to you. This is how God would love if He was living side by side with you. You want to know who God is? Let me paint you a picture.

You and I, as believers, are increasingly being transformed into that same image. "Beholding as in a mirror the glory of the Lord, [we] are being transformed into the same image from glory to glory."[592] "You laid aside the old self with its evil practices, and have put on the new self who is being renewed to a true knowledge according to the image of the One who created him."[593] "For those whom He foreknew, He also predestined to be conformed to the image of His Son, so that He would be the firstborn among many brethren."[594]

This trail that Jesus blazed, I am following along behind. He showed a watching world who God was, and it is that image that I bear, that picture that I paint.

This is what God would say if He was face to face with you. This is what God would do if He was walking next to you. This is how God would love if He was living side by side with you. You want to know who God is? Let me paint you a picture.

What picture am I painting?

If someone were looking at me to know who God is, they would see a picture of a God who is here one day and gone the next. Who is powerful and certain today, able to move mountains and conquer demons, and the next day is nowhere to be seen. If someone were looking at me to know who God is, they would see a God who shows compassion when it is convenient, who takes note of the suffering of others when nothing more important is occupying His attention, who puts principle over people, who demands perfection and condemns anything less, who keeps score of wrongs, who gives up on people when they no longer deserve His longsuffering. A God who loves conditionally, who forgives sporadically, who offers mercy to the deserving.

They would see a God nothing like the real thing. A God not worth serving, not worth trusting, and a God who, when hope is put in Him, disappoints every time.

Satan attacks me, and this is what my world thinks of my God. Satan may not have aimed at the heart of God, but that is exactly what he hit when he aimed at me.

2. An attack on my identity is a bushel over the light of Jesus.

There's a children's song taught in Sunday school classes across the English-speaking world, and it goes like this: "This little light of mine, I'm gonna let it shine. Let it shine, let it shine, let it shine."

It was prophesied that when Jesus came, He would come "to shine upon those who sit in darkness and the shadow of death."[595] Jesus said, "I have come as Light into the world, so that everyone who believes in Me will not remain in darkness. I am the Light of the World; he who follows Me will not walk in the darkness, but will have the Light of life."[596]

That's a lofty thing to claim. To be the lighthouse in the storm, the thing to aim at if you want to live and find solid ground. To be the flashlight on the path, so that you will not trip and stumble over every obstacle. If you want salvation, this is the one thing in the whole world that will show you the way.

And yet Jesus claims an even crazier thing. "You are the light of the world. A city set on a hill cannot be hidden; nor does anyone light a lamp and put it under a basket, but on the lampstand, and it gives light to all who are in the house. Let your light shine before men in such a way that they may see your good works, and glorify your Father who is in heaven."[597]

There's a second verse to that same children's song, based on the King James Version of that verse, where a "basket" is called a "bushel." "Hide it under a bushel? No! I'm gonna let it shine."

Jesus has lit in me a fire. When He, the great Light of the World, returned to heaven after His resurrection, He left little candle flames in all of us, to carry on what He was doing. To be to the world the same thing He was—no, not the sacrifice for sin. But the great big billboard pointing the way to salvation.

In a world of darkness, we stand out. We beckon. Like a lighthouse in a storm, we promise safety. Like a flashlight in a dark maze, we promise direction. Like a spotlight in a theater, no one sees the light and looks up at the light itself. They look at what we shine on. This is Jesus, your salvation! Come and be saved!

You want to know something Satan doesn't want you to know? He can't snuff you out. He can't dump a bucket of water on you, or tamp a fancy candlesnuffer down over you, or pinch out the flame that is you, or blow you out like a birthday candle.

But this little light of mine can choose to shine on top of a hill, or it can choose to shine under a bushel.

Satan attacks my identity so that I will let my life go by, quietly sitting under a bushel and not making an impact on my world. So that nobody sees me. Nobody hears me. Nobody notices me because I don't want to bother anybody. Still and quiet, under my nice, safe, warm little bushel, I live my whole life where the light in me shines on nobody, and nothing around me changes.

If Satan cannot defeat the army that is God's people, then he'd like us to sleep through the war, tucked away in our barracks. If Satan cannot destroy God's people, he'd like us to go through the whole war with our swords jammed securely in their sheaths and never strike a blow for truth. If Satan cannot snuff out God's people, then he'd like us to go through the whole war with our lamps hidden in our pitchers so the enemy can't make out our position, rather than breaking those pots wide open so that the light frightens the darkness away and announces to every captive that Jesus comes to save.

3. An attack on my identity is a roadblock in the path of good works laid out for me.

They say all roads lead to Rome. I imagine that was slightly more true before the first roads were built on continents separated from Rome by an ocean. But once upon a time, for the sake of argument, let's say all roads led to Rome. However, there were a thousand different pathways to get there, and which path you took depended on where you started and what you intended to accomplish along the way.

The purpose of every creation of God is singular: to put God on display. No ifs, ands, or buts. Every purpose. Every road. Every creation of God, good, bad, or ugly. All will glorify God.[598]

However, there are a thousand pathways that all lead to the same place, and which pathway I take is particularly, specifically, chosen by God for me.

Ephesians 2:10 says, "For we are His workmanship, created in Christ Jesus for good works, which God prepared beforehand so that we would walk in them."

God has plotted out a series of good works. My pathway of good works is uniquely designed just for me. Each good work has been fully prepared, obstacles foreseen, solutions provided. The pathway has been predetermined by a God who knows all, sees all, and controls it all with a loving heart and a powerful hand. And it is laid out in front of me, step by step, that I may follow. It takes into account all my strengths, all my weaknesses, all my needs, and all the ways I'm needed. No one else can do these good works quite like me, and I will never do someone else's as well. And it is designed *for who I am.*

Satan attacks identity so he can put roadblocks in this glorious pathway that God has prepared for me. If I lose sight of who I am, I also lose sight of what I'm supposed to be doing.

Only the workmanship that God crafted can possibly walk this pathway of good works designed for me. If I believe I am less than a masterpiece, a poor counterfeit that will never pass the expert's examination, I will shy away from the good works laid out in front of me, certain someone else can do them better. If I believe I am less than uniquely handcrafted by God for this work, that I am somehow a mass-produced garage sale reject, then I will busy myself with someone else's tasks, forever bemoaning the fact I will never do them as well as that other person. If I believe I am an ugly mistake on God's otherwise nice canvas, I will spend my life imagining myself to be worthless, useless, pointless, small. And, convinced I can't, I won't. I will behave as the thing I imagine myself to be, and that pathway of good works will be left untraveled.

If I allow Satan to put a roadblock in the pathway God has designed for me, I will end up lost and going in circles, wondering if I've passed this particular rock before. In this place, the sin I've already knocked down keeps coming back, and I am forced to deal with it over and over again. I pray and pray and pray for God to reveal His will for my life. I wallow in purposelessness and confusion. I waste my time on what doesn't matter and start setting artificial benchmarks for myself just to feel like I'm accomplishing something. All the while, the pathway grows less clear as I accept that I am not really who and how God made me to be.

This is exactly the kind of army Satan would like to be up against. An army not marching purposefully but wandering aimlessly. One so convinced of its inability to take a hill that it does not even try. One with so little direction that it is forced to retake the same hill over and over. One so divided and confused that everyone's trying to take everyone else's hill and the front never advances, the cause is forgotten, and the colors are muddied.

No, Satan can't defeat God. No, he can't damn me. But if I let him put enough roadblocks in my path, I will spend this war trapped in a hedge maze. That's as close to victory as Satan can ever hope to achieve. If he can only strike at God through His people, then there is no more vulnerable place than where I keep my very identity. If he gets that, then this army is neutralized without him firing a shot.

This is why identity is attacked. Given what Satan can't do, this is his next best option, his most potent weapon, his most effective attack, and the closest he'll ever come to getting what he wants. Therefore, this needs to be the place I put my greatest defenses, the target I need to most carefully shield, the assaults I most put my scouts on the alert for.

Up until a hundred or so years ago, war seemed to be something everybody participated in, one way or another. If you weren't pulling on your boots, loading your gun, getting on a boat, and shooting at the enemy, you were trading your skirt for pants and going to work in the factories making bullets or tanks. You were collecting cans instead of playing kick-the-can so that it could be turned into bullets or tanks. You were rationing so the soldiers could have what they needed. You couldn't walk down a street without seeing an Uncle Sam Wants You poster or watch a movie without a newsreel of what was going on over there.

But sometime after that, when wars weren't fought on the home front or in defense of the home front but began to be fought "over there," for reasons not everyone understood, war was no longer for everyone. There were soldiers. And then there were civilians.

There are no civilians when it comes to the war on truth. It's not being fought in the jungles of Africa or on the Amazon (the river, not the website). It's being fought in our homes, in our minds, for our hearts, and if each of us doesn't pull on our boots and do something, we're already losing.

Once upon a time, there was a fortress-city called Sardis, which sat on top of a cliff. On the one side, there was a gradual slope up to it, totally exposed, so that if the enemy attempted to sneak across the grass, they'd be seen and wiped out before they got halfway there. On the other side was an unscalable cliff. And for the centuries and centuries that people tried to overtake Sardis, it was only ever conquered twice, and both times for the same reason: Someone on watch fell asleep, and the enemy managed to sneak up unnoticed.

The very last time Jesus was on earth (a quick trip to dictate some letters to the last living apostle, John), He wrote a letter to the church that was located in Sardis. And His advice would have hit them like a gut punch, given their history and how important it was for their otherwise unassailable walls to be guarded by people who were paying attention. "I know your deeds, that you have a name that you are alive, but you are dead... Wake up!"[599]

These were people who looked like they had it all together. But complacency and rot were creeping in, and they were dying inside. And if they didn't wake up and start paying attention, their walls would be breached.

One of Satan's slimiest tricks is telling lies on both sides of the truth. Way over here, we have the lie that God is losing the war, which leads us to despair and fatalism, and we can't seem to drag ourselves out of bed to fight what is, after all, a losing war. And on the other side, we have the lie that it's all good, that I have my heaven ticket and my bags are all packed and there's nothing to worry about, which leads to complacency; so I sigh and snuggle back down into the pillow, still sleeping.

While identity is by no means the only thing Satan is attacking (he will attack on as many fronts as possible and any place he feels is vulnerable), it most certainly seems to be one of his favorites, and I need to be watching for warning signs that I'm falling asleep on this particular wall. When these thoughts start going through my head, I need to *wake up*!

- The "truth" of God's word doesn't really
  work in real life.
- What God says I am is different from
  who I really am.
- It doesn't really matter what I think
  about myself.

There's this TV show called *Burn Notice* where a burned spy uses his spy tricks to help the little guy against drug dealers and gang members and whoever. However, he insists that when you've captured a bad guy and need information from him, torture does not work. What works is to redraw his reality. And since you are the only link he has to the outside world, you can gradually convince him that out there, his friends have stopped looking for him, his cause is futile, and his boss is about to be captured with or without his cooperation, and he's going to spend the rest of his life in a CIA black site—when none of this is actually true. But a few days with no one but you telling him what to believe, he'll start believing it.

Maybe because God is the One who literally writes reality, and Satan wants to try his hand at rewriting it; maybe because God is truth, and therefore telling lies is the most direct assault Satan can make on the Person of God; maybe because Satan discovered on day one just how gullible the human race can be, one of his favorite things to do is paint for us an altered version of reality. One in which hell does not exist, God is in all of us, morality is subjective, and truth is relative. There are no sides, so there is no war. There is no war, so nothing is being attacked. Nothing is being attacked, so there is nothing to fight for. And as we hang our gleaming, unused armor on the wall and tuck ourselves into bed for the night, the fiery darts are hissing over the walls.

If Satan has waged war on me, and I refuse to believe that there is a war, then I am defeated before I even get out of bed. And if I do not understand the nature of the war I am fighting, I am in trouble just as deep.

The thing is, with enough darts getting through, and enough injuries and casualties, even a sleeping soldier is bound to realize his home is being attacked. If I have woken up and realized that my identity is under attack, then Satan would have me fighting for all the wrong reasons. He would have me believe that the war is about status, that the enemy is each other, and the only stakes are how I feel about myself. Running in circles, fighting the wrong enemy, we may as well still be sleeping, and Satan is free to sneak right in the back door and take the whole castle out from under us.

In every war, there are two sides and then there's the guy who plays both against each other. The war profiteer. He has a stockpile of weapons, and he's not choosy about who he sells to. In fact, the more carnage, the more he profits, because the more both sides come to him for more weapons. And both sides end up defeating themselves for the profit of the arms dealer.

Because Satan is just as invisible as God is, it's an easy thing for him to point out real, visible people and paint them as the enemy. It could be as simple as us vs. them, the believers vs. the unbelievers, those inside the city vs. those outside the city, and rather than seeing those outside the gates as those in desperate need of rescue—the very reason I venture out onto the battlefield in the first place—I start seeing them as the enemy, locking my gates up tighter and lobbing grenades over the walls at people I'm not close enough to see, let alone love.

It could be that Satan floats a rumor that there are traitors in my city, that my neighbors and friends have turned on me, and he creates two sides where there should be one. Just before the Apostle Paul goes into who our enemy is and how to put on the armor of God to fight against him, he describes how believers are supposed to live together. "Therefore I, the prisoner of the Lord, implore you to walk in a manner worthy of the calling with which you have been called, with all humility and gentleness, with patience, showing tolerance for one another in love, being diligent to preserve the unity of the Spirit in the bond of peace. There is one body and one Spirit, just as also you were called in one hope of your calling; one Lord, one faith, one baptism, one God and Father of all who is over all and through all and in all."[600]

As David said, "Behold, how good and pleasant it is for brothers to dwell together in unity!"[601] But usually that doesn't happen. Why? Because Satan's got a cart full of weapons to sell, and if we don't turn on one another, there's no profit in it for him.

And so Satan, the master of wrapping truth in lies,[602] of using the Word of God to tempt,[603] of redrawing reality so that we don't even know we're caught in his web until it's too late, points out all the ways my brothers and sisters are different from me, all the ways they think differently, act differently, put God on display differently, and he sells me the very Word of God to cut them down with.

As Jesus said, "Any kingdom divided against itself is laid waste; and any city or house divided against itself will not stand."[604] God's Word, an incredible and powerful weapon, is used in a manner it was never meant to be used for. We bloody each other, we ignore those outside, and the only one who profits is Satan, sitting on his empty armory cart while the hatred is flying, gleefully counting his coins as people are dying outside, and inside the gates is the very last place they'd imagine they'd find help.

There's a reason the Apostle Paul begins his discussion of the armor of God with a reminder of who our enemy is. "For our struggle is not against flesh and blood, but against the rulers, against the powers, against the world forces of this darkness, against the spiritual forces of wickedness in the heavenly places."[605]

Imagine the moment when, while obliviously pouring his coins into his coin purse while perched on his cart, Satan looked up to see that every single person suddenly recognized who the enemy was. Imagine if suddenly the gates opened and we began bringing people inside, wounded, yes, but getting help, as Satan frantically hops off the cart yelling, "No!" as people once bound for hell are now beyond his reach. Imagine if every sword turned on the true enemy as he ran from our cities, abandoning cart and coins, just to get away from us. It is a promise, folks. "Resist the devil and he will flee from you."[606]

There are soldiers who go off to war not knowing how the war even started. There are soldiers who go off to war not even knowing what they're fighting for. But, as far as I know, no soldier has ever gone off to war knowing, already, how it's going to end.

But we do.

We have a huge advantage. We know how the war started—Satan wanted to be like God, and went after His people as a way of getting at the God who loves them. We know why we're fighting—to put God on display so that a broken world knows where to come for healing. And unlike in every other war in human history, we know how it's going to end.

The book of Revelation is confusing to most people, myself included. There's a massive amount of symbolism, much of which is explained, much of which isn't, and I cannot for the life of me tell what's chronological and what's redescribing something already described but in new words. It's confusing.

Right up until you get to chapter 19. Then it's pretty straightforward.

"And I saw heaven opened, and behold, a white horse, and He who sat on it is called Faithful and True, and in righteousness He judges and wages war." This is Jesus, by the way. And it's a really hard thing to describe what Jesus, the Son of God, looks like in all His glory, but John gives it his best shot: "His eyes are a flame of fire, and on His head are many diadems; and He has a name written on Him which no one knows except Himself. He is clothed with a robe dipped in blood, and His name is called The Word of God. And the armies which are in heaven, clothed in fine linen, white and clean, were following Him on white horses. From His mouth comes a sharp sword, so that with it He may strike down the nations, and He will rule them with a rod of iron; and He treads the wine press of the fierce wrath of God, the Almighty. And on His robe and on his thigh He has a name written, 'KING OF KINGS, AND LORD OF LORDS.'"

Here's where it gets a bit gross. But it's war. You expect there to be blood. "Then I saw an angel standing in the sun, and he cried out with a loud voice, saying to all the birds which fly in midheaven, 'Come, assemble for the great supper of God, so that you may eat the flesh of kings and the flesh of commanders and the flesh of mighty men and the flesh of horses and of those who sit on them and the flesh of all men, both free men and slaves, and small and great.'

"And I saw the beast and the kings of the earth and their armies assembled to make war against Him who sat on the horse and against His army."

This is the climax. If this were a movie, it would be this moment on a poster, heavens split open, Jesus and His army blazing white and ready to ride, birds circling ready to eat the carrion, and every army left on earth, all assembled. Earth has been devastated, almost everyone is dead, and this is the final battle. The deciding moment. The last push to victory or defeat, no sequel forthcoming. If this were a movie, it would be here that the orchestra is at its loudest, the drums at their most insistent, the audience most on the edge of their seats.

If this were a movie, it would fail at the box office.

"And the beast was seized... and thrown alive into the lake of fire. And the rest were killed, and all the birds were filled with their flesh."[607]

In the space of two verses, the deadliest war in all of history comes to a close. The greatest enemy in all of history is defeated. The movie ends in all of twenty seconds. Jesus grabs Satan and tosses him away, while birds are feasting on the dead. You almost do a double take, wondering if there was something in the deleted scenes, if perhaps your crinkly-thin Bible pages got stuck together and you missed something. Nope. It's just... over.

There's a book series, The Twilight Saga, on which a movie series was made. Spoiler alert: The series ends with all the good guys lined up against all the bad guys in a field. The whole book has been building to this moment. We've been terrified of what these bad guys will do to us. They can't be escaped, can't be defeated, can't be dissuaded, and the entire book series ends with... a conversation. And everyone quietly part ways, grudgingly agreeing to live and let live. Let's just say the moviemakers recognized the problem with this and fabricated an entire battle to satisfy the audience.

And yet it is precisely the anticlimactic end of the world's greatest evil that *is* so satisfying to us as the audience. Jesus doesn't even have to try. There's no struggle, no darkness-before-the-dawn moment when it looks like our Hero might not make it. No. Satan was created, by God, as a tool in His belt, and when Satan's function has come to an end and it comes time to do away with him, Jesus tosses him away like the snake he always was.

When God does something great, something impressive, it is said to have been done by the hand of God. He sends plagues, destroys armies, empowers His people, leads the hearts of kings, makes rivers out of deserts, and saves souls. This is done by the hand of God.[608]

When God does something spectacular, something impossible, it is said to be done by the arm of God. The devastation of Egypt, the parting of the Red Sea, the destruction of Pharaoh's army, the fear spreading far and wide before the Israelites as they marched to their homeland. This is done by the arm of God.[609]

So, when the enemy attacks, what does God lift to crush him?

His finger.[610]

I have this image of Jesus, standing before Legion, countless demons who are cowering before Him, and Jesus just flicking them away like He's shooting marbles.[611] The enemy doesn't stand a chance.

We underestimate Satan. But we really underestimate God. And I have no intention of doing either.

Before the beginning, God chose me.[612] In the beginning, God created us in His image.[613] At my beginning, I was knit together in my mother's womb, fearfully and wonderfully made.[614] At my new beginning, I have been remade into the likeness of Christ, the old things have passed away, and all things have been made new.[615] And when all things come to an end, this is my confidence:

1. This battle will end.[616]
2. The war is already won.[617]
3. I am on the winning side.[618]
4. Satan will be crushed beneath my feet.[619]
5. I am an overcomer.[620]
6. Death has no power over me.[621]
7. I am destined to reign at Jesus' side.[622]
8. I will never be defeated.

"What then shall we say to these things? If God is for us, who is against us? He who did not spare His own Son, but delivered Him over for us all, how will He not also with Him freely give us all things? Who will bring a charge against God's elect? God is the one who justifies; who is the one who condemns? Christ Jesus is He who died, yes, rather who was raised, who is at the right hand of God, who also intercedes for us. Who will separate us from the love of Christ? Will tribulation, or distress, or persecution, or famine, or nakedness, or peril, or sword? Just as it is written, 'For your sake we are being put to death all day long; we were considered as sheep to be slaughtered.' But in all these things we overwhelmingly conquer through Him who loved us. For I am convinced that neither death, nor life, nor angels, nor principalities, nor things present, nor things to come, nor powers, nor height, nor depth, nor any other created thing, will be able to separate us from the love of God, which is in Christ Jesus our Lord."[623]

LIVING THE TRUTH

In what ways does God not change? (Make a list.) In what ways does Jesus change everything? (Make a list.) How does this change things between me and God? Am I fully living like this is true?

If a watching world were spying me out in order to see what God looks like, what would they conclude about the character of God? How is this different from God's actual character? What one way could I focus on living Jesus' character more in my life?

What does the "bushel" in my life look like? What would my life look like lived on a hill? What tempts me to hide my light under a bushel the most? What practical steps can I take today to start shining on a hill instead?

What is my pathway of good works? What roadblock is currently sitting in it? What do I need to do to push through that roadblock?

What propaganda does Satan try to sell me about the most pointless war in history? What lies am I most prone to believe? What effect is believing those lies having on my life? What is the truth? What would living that truth look like? How would my life be different?

How does the war end? When I am standing at the end, how will I feel about all the struggles and pain and suffering (see perhaps Philippians 1:21, 3:7–8 or James 1:2–4)? What current concerns, worries, or pursuits will simply cease to matter? When I am standing at the end, how do I want to look back over the time I spent in this life? Is there anything I need to change here and now to make that a reality?

The One Thing You Don't Mess With

" I n the beginning, God created the heavens and the earth,"[624] and then things get a little fuzzy.

They didn't used to be. But then Darwin introduced his ideas and evolutionary theory began to be taught in school and a great rift developed between people who believed that God created and people who believed that life evolved.

So, to heal the rift and allow rational scientists to still be good Christians and vice versa, two suggestions were made as to how the biblical account of creation might actually be an account of evolution, though primitive man didn't realize it.

The first theory is called the gap theory. "In the beginning, God created the heavens and the earth,"[625] and then a gap of millions of years went by. Presumably,

God created the heavens and the earth complete—fish, animals, birds, trees, what have you—and then, after millions of years of this, wiped clean the slate to start over: "The earth was formless and void, and darkness was over the surface of the deep, and the Spirit of God was moving over the surface of the waters. Then God said, 'Let there be light'; and there was light."[626] From there, things progressed as we were taught in Sunday school.

The second theory is, I think, more popular. "God called the light day, and the darkness He called night. And there was evening and there was morning, one day."[627] And this "one day," actually translates to millions of years.

Here is where folks get up in arms about the literalness of Scripture. If "day" doesn't mean "day," what next? Does "grace" mean "grace"? And the whole of Scripture goes out the window!

However, remembering, of course, that there are parables[628] and metaphors[629] and figurative language[630] all throughout Scripture, Christians *are* going to bump up against this problem at some point: How do we know when to take Scripture literally and when it's painting a picture?

"Day," in fact, means at least three different things. 1. The daylight hours. After all, God did call "the light day, and the darkness He called night…"[631] 2. A twenty-four-hour period. Obviously. For instance, when God told the people of Israel to work six days and rest on the seventh,[632] He was definitely talking about chunks of twenty-four hours. 3. An era of time. This is, of course, the tricky one. This is like your parents would say, "In my day, we respected our elders…" Even God Himself refers to things that happened in the days of certain kings.[633] Those guys certainly ruled longer than twenty-four hours.

Given this, I'm willing to say that okay, maybe "day" doesn't refer to a strict twenty-four hours. Maybe when God defines each of these "days" as an "evening" and a "morning,"[634] He does not mean a literal evening or literal morning. And on "day" four, when He created the sun and moon specifically to be humankind's way of measuring time, and He told them to govern day/night/evening/morning, however you want to say it… sure.[635] He could have been speaking figuratively.

And maybe when God tells Israel He will give up on them right after hell freezes over and pigs fly by saying "you're good until the fixed order of the sun and moon goes kaput,"[636] I suppose He meant that to sound a little more certain than that actually was. After all, the fixed order wasn't so fixed, and it went kaput eons ago.

Personally, I'm of the "day" means "day" persuasion. But if I must, I will give you all that. Here's where I draw the line.

We get our idea of millions of years from the fossil record. Fossils being the dead and preserved corpses of once-living things—trees, fish, T-rexes, etc. If, in our efforts to mesh the Word of God with the current scientific thinking, we place our millions of years—and therefore the fossil record—into Genesis 1... Houston, we have a problem.

"Through one man sin entered into the world, and death through sin, and so death spread to all men, because all sinned."[637]

God created the world perfect.

So how did death get in?

Sin.

How did sin get in?

"One man," namely, Adam.

But if we've got a whole pile of fossils *before* Adam sinned—actually, before Adam was created—then either death snuck in before sin or sin got in before Adam, and something is terribly, terribly wrong.

Since the dawn of time, manmade religion has appointed itself to decide who gets into the afterlife. Sometimes they call it heaven, sometimes Elysium, sometimes Valhalla—it doesn't matter. The question is how you get in. More importantly, how do you stay out of hell?

Almost universally, there is some version of a set of scales. Actually, in Egyptian mythology, it was a literal set of scales. They'd put a feather on one side and your heart on the other, and if the sins of your soul weighed more than the feather, Ammut would eat you. But that's neither here nor there.

The point is, it's almost ingrained in human psychology to think that my good has to outweigh my bad. That too much bad can never be balanced out. That God will judge me based on my actions, and I will either be found wanting or be found very lucky.

But this is absolutely not at all how salvation works. It's not how the world works. But everyone thinks it! And because it's so counterintuitive to think anything else, God has to go all the way back to Genesis 1 to explain how salvation *actually* works.

"For if by the transgression of the one the many died, much more did the grace of God and the gift by the grace of the one Man, Jesus Christ, abound to the many. For if by the transgression of the one, death reigned through the one, much more those who receive the abundance of grace and of the gift of righteousness will reign in life through the One Jesus Christ.

"So then as through one transgression there resulted condemnation to all men, even so through one act of righteousness there resulted justification of life to all men. For as through the one man's disobedience the many were made sinners, even so through the obedience of the One the many will be made righteous."[638]

Remember Adam? Well, he sinned, and when he sinned, every descendant he ever had got infected with that sin. I am condemned and going to hell because of *that* guy. How totally unfair!

Remember Jesus? Well, He died, and when He died, every child He ever had got infected with that grace. I am redeemed and going to heaven because of *that* Guy.

How totally unfair.

Crazy, huh? No scale, no balancing act, no condemnation for those who are in Christ Jesus.[639] God looks at my representative and declares me righteous. That is how salvation works. That's how the world works.

Assuming you believe that grace and its riches come from the One Person who did right on my behalf.

Assuming you believe that sin and its consequences come from one person who did wrong on my behalf.

If death got into the world before sin, then when Jesus saves me from sin, bully for me. I've still got a death problem. Frankly, I've still got a hell problem.

If sin got into the world before Adam, then when Jesus died on the cross, big whoop. My sin is still on me because *I* still haven't accomplished whatever I need to in order to rid myself of it. We're back to the scale again. And last I checked, my sin weighs more than a feather.

I can live with a nonliteral interpretation of the word *day*. I can accept that "evening" and "morning" are up in the air, too. I can even go along with God building on a graveyard and calling it "good." He does work all things—even bad things—together for good, after all.[640]

But I cannot give way on salvation. On how the transaction between my soul and that of Jesus Christ works. On how I became imbued with grace, subject to heaven. Or on how I became infected with sin, subject to hell. Because it's the same transaction, part of the same system. And if I give away Genesis 1, the system breaks down, and grace is no longer grace.[641]

Do I have to be naïve to believe this? Do I have to stick my head in the sand and ignore facts in order to have faith? Actually, no.

For a thing to be actual science, to qualify, it must be observable and repeatable (so says my eighth-grade science textbook). No one has ever observed biological evolution, and no one has ever repeated the big bang (sci-fi shows and comic books don't count). So, since no one's taken the theory all the way to the place of science, it's still just theory. Granted, I can't exactly argue with theory—your opinion versus mine, we'll be here all day. But then, if it's just opinion, I'm not really threatened by it, now, am I?

But the whole concept of a really old earth, of millions of years, comes from two things: the theory, and carbon dating, which uses actual science to date how old a thing is.

How do I argue with actual science?

Well, here's how carbon dating works (best I can tell). Living things start with a certain amount of carbon in their bodies, and when a thing dies, it begins to lose that carbon over time. This is a fact. I don't dispute it. Carbon is lost at a certain rate. And by knowing how much carbon the thing started with and by measuring how much carbon is left, you can figure out how long ago a thing died.

Great! Very rational. But it depends on one little assumption—that carbon has always been lost at the same rate.

If a police car points a radar gun at a red Ferrari, and that Ferrari is going eighty-five, and a few miles down the road, another police car catches him also going eighty-five, and ten miles after that, lo and behold, eighty-five, it would be pretty rational to assume that red Ferraris travel at eighty-five miles an hour. Period. From all we can tell, they always have, always will. They go from zero to eighty-five in the .05 seconds it takes to clear their garage doors.

But, obviously, having not clocked the Ferrari trundling down the neighborhood winding roads, the police cars would have no way of knowing that red Ferraris do not necessarily *always* travel that speed.

So, carbon always decays at the same rate, right? There's no evidence to the contrary. To my knowledge, no one has ever clocked carbon decaying at a different rate than scientists say it does. So, frankly, it's a very reasonable assumption to make, one I myself would make, and one everybody's pretty comfortable with. So, with the disclaimer that, yes, there is a bit of an assumption being made here, we can assume that carbon decays at a specific rate. Always has, always will.

We then measure how long a dinosaur has been dead and voilà! Millions of years.

Here's another thing that decays at a constant rate: the sun.

Yes, the sun is shrinking. Do not fear! It's happening very slowly. But, truth be told, last year, it was bigger than it is now. Ten years back, even bigger. A hundred years, a thousand, even bigger. And having clocked it last year, and ten years ago, and however long ago someone discovered that this was happening, it is safe to say that the sun shrinks at a constant rate. Always has, always will.

So, let's say both assumptions are true: carbon decays at a constant rate, and the sun shrinks at a constant rate. Carbon dating will tell us that the earth is millions of years old, and if we calculate backward...

Here's where I feel like I need a pull-down projector screen and old-fashioned slides and a pointer stick in my hand, perhaps a mustache on my lip so I look like a 1950s professor teaching naïve little students about the real age of the earth.

Slide One: Today. See the nice, round, yellow sun and our tiny little blue earth in the vast blackness of space, and that dotted line would be our planets' orbits drawn on there so nicely.

Slide Two: One thousand years ago. Note the slightly larger sun.

Slide Three: Ten thousand years ago. Really, folks, this isn't so long ago in the vast scheme of things, but see how big the sun is?

Slide Four: Millions of years ago, the approximate age of the earth according to carbon dating. Oops. (Gasps and oohs as the students see the bright sun filling their entire projector screen). Uh, sorry, students. See, uh, that pale blue dot *inside* the sun? Well, that's us, but that can't be... let me consult my notes. Class is canceled as I consult a slightly more accurate science Book.

So, one of our assumptions has to be faulty. Personally, I'm going with the one that contradicts Scripture. Maybe that's just me.

There are these things called body farms—yes, real thing—in which human corpses are placed under various conditions so that truly dedicated forensics students can observe with their own eyes what a three-day-old body looks like versus a five-day-old body, and how being in water changes things, and what it's like if they're in a compost heap, and what they're like if it rains, and so forth.

Sorry, yes, this is gross, but the point being that how a body decays is drastically affected by the conditions that body is placed in.

If we are to assume that something is making the carbon dating inaccurate and that carbon has not always decayed at the same rate, then we are making the rather ludicrous assertion that something affected every single dead thing on the face of the earth all at the same time, otherwise we'd have discrepancies everywhere and people would have debunked carbon dating a long time ago. I have no idea how to explain that, barring something cataclysmic like... a worldwide flood?

When God created the world, He made an expanse which He called *sky*. And He separated the waters that were below the expanse from the waters that were above.[642] Last I checked, there is not a giant layer of water wrapping our planet.

Best I can tell, this giant layer of water crashed to earth four thousand-ish years ago, causing a flood,[643] covering the mountains, changing the entire earth's ecosystem. A lot of things changed after that. Lifespans went from eight or nine hundred years to not much longer than a hundred. Something happened to the dinosaurs, too (which I do assume Noah loaded onto the ark next to the lions and tigers and bears, oh my). And—my guess—carbon didn't stay in the body quite like it used to. Therefore, anything that dates more than four thousand years old is going to be off. By millions.

This is a guess. A theory, if you will. Unproven, untested, but logical. None of us can actually go back to before the flood and point a radar gun at the red Ferrari to see if carbon was actually decaying faster back then. But knowing that the science of carbon dating is based on an assumption that directly contradicts an equally valid assumption and knowing that one of them has to be wrong, I can confidently say that I am not an idiot for presuming God knows better than we do. I am not naïve for supposing that our scientific methods are occasionally faulty. I am not sticking my head in the sand or ignoring facts. I'm choosing faith over assumptions, salvation over popular theory, God over man. Frankly, that seems to be the only rational choice to make.

I don't know the answers. I don't have the explanations. I don't understand the science. But I don't have to. That's where faith has the upper hand against all other schools of thought—faith doesn't actually *have* to explain itself. It just is.

Salvation is the fact against which other so-called facts shatter. If there is a fault in the machine, it is found elsewhere, because salvation stands. And because everything in the Christian life stands on salvation, that is the one thing you don't mess with.

ENDNOTES

Scripture in this book is taken from the NASB unless otherwise indicated.

1   Psalm 31:4–5

2   John 17:17

3   Genesis 1:1, 26–27, 2:7

4   Genesis 1:1, 26–27, 2:7

5   James 3:11–12

6   Matthew 19:26

7   Job 42:2

8   Jeremiah 32:17

9   Job 38:4–7

10 Jeremiah 1:10, 18:7, 9

11 Proverbs 21:1

12 Matthew 10:29; Job 38:31–33

13 Genesis 1:3

14 Genesis 1:14–18; Psalm 107:25; Mark 4:38–41

15 Matthew 8:28–34

16 1 Samuel 16:7; John 2:24–25

17 Psalm 139:1–4

18 Isaiah 46:9–10; see also any fulfilled prophecy in Scripture, such as Joshua 6:26 with 1 Kings 16:34.

19 Hebrews 4:13

20 Proverbs 15:3

21 Psalm 139:7–12

22 Philippians 1:6

23 Isaiah 46:11

24 Joshua 21:45

25 Psalm 139:14

26 Ephesians 1:9–11

27 Jeremiah 29:11

28 Romans 8:28

29 1 John 4:7–12

30 Nahum 1:3; Ephesians 2:4–5; 2 Corinthians 5:21; Romans 8:32

31 Romans 8:28

32 Isaiah 53:10–11, 5

33 Romans 8:29–30

34 Psalm 139:16

35 Philippians 1:6

36 Genesis 1:26–31

37 Genesis 1:26

38 John 4:24

39 Genesis 2:7

40 Genesis 1:29, 2:15

41 Genesis 1:12

42 Genesis 1:31

43 Daniel 1:8–16

44 Genesis 3:21

45 Matthew 10:29–31

46   John 1:1–3, 14

47   Mark 6:3; John 21; Mark 10:45

48   1 Peter 1:12

49   Revelation 12:4, 9

50   Matthew 25:41

51   Hebrews 2:14–18

52   Hebrews 2:18, 16; clarify via Galatians 3:28–29

53   Revelation 19:10

54   John 15:15

55   Psalm 8:3–6

56   Genesis 1

57   Genesis 2:7, 21–22

58   Isaiah 45:9

59   Romans 9:20–21

60   James 1:13

61   Psalm 139:1–4

62   Psalm 139:5–6

63   Ephesians 1:11

64   Romans 8:28

65   Isaiah 43:2

66   Psalm 139:7–12

67   Psalm 139:13–14

68   Psalm 139:16–18 NIV

69   Psalm 139:17 NIV's footnote

70   Psalm 139:17-18 NIV

71   Psalm 139:23–24

72   Romans 6:23

73   2 Peter 3:9

74   Isaiah 53:10–11, 5

75   Romans 9:22

76   Romans 9:23

77   Psalm 139:12; Romans 8:28

78   Romans 8:28; see also Romans 11:36; James 1:17; 3:11–12

79   Ephesians 2:8–9

80   Ephesians 2:10

81   Revelation 19:11–21

82   John 10:27–29; Romans 8:38–39; Colossians 1:13–14

83   2 Corinthians 11:14

84   Ephesians 6:12

85   Genesis 3:1

86   Genesis 3:2–3

87   Genesis 2:16–17

88   John 8:44

89   Genesis 3:4

90   Genesis 3:5

91   Genesis 3:6

92   Genesis 2:17

93   Genesis 5:1–24

94   Genesis 3:2

95   Genesis 2:25

96   1 Samuel 16:7

97   Romans 5:12

98   Genesis 2:18 KJV

99   Genesis 1:31

100 Isaiah 41:4

101 Genesis 1:26–27

102 Genesis 5:1–3

103 Genesis 12:10-15. Technically they were still named Abram and Sarai at this point, but they are better known by their God-given names Abraham and Sarah.

104 See Genesis 12:4 with Genesis 17:17

105 Genesis 3:7

106 Romans 5:12

107 See Genesis 3:18

108 Genesis 3:8–10

109 Genesis 3:15, 21

110 Genesis 2:22

111 Genesis 3:16

112 Matthew 22:1–14, 25:1–13; John 14:1–3; Ephesians 5:22–33

113 See Hosea

114 Genesis 1:3

115 Titus 1:2

116 Romans 8:27–28

117 Ephesians 1:11–12

118 Genesis 3:4–5

119 1 John 4:8

120 James 1:17

121 Matthew 7:11; see also James 3:11–12

122 Romans 8:28

123 Romans 8:32

124 Titus 1:2

125 1 Samuel 15:29

126 Isaiah 46:10

127 John 2:24–25

128 Jeremiah 29:11

129 Romans 8:28; Philippians 1:6

130 Ephesians 1:12; Romans 8:28–32

131 Genesis 1:1

132 Psalm 139:14

133 Isaiah 64:8

134 Romans 9:21–23

135 Isaiah 42:5–6

136 Psalm 139:7–12

137 Zephaniah 3:17 NIV

138 Isaiah 40:28–31

139 2 Corinthians 12:9–10

140 John 14:6

141 1 Peter 1:12

142 Isaiah 43:3–5

143 Psalm 130:7–8

144 Colossians 1:13–14

145 Revelation 19:16

146 John 18:36

147 Philippians 3:20

148 Romans 6:4

149 John 14:19

150 Ephesians 2:4–6

151 1 John 4:8; Ephesians 1:6

152 Matthew 7:11

153 John 1:12

154 Psalm 23:1

155 John 10:29

156 2 Thessalonians 3:3

157 Zephaniah 3:5

158 Philippians 1:6

159 Job 42:2

160 Romans 8:29–30

161 John 16:33

162 1 John 5:4

163 Revelation 2:7, 2:11, 2:17, 2:26, 3:5, 3:21, 21:6–7

164 Romans 8:31

165 Isaiah 43:1–3

166 Matthew 7:24–27

167 Psalm 1:3

168 Joel Houston and Matt Crocker, "Not Today," 2017.

169 Romans 16:20

170 John 10:10, 8:44

171 Genesis 1:1

172 Genesis 1:3

173 Genesis 1:31, 2:7, 21–22

174 Ephesians 1:4–5

175 Romans 3:10

176 Romans 3:11

177 Romans 3:12

178 Romans 3:12

179 Romans 3:13–18

180 Genesis 6:5

181 Exodus 20

182 Hosea 4:1–3

183 Romans 3:19–20

184 Galatians 3:24

185 Revelation 13:8 KJV. Please note: depending on your version, the phrase "from the foundation of the world" could either refer to the Lamb of God being slain (Jesus' death) or to having one's name written in the book of life (being chosen). If this is too ambiguous for you, take note that God was promising His Son as mankind's solution for sin as early as Genesis 3:15 and continued to prophesy both His coming and His death throughout the Old Testament. Either way, there is no way to imagine that Jesus was Plan B.

186 Starting in Genesis 3:15. Genesis 3:15 is the first Messianic prophecy (promise of Jesus), specifically that a descendant of the woman (Eve) would crush Satan and that Jesus Himself would be bruised in the heel (a reference to the crucifixion where Jesus' feet were nailed to the cross).

187 Romans 5:8

188 Romans 5:9

189 Matthew 20:28

190 Colossians 2:14; John 19:30.
     The Greek word translated
     into "it is finished" is the
     same one stamped across
     certificates of debt when that
     debt was finally "paid in full."

191 1 Corinthians 6:20, 7:23

192 1 John 2:2

193 Hebrews 7:26

194 Hebrews 7:19, 23–28

195 1 Timothy 2:5–6

196 Ephesians 2:5

197 Romans 8:28

198 Romans 5:8

199 2 Corinthians 5:17

200 Genesis 1:26–27

201 Colossians 3:10; Romans 8:29

202 Ephesians 2:1–3

203 Hebrews 7:25

204 Galatians 2:20

205 Philippians 1:6; Job 42:2

206 Ephesians 2:1–10

207 Exodus 3:14

208 Psalm 50:10–12; see also
     vs. 8–15

209 Genesis 1:1

210 Genesis 3:17–18;
     Romans 8:19–22

211 Genesis 3:16, 19; Romans 5:12

212 Matthew 21:33–39

213 1 John 4:8

214 Luke 3:22

215 John 17:22–23

216 Isaiah 49:6

217 Genesis 15:5

218 1 Corinthians 6:20

219 Psalm 19:1

220 Romans 8:19–21

221 Romans 1:20

222 Job 38–41

223 Romans 11:36

224 Romans 9:23; Ephesians 2:8–9;
     Matthew 5:14

225 1 Peter 1:10–12

226 Luke 19:40; Matthew 27:51–54

227 2 Peter 1:4

228 Romans 11:36; see also
     Philippians 2:10–11

229 1 Corinthians 10:31

230 2 Corinthians 12:9–10;
     2 Timothy 2:13

231 Romans 2:4

232 John 10:10

233 See Isaiah 59:9–15;
     Matthew 23:13–33

234 See Psalm 19:7–9; Psalm 119

235 Isaiah 42:6–7

236 John 17:2–3

237 John 14:16–17, 26

238 John 3:33

239 Zechariah 8:16

240 John 8:44

241 Isaiah 6:3

242 Matthew 5:8

243 Ephesians 4:27

244 Deuteronomy 7:9

245 Galatians 5:22

246 Exodus 20:14;
Matthew 24:10, 12

247 Nehemiah 9:17

248 Matthew 18:21–22

249 Matthew 18:23–35

250 1 John 4:8

251 James 1:19

252 1 John 4:8, 20; Romans 2:1

253 John 21:25

254 Frederick Lehman, "The Love of God," 1917.

255 Psalm 99:9

256 Exodus 34:6

257 Matthew 22:36–40

258 2 Timothy 4:3–4

259 Matthew 22:36–40

260 1 John 4:8

261 Ephesians 4:15

262 2 Thessalonians 2:10;
1 John 3:18

263 1 Corinthians 13:1–3

264 1 Corinthians 13:1–3;
1 John 4:7–8, 11, 20–21; James 3

265 Luke 18:10–14

266 John 8:32

267 John 14:6

268 Philippians 2:5–8

269 Isaiah 53:7; Mark 14:55–61

270 Peter Scholtes, "They'll Know We Are Christians," 1960s. Based on John 13:35.

271 1 John 4:19

272 Deuteronomy 7:7–8 MEV

273 Romans 9:11

274 Titus 3:5–7

275 Anthony Brown and Pat Barrett, "Good, Good Father," 2015.

276 Colossians 2:14

277 John 19:19

278 Colossians 2:14

279 Isaiah 53:10

280 1 John 4:18

281 Romans 8:1

282 Hebrews 7:26-27, 25

283 John 1:29

284 Hebrews 2:14, 17–18

285 Hebrews 5:8–9

286 Romans 8:2–4

287 2 Corinthians 5:21

288 1 Samuel 16:7; John 2:24–25;
Hebrews 4:12

289 Romans 8:20–21

290 2 Peter 1:4

291 Romans 8:5–8

292 Romans 8:9–10, 15–17

293 Romans 5:12–21

294 2 Corinthians 5:17

295 Psalm 37:4

296 Romans 8:8

297 Philippians 2:13

298 Philippians 2:13

299 Galatians 2:20

300 1 Samuel 17:31–40

301 Ephesians 6:14–17

302 Ephesians 6:13

303 Matthew 7:23

304 Isaiah 65:16

305 Titus 1:2

306 Exodus 33:18–23

307 Psalm 19:7–9

308 Jeremiah 1:12; Matthew 5:18; 2 Peter 1:3; Ephesians 1:11; see also Exodus 32 with 34:1; Jeremiah 36:20–28

309 Deuteronomy 30:11–14, 4:2, 12:32; Proverbs 30:6; Revelation 22:18–19

310 John 15:26, 14:16–17, 26

311 Note: God's Word does include figures of speech, metaphors, parables, and proverbs. And such things should be taken as the literary device they are. But some things in God's Word are historic, literal, and not up for debate. These should not be taken as literary devices. This is where grace comes in and gratitude that we have the Holy Spirit helping us to make what is sometimes unclear, clear.

312 James 2:19

313 Matthew 4:5–6

314 Matthew 15:8; John 9:41

315 1 Corinthians 8:1

316 James 1:22–25

317 Ephesians 6:11, 13

318 Ephesians 6:14 NIV

319 Isaiah 64:6 NIV

320 1 Corinthians 1:30

321 Romans 13:14

322 Colossians 3:12

323 1 John 4:7–11, 19–21

324 Galatians 2:20

325 Philippians 2:5–8

326 Luke 10:38–42

327 Ephesians 6:15

328 1 Corinthians 13:9–10, 12

329 1 Corinthians 13:9–12

330 John 20:29

331 John 1:18

332 Luke 24:50–51; John 14:2; Mark 13:32

333 Ephesians 1:4–6

334 Romans 8:29–30

335 John 1:14; Hebrews 7:25

336 Acts 7

337 Acts 17:16–34

338 Matthew 4:19

339 John 10:11

340 Matthew 13:3–23

341 Ephesians 6:15

342 Ephesians 6:12

343 Romans 5:5

344 Psalm 62:6

345 John 6:35

346 Zephaniah 3:5

347 1 Peter 2:6

348 Matthew 17:20

349 Mark 9:22–24

350 2 Timothy 2:13

351 Acts 19:13

352 Acts 19:15

353 Ephesians 6:16

354 Hebrews 11:8–10

355 Hebrews 11:17

356 Genesis 12:1–3; Genesis 16

357 Hebrews 11:19

358 Ephesians 6:17

359 Romans 8:29–30

360 Romans 8:31

361 John 10:28

362 Philippians 1:6 NIV

363 Romans 8:1

364 John 8:36

365 Romans 6:4

366 Colossians 2:14

367 Psalm 139:7–12

368 Galatians 2:20

369 Philippians 3:20

370 Romans 8:30–31

371 Colossians 3:1

372 John 10:28

373 Ephesians 6:17

374 2 Chronicles 20:15

375 1 Samuel 17:47

376 Deuteronomy 20:4

377 2 Chronicles 20:17

378 Proverbs 21:31

379 Numbers 20:8–13

380 Isaiah 61:1–3

381 Ephesians 6:12

382 John 13:35

383 Matthew 7:1–5

384 Ephesians 6:10–13

385 John 14:6

386 1 Corinthians 1:30

387 Ephesians 2:14

388 Nahum 1:15

389   Psalm 28:7

390   Exodus 15:2

391   John 1:14

392   Ephesians 6:10–13

393   Psalm 46:1–2, 6–9 NASB;
      Psalm 46:10 NIV

394   Exodus 14:13–14

395   All these from the Strongs
      KJV app as translations
      of the Hebrew word for
      "keep silent."

396   1 Samuel 17:47

397   1 Peter 2:6

398   John 14:18, 16

399   John 16:7

400   John 14:11

401   Matthew 11:28

402   1 John 5:1; Romans 5:8–11

403   Philippians 3:20

404   Ephesians 5:25–27

405   Ephesians 4:1–7, 12–16

406   Acts 17:6 NKJV

407   MaryBeth Eberhard,
      "Behold How They Love
      One Another," *All That We
      Have* (blog), March 31, 2020,
      www.marybetheberhard.
      com/2020/03/31/behold-how-
      they-love-one-another/

408   John S. Barnett, *Christ's Last
      Words to His Church* (Tulsa:
      Müllerhaus Publishing Arts,
      Inc., 2018, 105).

409   2 Corinthians 4:7

410   Luke 6:27–28

411   1 Thessalonians 4:13

412   Philippians 4:7

413   1 Corinthians 13:4–8

414   Ecclesiastes 4:9–12

415   Matthew 28:19–20

416   Acts 1:8

417   Acts 17:22–31

418   James 2:15–17

419   1 Corinthians 9:20–22

420   Romans 12:6–8

421   Ephesians 4:11;
      1 Corinthians 12:8–10

422   Romans 10:14; 2 Timothy 2:15

423   James 2:15–17; Matthew 10:42

424   Romans 12:15

425   Colossians 1:15

426   Colossians 2:9

427   Jeremiah 31:34

428   Romans 11:36

429   James 1:17

430   Philippians 2:13

431   Romans 8:29;
      Colossians 1:15, 18

432   1 Corinthians 12:4–7

433   1 Corinthians 12:12–14

434   1 Corinthians 12:15–16

435   1 Corinthians 12:17–19

436   1 Corinthians 12:20–24

437 1 Corinthians 12:24-26

438 See Galatians 5:13 and
     Romans 6:1–2

439 Ephesians 4:22

440 Ephesians 4:24

441 2 Peter 1:4

442 See Romans 14:23

443 James 3:17

444 Matthew 15:9

445 Galatians 1:10

446 Ephesians 6:6

447 James 1:27

448 1 John 4:7–8

449 Ephesians 2:10

450 Ephesians 2:10

451 John 16:33 NIV

452 Matthew 11:28–30

453 Matthew 5:16

454 1 Peter 1:16

455 Galatians 5:22

456 John 10:10

457 John 15:11

458 Romans 14:22–23

459 Matthew 23:25–28

460 Proverbs 23:7 NKJV

461 Matthew 15:11

462 See James 3:11–12

463 James 3:11–12

464 1 Samuel 16:6–7

465 1 Samuel 13:14

466 John 2:24–25

467 Psalm 139:4

468 Psalm 139:16

469 Jeremiah 17:9–10

470 Psalm 139:13–16

471 Genesis 1:27; Ephesians 2:10

472 Romans 11:36; see also
     1 Corinthians 12

473 Numbers 9:17–23

474 Numbers 9 as opposed to
     Numbers 13

475 Numbers 10:11

476 Judges 14:6, 19, 15:14

477 Judges 14:14

478 Judges 15:16

479 Judges 15–16:3

480 Judges 16

481 1 Samuel 9:2

482 1 Samuel 18:7

483 1 Samuel 15:17–19

484 1 Samuel 15, particularly
     verse 9; Esther 3, particularly
     verse 1

485 1 Kings 3:11–12

486 1 Kings 4:29–34

487 1 Kings 10:21, 27

488 1 Kings 10:23

489 The Bible is the best-sell-
     ing book of all time, and

Solomon's "Proverbs" and "Ecclesiastes," are obviously included.

490 1 Kings 11:3-4

491 1 Kings 12

492 Deuteronomy 6:10-12

493 Hosea 13:4-6

494 Matthew 5:16

495 Jeremiah 9:23-24

496 James 1:17

497 1 Corinthians 1:26-31

498 1 Corinthians 1:18-24

499 2 Corinthians 12:9-10

500 Judges 6:11, 14-16

501 Judges 7:2

502 Judges 7:16, 19-21

503 2 Kings 6:16-17

504 Isaiah 64:8; John 8:12

505 Philippians 1:6

506 See Isaiah 55:10-11

507 Isaiah 14:12-14; Ezekiel 28:17

508 Genesis 3:5

509 Proverbs 16:18

510 James 4:6

511 Proverbs 6:16-17

512 Isaiah 14:14

513 Isaiah 55:8-9

514 Matthew 7:21-23

515 Romans 3:10-18

516 1 Kings 18:25-29

517 See Proverbs 22:2 and 1 Samuel 2:7; see also Acts 5:1-11, particularly verse 4

518 1 Timothy 4:1-5

519 1 Peter 2:19-20

520 Colossians 2:21, 23

521 Mark 12:41-44

522 Matthew 6:24

523 Galatians 1:10

524 Romans 3:23

525 John 19:10-11

526 Romans 8:15

527 Psalm 111:10; Proverbs 1:7 as the foundation for the book of Proverbs

528 Psalm 139:16; Romans 8:28

529 Luke 14:26

530 Ephesians 6:1; Exodus 20:12

531 Ephesians 5:25-29

532 Matthew 22:37-40; John 13:35

533 Luke 14:26

534 Ephesians 5:29

535 Matthew 22:39

536 Philippians 2:4

537 Galatians 2:20

538 Philippians 2:3-4 NASB, Philippians 2:5-11 NIV

539 John 13:5

540 Psalm 18:7-19

541 Matthew 4:5–6

542 Job 42:5

543 Daniel 4:30–37

544 Isaiah 6:1–5

545 Numbers 12:3, 6–8

546 2 Kings 5

547 James 4:6–8, 10

548 Romans 12:3

549 Philippians 1:6;
Romans 8:29–30

550 Ephesians 5:27

551 1 John 1:8–9

552 Romans 2:4

553 James 4:8–10

554 2 Peter 3:9

555 Philippians 1:6

556 Isaiah 53:10

557 Titus 2:11–12

558 Matthew 4:4

559 Psalm 92:4

560 Isaiah 40:31

561 Psalm 64:9–10

562 Romans 12:15

563 Psalm 20:7

564 Psalm 66:16

565 Romans 11:11

566 Matthew 5:14–16

567 Jeremiah 9:23–24; 2
Corinthians 12:9–10

568 Philippians 4:4

569 2 Samuel 6:12–23

570 Luke 19:40

571 Luke 15:10

572 Genesis 1:1–13

573 See Joshua 2:10–11, 9:3–27;
Judges 7:19–23; 2 Kings 6:18–23;
Isaiah 13

574 See Exodus 15:8;
Joshua 10:12–14;
Numbers 22:22–30;
Exodus 7:14–21, Exodus 9–10;
Psalm 46:2

575 Leviticus 26:8

576 Joel 1:4

577 Exodus 33:22

578 Habakkuk 3:4

579 Ephesians 1:10

580 Isaiah 53:5, 10

581 Isaiah 30:18

582 Micah 7:18; see Hebrew
meaning for "delights."

583 Philippians 4:7

584 Matthew 14:28–31, 17:20

585 Joshua 6

586 1 Samuel 17

587 Genesis 3:1

588 Luke 14:31

589 Acts 26:18; Colossians 1:13

590 John 10:28

591 Colossians 1:15

592 2 Corinthians 3:18

593 Colossians 3:9–10

594 Romans 8:29

595 Luke 1:79

596 John 12:46, 8:12

597 Matthew 5:14–16

598 Philippians 2:9–11;
Romans 11:36

599 Revelation 3:1-2

600 Ephesians 4:1–6

601 Psalm 133:1

602 Genesis 3:1–5

603 Matthew 4:5–6

604 Matthew 12:25

605 Ephesians 6:12

606 James 4:7

607 Revelation 19:11–21

608 Exodus 9:3; Deuteronomy 2:15;
1 Kings 18:46; Proverbs 21:1;
Isaiah 41:18–20; Acts 11:21

609 Exodus 6:6. See also
Exodus 15:16; Job 40:9;
Isaiah 30:30; Jeremiah 27:5

610 Luke 11:20

611 Mark 5:1–20

612 Ephesians 1:4

613 Genesis 1:26–27

614 Psalm 139:13–14

615 2 Corinthians 5:17

616 Psalm 55:18

617 1 John 4:4

618 John 16:33; 2 Corinthians 2:14

619 Romans 16:20; James 4:7

620 1 John 5:4–5

621 1 Corinthians 15:54–57

622 Revelation 3:21

623 Romans 8:31–39

624 Genesis 1:1

625 Genesis 1:1

626 Genesis 1:2–3

627 Genesis 1:5

628 For instance, Matthew 13:1–23.

629 For instance, Revelation 12.

630 For instance, Psalm 63:1–8.

631 Genesis 1:5

632 Exodus 20:9

633 For instance, Isaiah 7:1.

634 Genesis 1:5, 8, 13, 19, 23, 31

635 Genesis 1:14–18

636 Jeremiah 31:35–37

637 Romans 5:12

638 Romans 5:15, 17–19

639 Romans 8:1

640 Romans 8:28

641 Romans 11:6

642 Genesis 1:6–7

643 Genesis 7